CLARK PUBLIC LIBRARY

3 9502 00147 5698

OFFICIALLY
DISCARDED
CLARK PUBLIC LIBRARY

956.7044   Collins, Jane,
Col        1948-
              For love of a
           soldier

# For Love of a Soldier

D1598741

**Clark Public Library**
303 Westfield Ave.
Clark, NJ 07066
(732)388-5999

# For Love of a Soldier

## *Interviews with Military Families Taking Action Against the Iraq War*

JANE COLLINS

LEXINGTON BOOKS

A division of
ROWMAN & LITTLEFIELD PUBLISHERS, INC.
*Lanham • Boulder • New York • Toronto • Plymouth, UK*

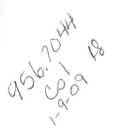

LEXINGTON BOOKS

A division of Rowman & Littlefield Publishers, Inc.
A wholly owned subsidiary of The Rowman & Littlefield Publishing Group, Inc.
4501 Forbes Boulevard, Suite 200
Lanham, MD 20706

Estover Road
Plymouth PL6 7PY
United Kingdom

Copyright © 2008 by Lexington Books

*All rights reserved.* No part of this publication may be reproduced,
stored in a retrieval system, or transmitted in any form or by any
means, electronic, mechanical, photocopying, recording, or otherwise,
without the prior permission of the publisher.

British Library Cataloguing in Publication Information Available

**Library of Congress Cataloging-in-Publication Data**

For love of a soldier : interviews with military families taking action against the Iraq War
/ Jane Collins.
   p. cm.
  Includes index.
  ISBN-13: 978-0-7391-2372-0 (cloth : alk. paper)
  ISBN-10: 0-7391-2372-6 (cloth : alk. paper)
  ISBN-13: 978-0-7391-2373-7 (pbk. : alk. paper)
  ISBN-10: 0-7391-2373-4 (pbk. : alk. paper)
  1. Iraq War (2003–)—Personal narratives, American. 2. Families of military
personnel—Interviews. 3. Iraq War (2003–)—Protest movements. 4. Peace
movements—United States—History—21st century. I. Collins, Jane, 1948–
  DS79.76.F675 2008
  956.7044'31—dc22                                           2007042857

Printed in the United States of America

♾™ The paper used in this publication meets the minimum requirements of American
National Standard for Information Sciences—Permanence of Paper for Printed Library
Materials, ANSI/NISO Z39.48–1992.

Clark Public Library - Clark, N. J.

# Dedication

This book is dedicated to the American troops and all the people who love them; and to the memory of my parents, Lawrence Sass and Roslyn Kleinfeld Sass.

# Contents

# Acknowledgments

I am indebted to Nikki Morse, Charley Richardson, and Nancy Lessin of Military Families Speak Out, and to many activists met at demonstrations whose names I never learned, as well as to the military family members I interviewed at length. I continue to be inspired by their courage and perseverance.

I would like to thank my dear friend Donna Southwell and my daughter Margaret Collins for their help in editing this book. Their close attention and wise counsel have much improved the manuscript, and their moral support mattered more than I can say. My husband and sons have also bolstered my morale throughout the project, and never once asked, "Aren't you done yet?"

Special thanks to Mary Susannah Robbins, who got me started on *For Love of a Soldier*, for her advice and encouragement. I urge readers interested in today's peace movement to read her book *Peace Not Terror: Leaders of the Antiwar Movement Speak Out Against U.S. Foreign Policy Post 9/11* (Lexington Books, 2008) which is comprised of essays by many of the movement's key figures, and includes excerpts from some of the interviews in this book.

Thanks also to Harvard University, which, quite unintentionally, finally gave me time to write.

# Introduction:
# Love the Soldier, Hate the War

Nearly all military families would support the war in Iraq if they thought it was necessary or even conducive to the well-being of the United States. However, as the lies that led us into the war are exposed, and the consequences of the war are now generally understood to be destructive to the long-term security of our nation, military families are speaking out against the war in ever-greater numbers.

The soldiers in the U.S. military today have made a commitment to obey the orders of their superiors. The voluntary nature of their service limits their ability to question those orders, even though some soldiers maintain that they owe a higher allegiance to the nation's Constitution and to their own consciences. Therefore, people outside the military bear much of the responsibility of protesting its misuse. Nobody cares more about such misuse than the parents, spouses, siblings, and children of the troops, with the possible exception of veterans.

It's a terrible sacrifice when family members in the military are hurt or killed for a noble goal, such as defeating Hitler and ending the Holocaust in Eastern Europe. But the sacrifice is most bitter when loved ones suffer for a war that harms America's security, liberties, and standing in the world, and, on balance, seems to hurt the civilian population it was supposed to help.

The fact that the Iraq War was promulgated on the basis of cherry-picked "intelligence," deceptions, and outright lies adds insult to injury. All Americans should be told the truth about the decisions and actions of our government, but in the case of the troops, the very least they deserve is an honest account of why they are being sent into grave danger and what they are meant to achieve. Such honesty has not been a feature of the Bush administration's prosecution of the Iraq War.

After every other argument it advanced for the war—that Saddam Hussein was a party to the 9/11 attacks; that he possessed weapons of mass destruction and was ready to use them; that the U.S. would bring democracy, peace, and stability to Iraq—was irredeemably refuted, the Bush administration fell back on ad hominem attacks on its critics, claiming that failing to support the war was the same as failing to support the troops. To an American public that is ashamed of how their country treated (and still treats) the veterans of the Vietnam War, this is a potent argument. It is a claim, however, that cannot easily be made against military personnel and their families. Their invulnerability to the last arrow in Bush's quiver has made military families and veterans extremely important and visible in the movement to end the Iraq War.

Activism by military families is not unique to this country or this war. The Mothers of the Plaza de Mayo is an organization formed by Argentine women trying to find out what became of sons and daughters who had been kidnapped, and then often tortured and killed, by their government during the internal Dirty War (1976–1983). They spent decades seeking justice for their children. In the process, several founders of the organization also "disappeared."

In 1997, Israeli women whose sons had been killed or wounded in South Lebanon formed the group Four Mothers, which became a grassroots movement dedicated to persuading Israel to pull its military out of the zone it had occupied since 1978. The movement had a strong effect on Israeli public opinion and, in 2000, succeeded in its mission. During Israel's renewed occupation of South Lebanon in the summer of 2006, the protest movement quickly reorganized under the name Waking Up on Time.

America's closest coalition ally in the Iraq War has been Great Britain, where the general public has never supported the war or their country's involvement in it. Bereaved British parents formed the group Military Families Against the War to call for bringing the troops home "quickly and safely," adequate protective equipment while they are in the field, and better physical and mental health care when they return.

Several organizations of military families have been formed in the U.S. in response to the Iraq War. The largest of these is Military Families Speak Out, to which most of the interviewees in this book belong. Gold Star Families for Peace was founded by people like Cindy Sheehan, whose loved ones have been killed in the war. Sheehan became an icon of the anti-war movement in the summer of 2005 when she camped outside the president's home in Crawford, Texas, demanding to know why the war was worth her son Casey's life.

The military family members I have interviewed for this book represent a broad range of political opinion and personal experience. Some, like Nan Beckwith, Dinah Mason, and Linda Waste, have proud family traditions of military service. Others, like Stacy Bannerman, Sarah Fuhro, and Jessica White, are long-time anti-war activists. Some initially supported the war, only gradually becoming aware of the false pretenses under which it was waged and the morass of problems it has created or exacerbated, and some started protesting the war before it began.

My own story is far less dramatic than many of those in this book, for which I am deeply grateful. My oldest child was an active-duty Marine from March 1998 through December 2005. He joined up during Bill Clinton's administration, a time when it seemed possible that the U.S. military would henceforth be used primarily for peace-keeping and rescue missions around the world. Like many other young volunteers, he was attracted by the chance to be a hero, as well as to travel, save money for college, and gain skills and self-discipline.

My son's decision was difficult for my husband and me to accept. My husband was drafted during the Vietnam War, which he was adamantly against. He managed to get himself the military equivalent of an annulment after six months. He and I were both active in the anti-war movement of the day. My husband and I tried hard, but we couldn't persuade our son that our cynical view of this country's recent military history had any relevance to his world.

Our son convinced us that he wasn't joining up out of any disrespect for our values; he felt that the Marine code of honor corresponded closely to the principles we had taught him. He also said that he reserved the right to make up his own mind about what the military asked him to do, and was willing to face the consequences if at any point he decided he couldn't go along with his orders.

Fortunately, before the Marines were pulled into the misadventure in Iraq, they discovered my son's computer skills, which made him more valuable as an office worker than as a mortarman. He didn't like this change in his status, but he had no say in the decision. While he worked on base, his original unit went to Iraq, where they suffered one of the military's highest casualty rates. Nearly one in three has been killed or seriously wounded. We know how lucky we are that our child was not among them.

Our son has only contempt for the Bush administration and its conduct of the war, which has cost his fellow soldiers so dearly. Still, he loves the Marines, and we've come to understand why. In the course of helping one another to endure material deprivation, physical hardships, and isolation from their home communities, people in the military form strong bonds. Their group solidarity, at its best, fosters trust, pride, and confidence. At its worst, of course, it can also foster shocking crimes, denial, and cover-ups; but the worst is rare.

The way my son feels about his "band of brothers" has helped me grasp the ironic fact that war—the most extreme expression of human hatred—actually runs on love. People are led, or misled, into battle to protect the ones they love at home. Once the battle begins, they fight to protect the comrades fighting beside them. Without love, at the first gunshot or bomb blast, everybody on a battlefield would just run for their lives.

Being the mother of a Marine gave me access to the people I interviewed for this book. The people whose stories follow this introduction are a random sample of anti-Iraq War activist military families, and, really, of Americans in general. Some have assumed leadership roles in the movement, but most simply show up at events, write letters to the editor, or make calls to their congresspeople. I met some interviewees at demonstrations, and they suggested more folks I should talk to. The good people of Military Families Speak Out sent a small tide of emails my way. I tried to follow up with everyone who contacted me, and greatly appreciate the help I have received from so many on this project.

Each interview is taken verbatim from long conversations on the phone or in person. I sent draft copies to the interviewees to make sure that my transcriptions were accurate, and to give them a chance to delete anything that they would prefer not to see in print. People opened their hearts to relate these stories, some of which were painful to hear and must have been very painful to tell. I have been astonished and moved at their eloquence, their thoughtfulness, and their passion. I hope that you, the reader, will be moved as well.

# Chapter 1
# Nancy Lessin and Charley Richardson

*Nancy and Charley founded the anti-Iraq War organization Military Families Speak Out. Both are professional educators in the labor movement. Charley's son and Nancy's stepson, Joe, joined the Marines in 1998 and went to Iraq in the spring of 2003. Joe is now out of the military.*

*Charley:* In the summer of 2002, I was outside a little store and heard three people arguing about whether or not to go to war in Iraq. Two customers, men, were saying we need to go in there, blow them up. The woman behind the counter was saying, "Wait a minute, don't you think we need to figure this out a little more?" What I would like to have done is go in and put a picture of Joe on the counter and say, "At least if you guys are having this discussion, do it looking at the face of someone who might be damaged by this war."

I began writing a letter that the two of us sent out to everybody that we could find. We had a picture of Joe that we included in the letter. It basically said that this isn't an abstract principle for us, it's very real. And if you're thinking about whether or not to do anything about this war, look at the picture, and think about the real people who are going to be involved. It made the rounds.

We also made a poster with Joe's picture that said, "Our son is a Marine, don't send him to war for oil." And it clearly affected people. Bush was in town in September 2002 and there was a demonstration. We had this poster, and a lot of people came up to us and thanked us for being there. That made it clear that the voice was important. We also began to run into other people who were having the same experience. It was actually at a demonstration in October that we ran into one other father, Jeff MacKenzie, whose son would soon deploy, which was the point at which we said, "Let's create an organization."

*Nancy:* I had done a little bit of exploration. A friend of mine was familiar with a group called Military Families Support Network that was
formed prior to the first Gulf War by military families speaking out in
opposition to that war. We were encouraged by this to try to start up an
organization of military families to oppose the new war we feared was
coming.

I believe there is a code of silence in the military that extends to the
families and that extends to the nation about not speaking out about military action, thinking of it as in a military situation where a command has
been given. But it's really a political decision whether or not to go to
war. So we chose the name Military Families Speak Out and then tried to
figure out how to reach other military families.

The real breakthrough moment was the first national press conference we did, in January 2003. An organization called Veterans for
Common Sense invited us to Washington. They were doing a press conference that was questioning the rush to war. Right before we went
down, Charley created a website, a very rudimentary one,
www.mfso.org, and we went out and bought an answering machine for
our home phone. We left a message, "If you want to speak with Nancy
and Charley, press one, and if you want to speak with Military Families
Speak Out, press two." We went on national television, and we got doz-
ens if not hundreds of contacts through that. Some of them were hostile,
but a lot of them were military families, in particular, moms, who wrote
saying—you just spoke with my voice, how do I join, this is how I've
been feeling, thank goodness there's something like this, I thought I was
the only one. To this day, four years later, we get emails that start out
that way, from someone who found us on the internet: "Thank goodness
I found you, I thought I was the only one."

One of the really important strengths of MFSO is that, though Charley and I have activist backgrounds, the membership—now over 3,600
families—is a very diverse group, with some like ourselves who have
protested other wars, and there are also military families who have never
spoken out and didn't have very much of a problem with any other war
that the U.S. has been involved in, except this invasion and now occupation of Iraq. There are pacifists who believe that there never should be
war, and there are those who believe that everything the U.S. has done up
until the Iraq war is fine, and everybody in between. And we have come
together on this issue of the war in Iraq. On social issues of the day, on
political issues, on the party we belong to, on how we view every other
war—we have incredible diversity. MFSO tries to be an organization that
is welcoming and nurturing in support of that diversity.

*Charley:* The only thing you have to do to join MFSO is to be against this war, and you have to have a loved one or relative in the military. We've held on to that very tightly, because we feel it allows people to join us who are split on all kinds of other issues.

*Nancy:* When we look back, we're standing on some pretty important shoulders. During Vietnam, the first Gold Star Mothers started speaking out and questioning the war in Vietnam. And right after we did our first press conference there was another big anti-war demonstration in Washington D.C. and Veterans For Peace invited us to march with them. There were around ten or twelve of us at that point. They gave us a place with them, by their side, and we've never left it. It's been absolutely an incredible, supportive place for us to be.

When we put together our contingents for demonstrations now, we have the veterans and families contingent, we have our anti-Iraq war cadences led by Veterans For Peace, we have our messages, our pictures of our loved ones, and it becomes a space where we do feel, as an organization, comfortable with our message and our purpose, and our collective reason for being there.

*[I ask about the fear of retaliation against loved ones in the military.]*

*Nancy:* Back in the fall of 2002, we didn't know what was going to happen with retaliation, but we had a good sense that if this nation did go to war in Iraq, Joe and so many others would be in harm's way in a way that makes other concerns pale in comparison. So if we could do something to prevent a U.S. invasion of Iraq, we would give it our all. But it was always with a sense that this may have some consequences. The reality for Joe is that he left on the deployment a lance corporal and came back a sergeant. He was elevated two ranks.

*Charley:* There are two kinds of concerns that people have. One is a concern about career, the other is a concern about safety. There are decisions made every day about who goes on what assignment. It's very possible for people to just get the worst assignments. So there are concerns about the conditions under which they would be forced to operate. Some people are very concerned about their loved one's career. Our concern was much more about safety. But we also figured we were so visible . . . There's that middle ground where you are visible enough to lead to retaliation but not visible enough for the retaliation to be noticed.

*Nancy:* We've heard a couple positive cases. One was the mother of a soldier, one was the wife of a soldier. The mother was another plaintiff in our lawsuit, filed in February 2003, that basically sought a temporary restraining order preventing Bush and Rumsfeld from invading Iraq, and her picture got in the paper. Her son was called in to his command's office, and the command put her picture in front of him and asked him, "Is this your mother involved in that?" and he said, "Yes it is," and the officer in command said, "Tell her for us—thank you." And the other was a situation where in Iraq, the husband got called into the command's office—his wife had been very vocal in speaking out as a member of MFSO, opposing the war—the command closed the door, and said, "I'm supposed to be telling you to tell your wife to be quiet, but between you and me, you can tell your wife, you go, girl." So early on, we had a sense that high up in the military, not everybody was happy with this war.

But we have heard other stories as well, of negative pressure. There's no doubt about it. A lot of MFSO members speak out, but other members are afraid. They say they want to be on the email list, but they don't want to talk to press, they don't want to do anything. When we get asked, "Will something happen to our loved one?" we write back that there are no guarantees about anything. This really needs to be a personal decision. I tell them the decision that we made to speak out was not one where we thought, oh this is going to be fine, nothing can happen; but the cost of not speaking out seems to us to be the higher price to pay.

*Charley:* There are a lot of members who've been in demonstrations who had never been to a demonstration in their lives. It's a pretty daunting step for a lot of people. There are people who have spoken who have never spoken in front of an audience. For them to arrive and see a group of people they can be with and become part of that group makes it a whole lot easier.

One MFSO member who came to one demonstration with a friend, she clearly had never been super active in things. As the weekend went on, we kept getting press calls, and we said to them, "Would you go on national television to be interviewed?" They thought hard, but then they said okay. This MFSO member ended up going to Italy in March 2004, the first anniversary of the war. We'd been invited to come to Italy and we sent her as the representative of MFSO. She was in Rome, a million and a half people in the street, and she was the opening speaker. A small shopkeeper from Indianapolis. She actually got up on stage and said, "Before I start my speech, there's something I gotta do, because my husband's never gonna believe this"—her husband was deployed in Iraq—and she stepped out from behind the podium, and she took a little camera out and took a picture of the crowd. The crowd went wild, they loved the honesty and openness of that. And then she gave her speech. We have hundreds of stories like that, of people just stepping out of their regular lives to make a point.

*Nancy:* It's so important—the support we give one another to get through the most horrendous experiences in our lives. If you don't experience it, you don't know what it's like to have someone in harm's way for no good reason. I think we share with all military families of all times the fear when a loved one is in combat, about what's going to happen. Nothing is as it was. The knock on the door takes on a new, sinister meaning. The phone ringing is a whole different experience. We share that.

But for those of us who believe that this war is illegal, it's immoral, it's unjust, it's unjustified, it's wrong, it should never have happened, to have our loved ones over there disrupts our lives in ways that are not comprehended by anyone who hasn't been in our shoes. What we have done organizationally is provide support for one another. It helps us get from day to day. It helps us to maybe do an action against the Iraq War in our community, but also to be with people who understand why we never turn our cellphone off, or why we can't function in a particular period of time because we haven't gotten an email from our loved one, and it keeps not coming. To have the support of people who have experienced that kind of fear, to be with each other, has been part of the ability to move forward and speak out.

The biggest single issue for those of us lucky enough to get our loved ones home is post-traumatic stress disorder [PTSD]. We have gotten emails from mothers who have taken the gun out of their son's mouth to stop them from blowing their brains out.

We get emails that say, "My husband is angry all the time." Or, "We're driving along the road and all of a sudden they'll swerve, thinking there's an IED [improvised explosive device]," or "My husband sleeps with a gun by the bed," or "I'm woken up most nights when he has nightmares." There are marriages that have disintegrated because of the anger and violence that servicemen have returned with. And there are emails we've gotten—one from a father whose two sons participated in the war, and he said, "It's like both of my sons are dead, one hasn't called us in over a year, another is drinking all the time and there's no relationship. That son's email address is walkingdead." Last Christmas, an MFSO member wrote, "Well, my son's body showed up for Christ-

mas, but I don't know where his mind was; we could not connect at all."
That devastation is not well understood.

When Joe came home, lots of people said to me, "Isn't it wonderful
to have Joe home safe and sound." And my response at that time was,
and it continues to be, those of us who have loved ones who participated
in this war, we don't know if our loved ones will ever be safe or sound
because of what they saw, what they did and what they were exposed to.
Whether it was depleted uranium that could negatively impact their
physical health for decades to come, or the psychological trauma of this
war, this war doesn't end when they come home. Now we're having
MFSO members whose loved ones are going on second, third, fourth,
and fifth deployments. If you're diagnosed with PTSD in Iraq now,
you're taken off the front lines for a couple days, given drugs, and sent
back.

*Charley:* We hear all the time, "They volunteered, so shut up." First, it's
not about whether or not they volunteered, it's about whether this was
the right political decision for our country and for the world. Secondly,
even if they did volunteer, how much can you ask of one individual or
set of individuals? If the nation has made a political decision to go to
war, the burden of that war should be spread across the nation. What this
nation has decided to do is to sacrifice a tiny percentage, and to ignore
that sacrifice because they're disconnected from it. What we're seeing is
that only a few are forced to really bear the burden of this war, and that's
why people have gone along with it, and allowed it to continue. It's not
because they think it's right but that it doesn't affect them.

A friend of ours from the Steelworkers Union once told me, "A just
war is one you'd send your own kids off to fight." That's the bar you
should have to get over to send someone else's kid off to war.

# Chapter 2
# Dinah Mason

*Dinah and her daughter Erika are both members of Daughters of the American Revolution (DAR). Dinah is an Army veteran; Erika left active duty after a tour in Iraq, but will be on Inactive Ready Reserve in the Army until 2010.*

I'm from a patriotic family. There are six in my immediate family and four of us are veterans.

I was born in Brazil, Indiana, a farming community, population around seven thousand. My dad was a pilot in World War II. He flew B25 bombers. He never went overseas but he trained pilots at an airbase in southern Arizona. About when he and my mom married, in 1946, they were starting to phase out the prop planes and go to jets. He got into my grandfather's house-building business in Indiana. He did farming and carpentry.

During Vietnam, my dad supported the Democrats but was pretty much pro-war. We went to Canada on vacation and saw all these hitchhikers. I never heard my dad cuss so much as at all those draft-dodgers. My dad's passed away, but I like to think he'd see this war differently. We had to go through Vietnam before we knew the whole story. It's incredible how many similarities there are. Too bad people aren't getting it faster.

My mother was a stay-at-home mom. She was born in Mexico and grew up in Arizona. She met my dad at an Army Air Corps base dance. They had four kids. I'm the youngest. My oldest sister, Phyllis, joined the Army in '68 or '69. She's ten years older than me. She studied communications and was a switchboard operator at the Pentagon. It was a difficult job. She put through calls to families when their loved ones were critically injured. While she was there, someone smuggled a bomb into a restroom on the next floor from her. She remembers the whole building shook.

My brother Gary, who's eight years older, is a veteran of the Indiana National Guard. He was on the Dean's List in his sophomore year at Purdue University, and he was married and had an infant daughter, but he turned down an educational deferment and decided to join the Guard instead of getting sent to Vietnam. That was a good thing. [Vice President] Cheney got three or four educational deferments. It's amazing to me that he got all those deferments; he must not live in the real world.

I joined the Army in '74, right out of high school, at eighteen. I studied Russian at the Defense Language Institute in California, in a forty-seven-week course. We mainly listened and transcribed. You can hear it spoken, write it down in the Cyrillic alphabet, and hand it to the translators. Vietnam was winding down. I knew I wouldn't get sent there as a Russian language specialist.

When I got out, I had cousins and an aunt and uncle in Los Angeles, and I rented a room from one of my cousins. They were really anti-war. I learned a lot, associating with them. They went to protests and stuff. I probably could have stayed in the Army if I'd wanted to, but I'd been visiting them enough so that I had a kind of awakening; I saw a different point of view. Indiana is such a conservative state. Partly I joined the Army to get away from that, see how other people lived.

I stayed in LA for around two years. I met somebody who grew up in Santa Barbara. He was into bicycling. We did a four-month bike trip in 1977, from New Orleans, to the Florida Gulf Coast, Georgia, the Smoky Mountains, Kentucky, and visited my parents in Indiana. When we got back to LA, there was a third-stage smog alert. My boyfriend said, "It's not as smoggy in Santa Barbara. Want to go there?"

We lived on a boat in the harbor. After about a year, we broke up. I kept the boat. I was still really into bicycling. A group of us would meet every Sunday for a breakfast ride. That's where I met my husband, in '78 or '79. We were married in 1984, and later that year my daughter Erika was born. In March 1987, Pete was diagnosed with colon cancer. The doctor told us if we wanted another baby we'd have to try before the radiation treatment started. So we tried, and it worked. His name's Terry Lee. Pete had ignored his symptoms, and it spread really fast. He passed away in July 1988.

I'd always wanted to learn Spanish. I found an intensive Spanish school in Costa Rica. We ended up staying there about five and a half years. One of my favorite things about Costa Rica is, they have no army. It's the smart thing to do, the moral thing to do. The people who live in that country are probably the most patriotic people I ever met. You can be patriotic and love your country and be against war.

I had my third child in Costa Rica, Alexa. My kids picked up Spanish right away. Then they stopped speaking English. I figured eventually they'd want to go to college, and I thought they should go to high school in the States. I was also kind of homesick. I missed my family. We came back to Santa Barbara in '95.

I found a school in Indiana where I could go through the Veterans Upward Bound program. They help vets find scholarships so you can go back to college. I went to the Herron School of Art, a branch of Indiana University. I did fine art and took some graphics classes. I transferred to Bloomington so we could live in family housing.

Then both my parents died, six months apart. I got pretty depressed and dropped out, and went to live near my sisters in Arizona. But it was kind of expensive there, and I didn't like the schools. I decided to move back to Costa Rica. We were all going to go down. But my oldest daughter—her aunt and uncle offered to let her live with them in Pennsylvania and put her in a good private school. My younger kids were going to go with me, but it was August, the middle of the school year in Costa Rica. Pete's sister offered to let them do the school year with them in San Jose. So I went down to Costa Rica and got things ready.

Because I'm a widow, I got about sixteen hundred dollars a month in social security survivor's benefits. My mother-in-law had sent us a lot of money to help us out over the years. Turns out my sister-in-law and her husband resented that. They had to have legal guardianship of the kids for him to be able to get them onto his medical insurance at work. They said they'd send the kids at the end of the school year. But he actually went to court and got legal custody. They took the kids and got my survivor's benefits.

That was a really nasty trick. I had to sell everything at a fire sale. I came back to Santa Barbara and worked two jobs, trying to save enough money to hire a lawyer to terminate the guardianship. It took me about a year to save the money. It was a nightmare.

By then my son had friends and didn't want to move. Alexa was at a borderline age; she wanted to join me, but the court mediator wanted to do a slow transition over a year. My sister-in-law and her husband worked hard to turn my youngest daughter against me. She told the mediator she'd changed her mind. It was just incredible. I was flabbergasted. She stayed with her aunt and uncle.

Going through the system, seeing how awful the court system was—my attorney didn't even want to look at the parental alienation thing that was going on—that led me to say, if I see something wrong, I fight even harder now, like to end this war. I see what goes on with the soldiers in the military; all their civil liberties are stripped away. Recruiters lie, and they keep getting away with it.

In the summer between Erika's junior and senior year in high school, she didn't like living with her aunt and uncle in Pennsylvania. She missed her brother and sister. She came to live with the same in-laws. He kept pushing her to college, but she wasn't ready. There was a recession in the Bay area; she could only find minimum-wage jobs.

She'd taken the ASVAB [Armed Services Vocational Aptitude Battery] test in high school. A recruiter contacted her. She went to the recruiter's office and they showed her videos that made the Army look really cool. The recruiters were very convincing. So she signed up. She called me when she first started talking with the recruiter. I told her not to do this. But she just wanted to get away. Her uncle was a control freak, kind of a jerk. She thought at least she could leave.

Her MOS [Military Occupational Specialty] was 92 Alpha, Automated Logistical Specialist, like a supply sergeant. She went to basic at Fort Jackson, South Carolina, the same place I went in 1974. She went in 2002. Then she went to Fort Lee, Virginia. This was after 9/11, before the war started. That's when she met her husband, Marco. He was also going to the 92 Alpha school there.

Then they went back to Fort Bragg, North Carolina. They were ready to be deployed. They got married in July 2003. He was in a different unit and got deployed before she did. He got deployed in January 2005 and sent to Iraq. He spent eleven and a half months in Taji. That base is about an hour from Baghdad, north. It's fenced off. They maintain and fix helicopters. The most dangerous thing he did was guard duty in a tower. Once in a while, Iraqis would drive by and shoot. It was a fairly secure base. That was before the insurgency was as bad as it is now. He didn't have much interaction with the Iraqis. He came back in January 2006.

Erika was deployed in October 2005, and came back in October 2006. She had been there three weeks on Thanksgiving, and she was on her way from the mess hall, heading to the warehouse where she worked. She stopped to talk to two friends. They heard a whizzing sound: a rocket hit the building she was walking to. It was a dud. It broke some windows but didn't explode. But if she hadn't stopped to talk, she'd be dead. They were constantly being shelled, had to go into the bunkers about twice a month.

She didn't tell me. She didn't want me to worry. I had a lump in my throat the whole year she was over there. My heart would skip a beat whenever the phone rang, especially before seven or eight in the morning or after nine at night. My heart would just stop.

I'm a member of Daughters of the American Revolution. My great-grandmother was a charter member. Last summer, Erika and I were elected as delegates to vote for our chapter at the Continental Congress in D.C. She was on R&R leave from Iraq. We got an email from MFSO before we went, about Operation House Call—putting pairs of boots in front of Congress, one for each soldier that died after they decided to continue the war. Erika didn't go to Operation House Call, but she was interviewed at the hotel. MFSO did a press release to say I'd be there, along with some Gold Star families and others. The press release said, "DAR member asks Congress to bring the troops home now." We got a good article published in the *Santa Barbara News Press* about me and Erika. It really ticked off some members of my chapter that I was against the war.

At the beginning of the evening ceremonies at the Continental Congress, they have an Army or Navy band play a medley of all the different branches' anthems. When they play your song, you stand up, so people can thank you. We look around. There are twenty or thirty thousand people in this auditorium. You could count the people standing on both hands. What happened? No DARs are veterans any more. All these people, they support war but they're not participating in it. There's something wrong with this picture.

On the way back from D.C., I met this gal "San Diego Suzy," a member of Code Pink and also a DAR member, the state chair for our overseas chapters. Since then, we go to protests together. So there's at least two of us.

When Erika joined the Army, she didn't really think about it. When Marco got deployed like that, she felt, "This is craziness." But when she was deployed, I sent her counter-recruitment stuff about Code Pink and Cindy Sheehan. She started going online, doing her own research. By the time she got back from Iraq, she was full-blown anti-war. She started a chapter of Iraq Veterans Against the War when she got back. She's a student at Santa Barbara City College. Veterans For Peace has a table there every Monday. She shares the table and hands out information.

She got out of the Army in January this year, 2007. She'll be on Inactive Ready Reserve for the next three and a half years. Marco decided to re-enlist last March. She told him she wanted to get out, and if he re-enlisted she'd file for divorce. The divorce will be final in a month. The Army isn't a good place to have a relationship. Out of the two and a half or three years they've been married, they were only together about five months.

He's in the hospital right now. He was driving a Humvee near Fallujah on April 14 and he was hit by an IED. The gunner and the guy in the passenger side were killed. Both of Marco's arms were broken, and both bones in his lower leg. He had several surgeries in Germany. They were able to save his leg. He just got his Purple Heart.

He's originally from Bolivia. Latinos are pretty macho. He's telling his commander he wants to go back to Iraq and finish the job. But sometimes he talks about, they'll have to give him a desk job. He'll probably walk with a limp. He'll need lots of surgery on his arms; he'll only have about seventy percent use of his right arm. They haven't tested him for brain trauma. He's been getting fevers, infections in his leg.

He's a nice guy. He was really upset about Erika filing for divorce. I keep telling him, "You're really lucky that you got through this." He was promised U.S. citizenship when he enlisted. It's been five years and he still hasn't got it. I called the representative from Fayetteville; someone from that office will help him get citizenship.

They kind of jerked him around. All his personal items are still in Iraq. His captain said he couldn't just send him his laptop and cellphone, they have to send all or nothing; typical Army crap. They don't know if he's going back yet.

The Secretary of the Army gave him his Purple Heart. He said, "If Bush was going to give it to me, I'd save up my bedpan for several days and throw it on him." I proudly wore my Veterans For Peace button to the hospital. Everybody was really nice to me.

Nobody out there can say I'm not patriotic. The part of MFSO I like is, "Take care of the vets when they get here." I do a lot of that through DAR and the American Legion.

Some of the people in the movement, I'm a little bit disappointed. If we get so far left we can't relate to anyone, that's not a good thing. We have to understand how people think. We have to find the common ground where we can meet.

I go to church and sing in the choir. I haven't been going too often; there are a lot of outspoken right-wing people there who know I'm an anti-war activist and they give me some flak. Once in a while they'll send me an email by mistake. I write right back; I hit "reply all." When the post office came out with that Arabic stamp, this person sent out a thing to boycott the stamp, grouping all Muslims together. That's racism. It was a small fraction of fundamentalist Muslims doing these attacks, and you can't just put all Muslims in one bag. You can't blame all Muslim people for what a few of them have done.

When Barbara Walters had Jane Fonda on her program, they sent out an email bashing Fonda. I wrote back and said, "I'm a Vietnam vet and I think Fonda is a great American." We just have to stand up to these people. We can't just sit here with smoke coming out of our ears.

I'm not afraid of anybody any more. Having a daughter that spent a year in Iraq . . . Every time I meet someone who's rah-rah Bush, I ask them if they have a family member in Iraq. Of course not. They never do.

# Chapter 3
# Jessica White

*Jessica is a teacher. She met her husband just before his first deployment as part of the first invasion force in Iraq. He served another tour in Iraq, and now provides mental-health counseling for other veterans.*

Before my husband and I were even together, I had a history of protest: workers' rights, student rights. I came to UMass Boston for my undergraduate degree in 2000; I tried to unionize the cafeteria workers, unsuccessfully. I've always tried to tie human rights to the bigger picture. We spend so much on the war, and there are forty-seven million Americans without health care.

My husband joined the Army Reserves in December 1998 as an adult, twenty-seven. He joined for a few different reasons: he was patriotic; he wanted to pay off student loans; he'd been out of college, working at lower paying jobs, and didn't have a direction. We met on the weekend when he was first deployed. It was a fluke situation. It was January 2003. I was looking for a new apartment, and there was a room available in his apartment. He'd just come back to pack a few things before leaving. He was going to Fort Drum for two months, then Iraq; he was there for the invasion in 2003.

It was love at first sight. I got his email address and we corresponded.

None of my emails were political. I did support, morale-boosting, thinking-of-you, shooting the crap. I didn't know where he stood. I remember feedback from the protests in February of 2003, hearing from soldiers that they didn't like "how the American public is treating us." I was never against the people in the military, just how the U.S. government uses the institution. We can't blame the people in the military, they're just doing their job. Just like I get up and go to teach.

He emailed back. We kept it basic. We barely knew each other, we'd just met for about five minutes. It was just friendly back and forth, sporadic. Once he was in Iraq there was no internet access. He just emailed from Kuwait or Fort Drum. The first time, he was in Iraq for thirty-two or thirty-three days.

When he came back in June 2003, we hit it off immediately. We've been together ever since. I've never been so sure in my life. He had left his job about a week before deployment, came back without a job, and did construction for about a year. We were trying to save up for a house. Now he's a mental health counselor, trained in the military, in a vet center in Connecticut, counseling GWOT (Global War on Terrorism) veterans, mostly. The work comes naturally to him. That's one of the good things to come out of the military; he had first-hand experience from Iraq, and now he has training and experience.

It took him a little while to talk about the invasion. His team was with the Third Infantry. He saw some pretty rough stuff in 2003. He wasn't right on the front lines, but soldiers from the front had to be counseled after major battles. He was embedded. Guys who had just killed however many Iraqis, killed children—he wasn't fighting, but he was talking to them.

On April 15, 2003, they were sleeping in Saddam Hussein's brother's bombed-out palace. There were mortars flying in the middle of the night. They didn't think they'd live through that raid. They had no electricity. They were vulnerable, sleeping on the floor. What got him through was thinking of people back home that day, standing in line at the post office to pay taxes. It helped him get through the night. It was the most frightening night of his life.

I was still active, back in school; I graduated in July 2004. Almost accidentally, I found MFSO. I wanted an outlet, wanted to meet people in similar situations to me, that had loved ones in peril. By other military wives, I was looked at as a traitor. It's kind of one of the rules: you don't talk about politics. But I'm such a passionate person, I can't help it sometimes. They'd say, "Our men could go back to war, why don't you support our president?" I said, "All the more reason."

I knew there'd be more people like me. I don't know how I found them. Nancy [Lessin] emailed me back almost immediately. I felt such a sense of relief: finally, somebody who understands. I got on their email list and heard about events.

In April 2005, I heard of his second deployment. It's never a good time to be deployed. We already had a wedding planned for May 2006, but we pushed it up to July 2005. We got married two and a half weeks before he left. We had two months to plan the wedding. There were all these life-changing things: graduating, moving to a new place, getting married, deployment.

We didn't know anyone where we were moving, in Connecticut. I would get a teaching job, he'd be at the vet center. He left August 17, 2005, for Fort Dixon, New Jersey, and went back to Iraq in October 2005. He was there just under a year. His original eighteen-month deployment was shortened to fourteen months. If they're in country for a year, they have to get paid an additional thousand dollars a month. So, many get less. I'd much rather have him home than have the money, but it's pretty sneaky that the military does this.

It was terrible. It was a real challenge every single day. Teaching was tough. I didn't have any friends in Connecticut, or family or support network. It was extraordinarily lonely.

We spoke almost every day. He worked in a clinic with internet access and a global cellphone. That was unbelievably comforting. He had his days. He often had to be my cheerleader, I was having tough times. He had to support me; it should have been reversed. Luckily, his best friend was running the clinic with him. That was just a blessing.

But some days, he'd break down. His emotions weren't going to go on pause. I'd always remind him he had to let it out, talk about it. He tries to tell people it's okay to have these explosions but you have to learn a better way to deal. It was relatively safe where he was, on base, not traveling. He had a bed, air conditioning, plenty of food and water. He was right in Baghdad, but the base was huge. He was just outside the Green Zone, in Camp Victory, about eight miles down the road. This time, they had gyms and swimming pools. It was better than the first deployment.

I just found out an incident last night. He was with his best friend, and they thought they were being raided. Bullets came very close, hit the trailer next to them, for half an hour or forty-five minutes. They found the Iraqis were watching a soccer game and were celebrating whoever won. They had helmets on. They didn't know if it was an attack. They were screaming, panicking, planning what to do if insurgents came to the door. Now it seems kind of funny. One soldier did get injured, but not badly.

He was never against my politics or me speaking out. Usually he agrees. He'd hear buzz about what was going on. He learned to take things with a grain of salt. He'd tell me, "Jessie, don't watch the news, it'll just get you upset." He knows I always have news on in the house. He said, "Please, try not to get so caught up and be a bundle of nerves."

His training as a mental health specialist helped. Many people are emotionally scarred. I'm sure there are things he'll have to deal with, but he knows coping mechanisms to get through.

He's very angry and frustrated now. He didn't see the point of all that's gone on. Too many have been hurt, and for what? There's no good coming out of this war, just so much chaos. It's been three years, and nothing is getting better. He's pretty much on board with me. He's been in the military eight years now. He's been burnt several times by the military, constantly being told one thing, and then something else happens. He's been fighting with them for three years about student loan repayment. They paid a huge lump sum for three prior years. Then we had to pay taxes on that, and he had to pay the school. It's a constant game. You need to talk to this person, fill out this form. It's hard to fight the government.

He's leaving in December. They tried to pull this crap: if you re-enlist, everything will be taken care of. While he was in Iraq, he was supposed to get a promotion. Then they said he wouldn't get it unless he re-upped. But his contract is up. He's not re-enlisting.

I've done some interviews. The *Hartford Courant* used the title *The Anti-Military Wife*. Some woman came up to me and said, "You're betraying our country, betraying the military." She took the simple-minded patriotic view.

I don't want any wife or husband to go through this constant worrying for a war like this that's unethical and immoral. I know how it tears people up if they feel like they've been duped. At least my husband and I knew going into it that we were against the war.

His first deployment, his feelings were different. He needed to be in survival mode, see black and white. On his second deployment he was much more jaded and cynical. His line of work is a necessary occupation. That kept me going: he's helping someone today. That was the only thing I held on to.

One of my students last year said, "Is the war still going on?" I said, "If you weren't so busy watching video games, you'd know."

It won't be until the draft is re-instated that people will get involved against the war. Now it's not personal enough. You can't change people, just try to educate and enlighten them. The apathy is mind-blowing.

# Chapter 4
# John Fenton

*John and his ex-wife live in New Jersey. Their son Matthew, a Marine, died in April 2006 as a result of severe head injuries inflicted by a suicide car-bomber in Fallujah.*

I was born in Ireland. I was two years old when my mother and father brought me here with my two older brothers. We grew up in Nyack, New York. My younger sister was born here. My dad worked in a small town, in a big pharmaceutical plant. My mom worked part-time. When we were older, she became a supervisor of the janitorial staff in a hospital. When we were young and wild, I don't know how my mom did it.

I went to Temple University in Philadelphia for two years. I didn't like Philadelphia. I always thought about going back to school but I never did. I've been working for the postal service for twenty-four years; I'm hoping for early retirement shortly.

I would have been drafted during Vietnam but my number was high, 252. I was relieved. My oldest brother had a student deferment until the end of the war; he was going to Columbia. My other brother failed the physical. He had high blood pressure. He would have gone to Canada. I don't know what I would've done. I wasn't volunteering. There's no military blood in me. I'm not sure where Matt got it from.

I met Matthew's mother at work. We got married in 1980. We separated in 1991 or 1992 and now we're divorced. She lives down the road from me about half a mile. We used to get along pretty well, but not since Matthew's death. Now we don't even speak. My daughter is stuck in the middle because of Matt's death and all the hard feelings. It's a shame.

Matthew was born in 1982. He was a typical boy, into everything. He could wreck a house. He was a sweet, soft-spoken kid, a little on the shy side. He certainly got over that. He got kind of boisterous later on.

There'd be a ruckus going on, and he'd either be the cause of it or in the middle of it.

He did very well in school when he was younger. Somewhere along the way, he lost interest. He struggled through high school. He didn't have a sense of where he wanted to go. In his junior year, he told us he was thinking of joining the military. This was pre-9/11. I thought it was a good idea. There was no talk about college then. In the Marines, he started taking courses, but after 9/11 those courses were cancelled.

He went in September 2000. I remember saying to myself, "There's nothing going on anywhere in the world." He was in supply and something, I forget the phrase. When he got to Iraq, it didn't seem to matter. He was a regular grunt. He was in administration for his first MOS; he went to Fort Deven in Ayres, Massachusetts. He was a lower-level liaison between the Marines and the Army. He was always working on computers. I'd ask what he was doing, but I didn't understand it.

He would come home quite often. He was dating a girl here and actually got married. They'd come by about every other weekend. His wife walked out on him; she decided she didn't like the military life. That was quite a blow to him. She was nineteen. She was just too young.

He was told around Thanksgiving 2005 that he was going to Iraq. He had to go to Twentynine Palms for desert training. He came home for Christmas and went back. He was only in Iraq for six or seven weeks. It was his first tour, in early March 2006.

Matt called me once. I remember he was outside of Fallujah. He said it was absolutely beautiful, there were mountains in the distance. But in the city, it was disgusting. The city was in shambles, dirty, just a big mess. I believe we did that: leveled Fallujah. It was a disaster area. They say Fallujah is under control now, but there's nothing there to control.

He was in touch with his mother through email. I didn't have a computer. A year ago, I didn't know anything about email, I couldn't turn on a computer. Until he died, I didn't know how far out of touch I was. I could have emailed him if I'd known. I'll always regret that. I did write him a letter that, as far as I know, he never got.

*[John wrote the following about his son's death.]*

On April 26, Matthew, twenty-four, was the gunner on a Humvee protecting a Marine convoy on the outskirts of Fallujah. A suicide car bomber attempted to ram his Humvee and he got off a few shots at the vehicle. From what I have been told it is common practice for these bombers to detonate their bomb if they come under fire. Matthew was the only Marine injured in the attack. Later that same day I received a phone call telling me that Matt was seriously wounded and that it was a head injury.

The next day we were informed that Matt had been flown to Germany. Matt's mother, Diane, and I prepared to go to Germany. But in the middle of trying to get a flight, we received another call saying that he had stabilized and they were going to fly him to the United States. We were all lifted by this seemingly good news.

Diane and I flew to Washington the next day and were met by a uniformed Marine and driven to Bethesda. What awaited us there is still shocking to me now. We met with two doctors who laid everything out for us. Matthew's injury was a devastating one. Shrapnel had entered his head just above his left eye, traveled diagonally through his brain, and exited the right rear.

Surgeons in Baghdad had removed two plates from his skull to help relieve the pressure from the swelling of his brain. The frontal lobe was destroyed, so they had removed it. It was explained to us that the frontal lobe is the center of personality, the place where someone is aware of themselves. The Matthew that we knew and loved was gone and would never come back.

As we struggled with that staggering news there was more to come. The shrapnel had done severe damage to both sides of Matt's brain because of the angle that it traveled through. The doctors told us that if this had happened in Vietnam, there would have been no surgery. If this happened in front of the best hospital in New York City, there would have been no surgery. His chances of ever having meaningful movement were less than slim.

Why, we asked, was the surgery done in Baghdad? The answer was that surgeons do whatever they can to keep a soldier alive. They do not decide life or death.

We were then led down a long hospital corridor toward my son's room. This is the moment that I will never forget until the day I die. He was unrecognizable. His head was completely swollen, like some cartoon character. There were maybe hundreds of metal staples in his head. There were of course tubes coming and going everywhere. There were drains running from the site of the surgery. And there was the ventilator. I immediately snapped at the doctors. Somewhere along the line I had been informed that Matt was breathing on his own. Nine years ago I watched my father die after having lung cancer surgery. He never got off of the ventilator, and I flashed back to that time.

Matthew was able to breathe on his own, the doctors explained. The ventilator was only assisting. His heart and lungs were perfect. There had been no damage to his brain stem, which controls involuntary actions like breathing and the heart beating. So there we were looking at our son, not recognizing him, not a scratch on him below his eye, but his face and head mangled and inflated. This must be a nightmare, one that we will never wake up from.

For days we made that walk down that long hallway. It took some time but I finally was able to look at some of the other Marines on the ward with Matthew. I wish to this moment that I hadn't. Kids with horrible injuries.

One had been in the ward for eleven months, after seven different brain surgeries. His wife refused to let him go. She was praying for a miracle. He had parts of his skull removed also, but all the swelling was gone now and his head had sunken in where they had been removed. He did not move at all.

Across the ward another Marine was in his third month, and his head was all sunken in. This is what lay ahead for Matthew. Also across the ward was another Marine who was there only a few days before Matt. He was lucky; he had damage to only one side of his brain. I became friendly with his father, Jim, from Tennessee. One day there was an uproar from his son's room and I looked over and made eye contact with Jim. Maybe an hour later we met in the hallway and he apologized to me. His son had opened his eyes for the first time and his family just responded. There was no need for an apology as I would have jumped for joy if Matthew were to open his eyes.

All that was left was to decide when the life support would be removed. That final decision rested in the hands of his mother. There was no disagreement on what course to follow, just when.

On May 3, the Marine Corps commandant presented Matthew with his Purple Heart. On May 4, I noticed that the swelling of Matthew's head was going down. By the end of the day the indentations where pieces of his skull were missing were becoming noticeable. The next morning I was dreading what he might be looking like. And, yes, there was his head becoming very odd-shaped.

I prayed that Diane would find the strength to let her son go today. I did not want to see him decline another day. Another day of watching his head sink into his skull. And neither did she. Sometime around noon on May 5, Matthew was moved from the ward to a private room. Behind some curtains they removed the ventilator and most of the tubes. He was kept on the morphine, and we were assured he would not feel any pain. Now he was breathing all on his own. Diane got into the hospital bed with her son, and I held his hand and we all waited and watched for Matthew to pass.

But he would not go easily. After three hours of labored breathing, I asked the nurse if there was anything that she could do. No. I asked God to take him now. No. His mother told him to go. I asked him to go. Go to some peace. A half-hour later, he finally took his last breath.

I met two people in Bethesda. One was [then-Secretary of Defense] Rumsfeld. He happened to be on a visit to the hospital while my son was there. His room had a glass wall. Rumsfeld approached my son's bed and stopped and was looking at him. He was pretty hard to look at. Rumsfeld said, "Oh, my." He turned and asked if I was the father. "I guess you're having a tough time." I wanted to grab him and choke him. That was the most asinine thing he could have said. It seemed like such a cold comment. He was surrounded by security. I leaned in and said, "You have to put an end to all this." He said, "We're trying."

A few days later, this man comes to the bed. He shook my hand. Looking down at Matt, he said, "This is terrible." He said he was sorry he hadn't been able to stop it, but he was trying. It was Jack Murtha [the Democratic representative from Pennsylvania, best known for calling for withdrawal of American troops from Iraq].

These two men . . . One did not care about Matt; Rumsfeld was so flippant. Murtha came in with nobody around him; he said Matt this, Matt that; he knew his story. He cared enough to find out. We'd decided to remove Matt from life support. Murtha said, "You're doing the right thing for Matthew." He took the trouble to find out what was going on.

Before Matt died, I read the paper and watched the news. Like a lot of people, with the WMDs and 9/11, I thought we had to go. When the truth started to come out, I changed my opinion. By the time Matt went, I thought we should already have gotten out of Iraq. I'd never speak out. I might get into a heated argument, but would never go to a rally. It never entered my head.

A couple of months after Matt died, my brother, a lawyer in Indiana, wrote a letter to the editor of a paper out there about Bethesda. Somehow, the head of the local MFSO here picked it up and called me, asked if I'd be interested in joining. This was about four months after Matthew's passing. I met her and another woman at a restaurant, and we talked. I started going to the vigil every Wednesday night at the Teaneck Armory. I've been there pretty much every week. People hold signs. I just hold my son's picture.

My daughter will be nineteen in November. She just finished her freshman year. She's come to the vigil once and stood with Matt's picture. She feels kind of in the middle, and I don't want to pressure her.

I go to a doctor at the VA about once a week, a counselor. Since I'm not a vet, I wasn't sure I could. He told me, "You need to talk about it, display your emotions." When I joined the group, that's what I did. I've done public speaking, written letters, been on television. I just talk about Matthew and what happened to him.

If they make it to Bethesda, they usually end up surviving. Not too many make it to Bethesda, and then—nothing. He was so far gone. There was no hope. I got to see those other kids and it was so disturbing to me. I need to talk about that. I definitely feel better. These people have listened to my story and they're very supportive. I've become friends with a good number of them.

The head of our chapter is a throwback to the peaceniks of Vietnam. When she told me she went to demonstrations in D.C. in '67, it didn't surprise me. She's a sweetheart of a woman. At first she protected me, wouldn't let me get too involved. She watched out for me with the media. She's been a great help to me.

I was in shock for months, numbed to everything. I'm out of that. I'm proceeding along day by day. That's all I can do.

I've been asked, do I think we need to stay in Iraq to honor my son's memory. That's the biggest bunch of hooey I ever heard. I need more kids to die to make me feel better? I don't get that.

The differences between me and my ex, that's one of them. Me holding up Matt's picture has shown up in the paper on occasion. Before we stopped talking, she asked me not to use Matthew's image in my antiwar activities. I couldn't agree to that. That's all I have.

I certainly know I'm not dishonoring him in any way, shape or form. She's against the war, but she doesn't want to dishonor Matthew's choice. I honor his choice to join the military. But he shouldn't have been where he was, and these other kids shouldn't be there either.

# Chapter 5
# Sarah Tyler

*Sarah's son Ben is a combat photojournalist. He has served two tours in Iraq with the Army Third Infantry Division, Second Combat Brigade, and is now a sergeant. His most recent tour has been extended from one year to fifteen to eighteen months.*

I grew up in the Boston area, in Wellesley. My father was a minister. That came with its own set of expectations. He wasn't paid very much, so we were not part of Wellesley society, although my parents' friends were pretty influential people. My father was the assistant rector at Trinity Church in Boston, so he had a big job and a lot of people were attracted to him because of that, and his personality. Growing up in that environment and with my father's position, there were high expectations in terms of behavior, education, so we all have been very well educated.

There were four kids in my family. A pretty dysfunctional family: both parents alcoholics, verbally abusive. Since my father was a minister we were always expected to present this perfect front, the four of us, and it was far from perfect. So it was not a very good childhood. I vowed that it would be better for my kids.

I married a lawyer, had two kids, found out he was having an affair, and got divorced when the kids were very little. So I raised the kids pretty much single-handedly, Benjamin and Elizabeth. It was very hard, even though I was lucky that my husband, as a lawyer, made a lot of money, and financially we were okay. The kids were able to go to the best schools. He always felt very strongly about education too, so he certainly did provide for them. But it didn't make for a very stable growing-up.

Our divorce was very difficult for my kids, especially for my son Ben, the soldier. After he was in fifth or sixth grade, he got in all this trouble at school, basically not doing any work. He was bored by everything. He was extremely bright, had an off-the-charts IQ. He had a very rough time. By the time he was in ninth grade, he was kicked out of two schools I think, but his father and I found a wonderful school for him in upstate New York, Darrow School, that really turned his life around. Even though he got into a lot of trouble there, nothing malicious, just doing the crazy pranks and things that boys do. I think the headmaster's happiest day was the day that Ben graduated.

Then Ben went off to Goucher College. He wanted to go to Bennington, but in his typical contrarian way, he didn't answer the essay question on the Bennington application. He wrote a different essay that was very good and well-written and everything in its own way but had nothing to do with what they had asked for. I was very disappointed that he did that, but that was just the way Ben was, he would always be the contrarian and do the opposite.

So he went to Goucher and ended up flunking out there. I don't think he ever went to any classes. But he had discovered photography when he was at Darrow School, and he decided to go to New England School of Photography in Boston to try to get some credentials to develop his interest. He did make it through that, he did really well; he liked it a lot. But then he spent a year kind of flopping around the Fenway, working in a photo store, developing friends and things like that. And he realized that in the field he wanted to be in, photojournalism, it would take him years and years and years to become a photojournalist.

So when he was about twenty-three, after thinking about it for a long time, he decided to go into the military with the specific goal of getting a job as a photojournalist. The military actually has those jobs; they have very few. But he interviewed with the Marines and the Army; I think that was it. He decided he didn't want to be a Marine because he felt that they just wanted killers.

The Army at that time just had one slot for a photojournalist in the entire country. Ben's father and I were very, very upset, totally against it, we couldn't believe it. The recruiter couldn't believe that he was getting a boy who had been very well educated, gone to prep school, came from a fairly affluent background. He said they just don't get kids like that. He was trying to dissuade Ben from doing it. He was trying to play the devil's advocate, because he didn't know if it would be a good match. He didn't realize that when Ben makes up his mind to do something, he's gonna do it all the way, and he's already thought the whole thing out, and had studied it—which he had.

He took the test and of course he passed everything. He got the job as the combat photojournalist, in 2003. He was kind of nervous that they might have just used it as a ploy to recruit him. At the same time, the recruiter was very skeptical of Ben, even though he's physically fit and everything.

Anyway Ben went in, went to boot camp, and absolutely loved it. He said it was the only time in his life he would ever get that chance to be so fit. He absolutely loved all the crazy things they make them do, the endurance, all the tests. His friends said, if they didn't have to stay in the Army, they'd do it for the boot camp. When they're that age, they want to do it; it's a big challenge. They're young and healthy and they can meet it, eventually they can become that physically fit.

He went to Army journalism school just outside of D.C. He ended up at Fort Stewart, Georgia, in public affairs, and ran the Army newspaper for the base there, and also contributed to other Army publications. He did a lot of photography. He got some awards for it. He continued to get really good training, and did all the combat training.

He was lucky that he went in when he did, because he had two solid years of very intense combat training, urban guerilla warfare, desert warfare. He loved all of it. He loved going out to the Mojave Desert and sleeping on the ground.

I left out one thing about Ben that's kind of important, and in a way encapsulates the kind of guy he is. The winter before he decided to go into the Army, in 2002, Ben was foundering. He never wanted to take up any space or move in with anyone, so he ended up camping out the entire winter on a mountainside in upstate New York on the grounds of the school he had gone to.

He had friends there. One of the teachers there and his family had become really lifelong friends, like a second family, or maybe his first family. I think he'd say they were his first. They at least had a house there; he could go in and take a shower or sleep on the couch or whatever. But he literally lived on this mountainside all winter. I went to his campsite. Sometimes he would call me on his cellphone.

He absolutely adored it. It was very hard. It was a very cold winter and we had a lot of snow. But that was just part of Ben's conditioning himself. He's very iconoclastic, doing his own thing. He's not a compromiser. There was nothing I could do about him; there's never been anything I could do about him.

He had great training. Then we became more and more involved in the war. It was pretty clear that Ben was going to go to war. Then in the summer of 2004, Ben's father died, very suddenly. We just found out he had metastatic liver cancer on June 15, and he was dead July 15. Both of the kids were on their way to see him when he died. They had seen him a week before.

Ben had a very ambivalent relationship with his father. His father never did anything with him. Even though his father was a huge baseball fan and fisherman, he never did any of that with Ben. I think the preparation for going to war blocked out any chance to grieve.

He was in the Third Infantry Division that flew into Baghdad in January 2005 and returned in December 2005. The entire time he was in combat with the Second Combat Brigade. He did over 130 raids. He was a combat photojournalist. He wasn't over there in khaki pants and a blue polo shirt, he was fighting alongside his buddies, with the same weapons and everything; he just had a big camera as well. He took a lot of incredible photos of Baghdad and the war. A lot were classified and I've never seen them, but he was able to send a lot home through the internet.

Being a photojournalist, he had his own computer satellite hookup, which was very convenient. He lived in a bombed-out Iraqi Army base with his buddies. He shared a room with three or four other guys. One was his senior officer, who he got along with very well. This was in Baghdad, Sadr City.

It was very intense. They had some rough times. He wrote me at one point they were surrounded by an angry mob that was armed. I think there were about seven soldiers; they were armed too. But it was a huge, huge, angry Iraqi mob. They had been trained in some kind of crowd evasion maneuver, but they tried that and then they really thought it was going to be the end, but then the next thing they knew this huge Bradley tank came rolling up and they were rescued. But the fact that they did 130 raids and in every single raid he could have died, so many of these soldiers were dying—I was out of my mind.

I went into such a deep depression, I could hardly stand it. I ended up having to go get a lot of medication, just to be able to get through it, because I was just barely functioning. Luckily I was able to do my job. I've always worked in healthcare and healthcare administration. It was very familiar to me so it was easy for me to do my job. I was so, so busy all the time with my job, I didn't think about it that much during the day, but the rest of the time I felt like my entire life was on hold. I never took any vacation. I just couldn't imagine going on vacation while my son was being shot at. They were targets for the snipers.

He really was in the middle of the whole thing. Another thing about Ben is, he never ever complained about anything, except maybe about dust storms or drinking warm bottled water.

He came home in December 2005. My daughter and I went down to meet him in Georgia. It was the happiest day in my life aside from the day he was born. I didn't want to let him out of my sight. It was quite a sight to see these three hundred soldiers marching in formation on this huge football field at Fort Stewart.

He'd gone through so much in his life because of his father's and my situation, and his general rebelliousness, and getting kicked out of school, that kind of thing, and he's very, very sensitive, and I was very worried about him. He was absolutely fine. But I know he saw horrible things, indescribable things. He would never tell me, but he did say blood was running in the streets. I know he saw it all. He saw his buddies shot. But Ben was the same old Ben. He's just a totally wacky guy, who will tell you the worst thing you could imagine and be laughing the whole time. He usually enjoys the ridiculousness of the situation. He's got a great sense of irony. He just has incredible reserves. He was actually fine.

His first stop was the cellphone store. The next stop was to buy batteries for his car. Then we went into Savannah. My daughter and Ben and I spent a weekend there in an apartment. He just gloried in taking a shower that wasn't a hundred parts sewage or something, and sleeping in a bed with comfortable pillows. I remember we went out and bought pillows for Ben so he'd have just the right kind. We cooked his favorite things. He was happy as can be; he was just fine.

For the next year, he was at Fort Stewart working on the newspaper. Actually for the first five months after they arrived, they didn't have anything for the soldiers to do, so he didn't even have to show up for work, although he did show up—there would be some kind of formality, he would do PT [physical training], but he was basically on his own. And that was fine with him, because he had rented an old dump of a home out in the middle of nowhere in rural Georgia, the kind of place where everybody lived in trailers, except Ben had a house that seriously would have been condemned if it hadn't been so far out in the country. So he lived there, did a lot of gardening and things like that, fishing, canoeing, kayaking. Then they had to go back to work after about five months.

He was running *The Frontline*, the base's newspaper, again, and had a couple of people working for him. Then they started getting ready to go back to Iraq. Actually, he knew that he was going back to Iraq the second time before he left Iraq the first time, except it was supposed to be June or July 2007. He left on March 13. Then they became part of the surge.

Ben's amazingly strong, and he went back over there uncomplainingly, except that he was working twenty-one hours a day—they were compressing three months of training into three weeks. Ben's concern was that the younger soldiers, who had just enlisted, wouldn't get the full benefit of combat training the way he did. He was very concerned about that.

I guess the way I can describe him now is, when I dropped him off at the Army recruiter's in February 2003, he was a skinny, gangly, bald-headed kid, and he's turned into a completely responsible, strong man who is very concerned about other people and concerned about doing the right thing. I attribute that to growing up; and of course going to war changed him, in the sense that it forced him to really grow up and become a real man. And he is. He's a sergeant. He takes responsibility now for himself and for other people, and feels very protective of the soldiers who work for him. I think he's very grateful that he's had the training that the Army's given him.

So I'm very lucky. I think Ben went through PTSD when he was a child, I really do, despite how hard I tried to make those things not happen.

Now I don't have to worry so much because he's on a base, at Camp Victory, and his lieutenant colonel decided to have Ben work at headquarters for him in public affairs. Also they do a lot of strategy. I don't think Ben's involved in strategy so much, but I think he's involved in transfer of information. He's very disappointed that he's not in combat. He knows how happy I am. But I think once they've gone over there, they miss that adrenaline rush. That's what they want. I know he missed it when he came back. He wanted to go back in combat again. But his superiors reassigned him. So he's there. They're sleeping in big tents. He doesn't complain about anything except that he's bored silly with his job.

He won't talk to me about the war. He really gets annoyed. Even though he knows the war is a huge mistake and based on lies and everything else, he says, "Once you get over there, Mom, it's different, and civilians can't possibly understand." He really pushes me away whenever I ask him any questions. He knew right away the fallacy of the whole thing. He referred to it in one email as the administration making pawns of the Iraqis and the soldiers for George Bush's failed energy policy. He reads a lot, and he gets it. And his officers get it too.

When you think that all of this bickering in Congress now over funding something that has been proven to be based on fabricated, deliberate lies—every reason for going to war has been disproven, and there's more and more coming out all the time—I don't know why somebody can't just stand up and say, "Whoa, let's go back, why did we go over there?" Okay: the uranium from Niger, that was a lie; the Weapons of Mass Destruction, that was a lie; Saddam and Osama bin Laden, that was a lie;

the aluminum tubes, that was a lie. It was all a bunch of lies. To me, that invalidates the resolution [allowing Bush to go to war].

Ben's deployment has been extended. He's in for fifteen to eighteen months, but I have a feeling it'll go longer. At that point he'll be part of a stop-loss; he will have exceeded his time, five years, that he signed up for.

I was never politically active, even though I was in college in the late '60s when everything was going on. I think the reason I wasn't was because I was very afraid. A lot of it was very dangerous. A lot of the protests became violent, and there was shooting and everything, and I was afraid of it. But I was always against the Vietnam War.

And I was definitely against Iraq, right from the very start. The whole idea was so preposterous to me. I read a lot about it before the war happened. I read some of *The Nation* articles that brought up all the reasons that had been disproven even before the war. I was paying a lot of attention. I was very much against it. But I would never, ever have believed that we could have gotten to this point where we are now, where we're perpetuating this huge lie, when we know it's false. It's hard to even imagine how we could do this, that we could not have people speaking out about it, except of course for writers, op-ed pieces, that sort of thing. I'm not sure the American public gets it. They don't want to know. That's my feeling: they just don't want to know.

Right after Ben got back in January 2006, that's when I found out about MFSO. I had had no support during that first deployment. I didn't know anybody who was in a similar situation, just because it's Boston, and there isn't a lot of military awareness here. There just wasn't any support. It's not part of people's daily lives.

In September 2005, before Ben came back, I was down in Washington D.C. for the big march, and MFSO was there. It was wonderful, I really loved it. I got in touch with them as soon as I got back home. Last summer, George W. was in Kennebunkport, Maine, for a family wedding. We had a very peaceful march, probably about a thousand people. It was a beautiful day. The chief of police led the whole march in his police car with the little blue light going. There were scary-looking secret service men all along the way, but there weren't any other police.

It wasn't like in Boston, where they bring out the motorcycle brigades, they bring out the biggest horses they have, they bring out the helicopters, and I just want to say to them, "This is just a bunch of middle-aged parents and we're sick about our kids."

So much money, almost four hundred and twenty billion dollars so far, could be going into healthcare, health insurance for people who don't have it. We could house the homeless; we could feed the hungry; we could upgrade our schools; we could develop and expand all kinds of youth programs. That of course is on my mind, because I feel that crumbling. So much money has been diverted. I think what really got me going was just the total injustice of this whole thing. I was just infuriated by what this administration has gotten away with, and to see my child and other people's children being put in harm's way by a simple-minded president, and horrible people who work around him, for their own personal goals—the whole thing is inexplicable, it's mind boggling. That's why I'm active. I'm so angry.

And then it was a way I could be with people who are experiencing the same thing. Because outside of MFSO, it's just life as usual. Life goes on. I feel, and I think other people feel it too, that with your kid over there, your life just goes on hold.

Ben's joining the Army—he really had a goal, to jumpstart a career, so he would not have to go through what anybody else would have to go through to be a photojournalist, he would not have to take pictures of weddings or children or whatever, and so that he could get the training. And because of the training and the fantastic experience he had, plus the fact that he's been conditioned and hardened in combat, in a war zone, he's got a lot of credibility now. He certainly feels that he's made incredible contacts with all the wire services and the news groups that come over—he has usually ended up either taking people around his base in Georgia, dignitaries or the press—to Ben, it's a totally practical thing. He wanted to be in the worst place in the world.

I have a feeling that he's going to be doing this for the rest of his life. So I just have to harden myself to it, because he's really happy with what he's doing. He is not happy about war; he doesn't like the war, he doesn't like what they had to do; but he has no regrets. So I'm really lucky. It's been a great experience for Ben. Going down the road, I'm sure that it will come back and haunt him in a way, it has to eventually, but I'm confident that he's strong enough to handle anything.

# Chapter 6
# Sarah Fuhro

*Sarah lives in Natick, Massachusetts. Her parents were radicals, and she has been politically active in left-wing causes most of her life. Her son served in Iraq for a year with the Army Reserves.*

My son was born in 1971. We also had a daughter from my first marriage. Our children were raised amid anti-war, civil rights politics. My son went to demonstrations in his stroller. He shared those values all the way along. He wouldn't even sign up for selective service registration when he was eighteen.

School for him was really hard, although he graduated with decent grades. A friend kept saying, "I think he's ADD [attention deficit disorder]." He had no behavior problems at school, so teachers wouldn't catch on at first. But he did no work. He would be great in class, being in discussions, having great ideas. I would always get all these wonderful reports, but then they would say, "But he hasn't handed in a book report for six weeks." He was wonderful at home. We had no idea he wasn't doing his homework. He said he had done it.

After high school, he took a series of odd jobs. He was a tournament champion fencer. He would do things like coaching fencing, but when I would say something like, "Well, why don't you go to Brookline High and suggest that you become a fencing coach, so you would have a real job and a real salary," he'd say, "They don't have coaching." I'd say, "They might get into that; you can do this—having always been an entrepreneur." "No, no, no, no."

He didn't go to college right away, and then went to Arizona State University in his mid-twenties. He came out with a huge debt. It was like the homework; all along we kept saying, "Do you need money for tuition?" "No, I'm fine, I don't want you to pay, I'm going late, I can take care of it, I have a job and I'm getting financial aid." The financial aid turned out to be huge loans. We were totally out to lunch. We just heard

33

him saying that it was okay, he was doing what he needed to do. And he wasn't.

We said, "Okay, we'll take out a loan against our house." He said, "No, I don't want you to do that." The next thing we know, he's joined the Army Reserves. And that's gonna solve everything.

He said, "I'll learn mental health training and they're going to pay my loans. And then I get college tuition." But any time he tried to go to school, first of all, the Army never pays until a year and a half after you're done. So he was supposed to get this money up front somehow. Again, refusing to take our money. I still don't know what to do with him. He's my grown-up son, and he's still a mystery to both of us. We can't figure out how to help him. We can't figure out how to get out of his way.

The mental health training turned out to be great. For about three years, he worked with mentally-ill teenagers, and did very well at that. But he was making twelve dollars and fifty cents an hour, part-time, barely skimping by.

He loved the Army; I could see that. It gave him the kind of structure that an ADD person needs. He hated going to camp, even, and suddenly he loves the Army. It was very confusing. I still have his camp letters: "Get me out! My upper-bunkmate is a knee-biter!"

At this point, he didn't really expect to be called. He joined before 9/11. Iraq was going to be a fast war, and he was in the Reserves. But it made me feel like, my son is putting his life on the line for this country in the way that he thinks is right, and I need to put my life on the line for this country too, and this is how I need to do it, to get very involved in the anti-war movement. I didn't know about MFSO until he got his deployment notice. I was just involved in the general vigils or writing letters.

Meanwhile, I get arrested the first day of the war, in Natick. I'd just moved there, and that's how I got to meet all the people I really wanted to meet in Natick, getting arrested and going to jail with them. I'd been vigiling with this group of people on Saturdays for almost a year against the war coming up, and when I went to the Common, they said we're going to go down to this Army base. It turned out these people from the Peace Abbey had already planned to be arrested, and had told the police they would be. They did peace prayers from different traditions. Then they said they were going to go liberate the soldiers from the fort by walking into the fort when they'd been told they couldn't go in. So the police arrested all of them, and then three more of us said, "You should arrest us too." So we joined up.

We had a big trial that went on all day long with this wonderful judge who let us ramble on and on. The district attorney was so mad at her. In between, she'd handle shoplifters or domestic violence or whatever needed a pretrial hearing. We were found guilty. Then we did community service.

For the first time, my son and I had a painful run-in about the issue. Not because I got arrested; he was fine with what I was doing. But he wanted to say that somehow the war was okay, that Saddam Hussein had been bad for the Iraqis; he was really having trouble with it. If I would try to say anything back to him, he'd say, "Okay, I know, I know."

I had to learn to just listen to my son's way of looking at things. I couldn't address it, really. He didn't want to quit the Army. He wanted those things that it offered him, and I understood that. Then it was several more years before he was going to be called up. He'd already told me it was inevitable. He was going to go with his mental health unit, and they were going to be helping people with stress. He clearly wanted to go.

I brought him to talk with the guy at the Peace Abbey, because I felt like he should know what his legal rights are, and what other people's legal rights are who he might be counseling, who might feel like they should not be there. I think he was trying to project his idea of what I wanted onto me, and I was trying to project something else onto him. It was hard. As much as we really get along very well, and enjoy each other's company, it was difficult. When he left for Iraq, I had no idea how bad it was going to be. I always say MFSO saved me.

One of the things that hit me was, he went off for training in July of '05, and while he was there, Katrina came along. Here are all these stress workers—he's trained as an EMT [emergency medical technician] for the Army too, and there's a medical unit, and he says to his captain, "Aren't we going to go down there to help?" And the captain said, "No, we're not; that's for FEMA [the Federal Emergency Management Agency]. They have stress workers too." They have two, for the whole Gulf.

Just before he left, there was a big demonstration in Washington that I went to with my grandson. That was really wonderful, to be there; that's where I met the MFSO people, I think.

Emails were very sparse, very tersely written. He called once, and that was a very bad connection. I asked him if I could send him a telephone card so he could call more, and he said no. So that was that.

Whenever he talked about the war he said it was bad. But he couldn't stand to have me say that it was bad, even though he knew enough about me to know that was inevitably what I would say. I had to stop sending him anything to do with the war. That was all I thought about and all I talked about; I was wearing everybody else down with it too. I had to just stop it. So that meant I'd send him cute animal pictures or a picture of his nephew.

He was stationed in two places. One was a big base with a big hospital on it. He got to see that whole thing with the contractors and the swimming pools and the golf courses and drinking, which the soldiers are not allowed to do—you can't have a beer after work.

I came the closest to having a nervous breakdown that I've ever had. I think a lot of that energy went into MFSO work. I'd constantly be meeting other parents in much worse situations: either their child was dead, or their child was there for the fourth or fifth time, or their child was wounded. I came to have so much admiration for these people, many of whom are from the military or support the military. Every time I'd go to something that had to do with the Army, like graduation from medical training, it was a real diverse group of people, and a lot of wonderful people, and I appreciated that he loved that, and that he felt he was dealing with people who really needed help from his mental health unit. I went to Washington a couple of times, to talk to Congress and see how politics works or doesn't work.

Then his year was up. When he came back, he was so armored, and so stressed. My son was just exploding with anger. And then when I would say anything against the war, he would turn on me and scream at me. It was really bad. I never saw him like that before. He apologized to me two or three times after that happened, but it was very difficult. He stayed with us a couple of days before moving back in with his cousin, and the second night he was there, my husband got up early in the morning and looked, and there was water coming through all the electric fixtures. Our kid had turned on the faucets in the bathroom with the plug in and never turned them off. It felt so symbolic of the amount of emotion that couldn't go anywhere.

It was really hard for him to come to Thanksgiving because there were too many people. He had to see people two at a time. He was totally stressed out in every possible way.

He's just living on unemployment. When I ask him, doesn't he want to look for work as a mental health worker, he says, "I can't do it." So I don't know where he's going, what he's going to do.

If you met him, you wouldn't get any of this, though. He's thirty-six. He's a grownup. He saw a therapist through someplace called the Vet Center, a student social worker. He said, "This guy has no idea what he's doing. But it's someone for me to talk to that isn't involved with me; I just need to talk." Now he says he's going to join a veterans from Iraq group, which is a really good idea.

He has three more years in Reserves. This is what they threaten you with, okay? His term was up in Iraq, which meant he would have had to stay on but not really be in the Army. They don't send you home when your term is up, you have to stay on. But it's now known that you're not re-upping. So you're really treated like shit, first of all. Secondly, you can be on call-up Reserve, reserve Reserves, indefinitely if you do that. Whereas if you sign up again, you're not on the bottom of the shit list. They promise you that the end of three years will be the end; you won't be on the shadow Reserves, you won't be back-door-drafted.

He was in Iraq from October 13, 2005; he went on Yom Kippur, and came back October 15, 2006. He's just now starting to do Reserves meetings again. Reserves is a crime to him anyway, they do nothing. They sit around on a bench. They're supposed to work in a mental hospital, but they don't. They tell you you're going to do all these really helpful things and then it's nothing. They once spent an entire Reserve weekend telling them how to wear the new beret, what were the advantages of the new beret.

My husband does some things with MFSO. He doesn't like to do groups or organized stuff. He's very much against the war, but he's also very supportive of our son. He's cheerful to relate to, for our son, on the level of, "Let's play cribbage." It's very hard for him too. It just tears your body apart. You think you're not thinking about it . . . I lost fifteen pounds. I couldn't sleep. I was completely wacky. Luckily I have good friends at MFSO where people were even wackier. And they could keep me very busy. I started doing a lot of writing and publishing. I upped my client list a lot; I work as an astrologer and flower essence practitioner. If I was with a client, I was in a totally different space, and that was good.

*[I ask how she responds to the idea that you can't support the troops without supporting the war.]* We don't send people to their deaths to support them. Our sons and daughters have chosen service to their country, and this war is not service to our country; it may be hurting our security. They are really hurting their souls and their hearts and their psyches. If this were a straightforward thing, and they felt fine, if my son told me that they were doing great things in Iraq, I would have nothing to say about that. What he used to say to me was, "Really, I know less about the war than you do because I'm cooped up here." He would occasionally go out and get people who needed help.

In a sense, when I do MFSO work, I'm working along with my son, because I'm with the families of other people who were there. We've been tremendous support for each other. MFSO really has allowed people's creativity to come out, and to blossom. I've seen people who've never done any political work before getting up there and making speeches, doing all kinds of amazing things. I have to say how much I respect the Gold Star families. I can't imagine, if my son died, that I could just go on day after day. They're some of the most active people. They say they do it because it's the only way they can heal their grief, but I still admire them for being able to do it.

# Chapter 7
# Tiki Fuhro

*Tiki, a middle-school drama teacher in Maine and mother of two, is Sarah Fuhro's daughter. I met Tiki and her daughter at a peace march in Boston. Tiki's brother served a year in Iraq and will be in the Army Reserves until 2009.*

I'm a lot older than my brother, about nine years. We're not close in the traditional way. I was like a babysitter/extra mother for him. From when he was born until I went to college, we spent a lot of time together. I just adored him, but as a teenager I went off to do my own thing. When I went to college, I was seventeen and he was in elementary school. When I left, it was a problem for him, being an only kid.

Our day-to-day relationship became diffused by distance. I never lived at home after that for a long period of time. As a result, he has a peer group that feels like a different generation. There have been times when I've thought, "Oh, I'm just another mother, I take on a parental role," and so I don't say anything.

I went to NYU and studied theater. I continued to live in New York City and Brooklyn for about twenty years. I started as an actor, and transitioned into teaching theater in a program for middle and high school students. Now I'm a summer arts camp director and teach middle-school drama part-time in a private school. I have two children, fourteen and eleven. They're close to my brother. My son, especially, looks up to him. They have similar interests.

My brother has unusual talents. He was a fencer and did martial arts in high school. He continues to be a referee in fencing. My son just started first-year fencing. He's interested in history and politics. My daughter enjoys her uncle but is not as connected through interests. At different points in their childhood, he wasn't living close by. We moved back to New England seven years ago.

Until recently, I was just a little bit politically active. I started teaching in a poor neighborhood. I channeled my social consciousness through my work. I worked for a foster care prevention agency; they did a lot of preventive programming, and arts were part of that. There was a lot of fulfillment in my work, enriching kids' lives through an environment that wouldn't have existed otherwise.

When we moved to Maine, I got a job at a private school. I had no familiarity with that, but I could teach what I knew how to teach. I kept volunteering at the public school where my kids were. I wasn't political until my brother went to Iraq. Him going to Iraq, plus the current climate, has woken me up to being more politically active and aware.

As a parent, I'm always having to make decisions that seem political in regard to schooling and social issues. People ask why my kids go to public school. It's part financial; but private school is elite and it isn't fair. I've also stepped up in a local way, on school budgets, that kind of thing. If it's in my face long enough, I'll write a letter or something.

*[I ask when she knew her brother would join the military.]* We knew at least five years before the war started. It felt like, for him, joining the military was a pragmatic decision, taking care of very bad debts he'd accumulated over the years. The concept of a war that would put him into combat as a reservist seemed very remote. I was pretty shocked by his decision initially. My mother was upset.

Different people in my family talked to him. We're a very peace-oriented family. We're social activists. The thought of being part of the military is way off. Maybe we've had the luxury and means to live that way. The way my brother struggled with finding a place for himself, he needed a place to help him get focused and learn skills. Military training gave him a lot of self-confidence. It was clear from the beginning that he was a star. He was well-educated, older than a lot of people there. For a long time, I thought this was really a great thing for him.

His medical and psychological training—he was doing so well with it. It made him feel very successful. He sacrificed a lot of personal time for all his training. He hadn't succeeded in the traditional academic path that others in our family have. He felt, "This is something I'm doing well." He felt good about himself regarding his military experience.

When 9/11 happened and Bush went into Iraq, the prospect of my brother being involved with the conflict still seemed remote, but alarm bells went off. Initially we didn't think the war would last that long. His unit had just returned from Bosnia; they were held for a while, but we were told they would go. It was a couple of years into the war when he got the announcement.

He got his orders probably four months before he went, in the winter or spring of 2005. He told us and we freaked out. We were all upset. My uncle called from California and said we need to stop him from going. I was upset about that call. What, he goes to jail? "Jail would be better." Easy for you to say!

I've never been in a situation where I had no control over my choices. You're going into an unknown, and you could see or experience unspeakable things. I had a hard time wrapping my brain around that. It made me feel really sad for my brother. This is a whole chunk of his life; he has to do it, he can't get out of it. His contract was almost up. He signed up again. I don't know exactly why. He wanted the full benefit of going, if he had to go.

It was really shocking for my kids, particularly for my son. He wanted to get active at that point; he was turning thirteen. He went to D.C. with my mother. He was really upset. Absolutely, he was going. They took a plane for the day, protested, and came back that night.

When he was called up, we asked my brother what we could do for him, as a family. He said, "Protest the war." That's what we did.

The year he was away, I worried about him periodically. Mostly I stayed in a state of denial. I realized anybody in the military can be a soldier if they need to be, but I knew he'd probably be in a hospital on a base. Mostly I think that's been true. I didn't have a lot of people I could talk to about it. I often didn't mention it. It was such a hot topic; I didn't want to get into it. At the private school where I work, war was a pretty distant concept for people. It gets more in our faces as it wears on. Nobody I knew had family or friends in the military.

We did little things. Sending Brian to march was a big thing. I supported my mom; she was very active. She was very involved with the Peace Abbey in Sherborn, Massachusetts. We visited there regularly. We put signs on our car. Little things. My husband, who works in a high school in Bath, Maine, the home of the Bath Ironworks, wore a peace button every day. He invited regular dialogue with his students, many of whom were considering signing up. Many of them come from military families. The town has a base. It's very pro-military, a working-class area. A lot of his students had always planned to enter the military. College was maybe out of sight for them.

My husband was very vocal. Sometimes I'd bring up the war in social situations because I felt like, hey, someone needs to bring this up. Sometimes I felt people were annoyed by it.

When my brother came home, my first reaction was just to say thanks to him. He'd dedicated an entire year of his life to helping people, helping soldiers. I wanted to let him know that I appreciated him doing it, and doing it without complaint. I wanted to give him a chance to talk if he wanted to.

I feel the ridiculousness of the war has gotten worse and worse. It's harder to ignore at this point. My husband's niece said she's interested in the military; she's interested in aviation. I confronted her at a family event. I wouldn't have done that a year before. I said, "You really need to look at the bigger picture here; you can learn to fly without being in the military." Everybody was surprised, and I said, "Okay, I'll get off my soapbox now." But they said, "Don't get off your soapbox." I was the first to say to her, in public, "That's a dumb idea."

Since my brother's been back, he seems upbeat. He's continued to be unemployed. He goes to fencing tournaments on weekends. He treats himself well, he's enjoying himself. He's still recovering from being there: "Oh my God, I got through it, I'm going to enjoy life now." One of the teachers at my school has asked if he'd come and talk with the kids about it, and he agreed. He hasn't given me any details of what happened over there. He's talked about the endless time put in, working, working.

I've overheard him talking; he described it as a year in hell, not to me, but to someone else. I think he meant that. He's been seeing a counselor through the veterans' hospital to talk about things he heard from his patients or saw, and to process his feelings. But the person is a twenty-year-old kid, never deployed—maybe not the best person to talk to.

I have a feeling he'll be dealing with this for a long time, but in subtle ways. He's hooked on the structure the military provided; he's not used to doing without that. That'll be hard too. He may be deployed again, I don't know. I have a little sense from him that since he doesn't know what his life is going to be, he's living in a temporary way, not making any big commitments. He's in the Reserves until '09.

I joined MFSO and have a pipeline of information about things going on. I went to one Boston peace march with my daughter. It surprises me how little media coverage there is.

The action I'm taking is more personal. It comes back to the way I'm raising my children. I'm more adamant about images they get from the media, more adamant about an educational setting where they won't compromise what they want for themselves in any way. I'm adamant that they're savvy about what's going on in the world, that they can be politically active and more involved. I'm trying to be more informed too, like about sustainability. I think it's all connected.

I've made changes in my own life, so I'm acting how I feel rather than just saying it. I'm being on a bit of a soapbox. I tell my kids why I don't buy certain things. My son is going to a school that's smaller, just formed. I encouraged him to break away from the regular high school; I felt he was falling into a trap there, around boys and men who were into being tough, thinking that feelings are not important. He was playing football. I pushed him a little into team sports; I wanted him to feel accepted. Then, when he wanted to stop, I said, "Great, don't do it anymore." I think a few years ago I wouldn't have said that. I need to give him permission not to conform in that way. Playing football—the culture of it wasn't healthy enough.

My daughter is eleven. She's principled. The peace march was a great experience for her. She's in the middle of a struggle with me being a liberal, progressive mom in a community where she gets the message to be something different. For a few years, I didn't present a real opposition to some things she wanted. But now, I've taken on the politics of this culture that supports the war, not thinking about your choices, doing what everybody else is doing just because they're doing it, and I'm challenging it. I'm trying to question more myself, and teach my children to question more themselves.

It seems to me that the troops know there's a lack of mission in the war. They're being sacrificed and they don't know why. It's not clear to them why they're fighting, who they're fighting, and their leaders are not helping them with that. They're not getting medical help, psychological help, when they come home. People are sent over and over. It's a horrible way to treat people who have volunteered for their country.

# Chapter 8
# Stacy Bannerman

*Author of* When the War Came Home: The Inside Story of Reservists and the Families They Leave Behind; *Continuum Publishing, March 2006. Stacy's husband Lorin, a member of the Washington National Guard, served a year in Iraq and returned with PTSD.*

I wrote a bill of rights for my elementary school when I was in the third grade. I suppose that's where it all began. Things like a longer recess. They used to bring a little cart around with milk cartons in the cafeteria, and by the time we got them the milk was warm and icky. I asked for cold milk. I also wanted equal opportunity in sports. At this time, Title IX was in the process of getting passed. That was on the list. I talked to my classmates about what they'd like to see different. I had them sign with their crayons and pencils. I gave a copy to the principal and we had a sit-down meeting. No idea where this came from.

I recall the televised coverage of Nixon's resignation. My parents made us watch that. They said it was history in the making. My dad was a high school biology teacher. He was very involved in environmental issues in the '70s, before most people were thinking about them.

Then they did pass Title IX. They had to let me wrestle. There was no team for girls, so I was on the boys' wrestling team. I placed third in the state one year.

My undergraduate study was political science/international relations. I got a graduate degree in women's studies and sociology. I worked in a non-profit as a volunteer at a shelter in 1990, for women victims of domestic violence. Then I worked part-time for the Minnesota Committee for Prevention of Child Abuse.

Then I began working at Genesis 2 for Women, an alternative-to-sentencing agency. We worked with women offenders, including felony offenders, many of whom were mothers. Their children had pretty significant issues of abuse and neglect. We worked both with mothers and

45

children as part of the sentencing process, to provide therapy, education, skill development for the women, and help for the kids. We worked with a community-based justice model and restorative methodology.

One summer on sabbatical, I was house-sitting in Idaho for my father and stepmom, and I saw an ad for my dream job as executive director for the Martin Luther King Center. I applied but thought I didn't have a chance. Next thing, I got hired as the first-ever white executive director of the MLK Center in Spokane, Washington, thirty miles from the Aryan Nation Headquarters in Hayden, Idaho.

There were a lot of people in Spokane, a large portion of the black community, that didn't want a white executive director at all. There were a lot of black church leaders and previous employees of the MLK Center that literally slammed the door in my face, refused to return phone calls. I got hate mail and death threats from blacks and whites, harassing phone calls, people at every turn trying to make my job more difficult than it already was.

In January 1999, on MLK Day, I had spoken at a church and I was stopping by the Center to pick up some things for the afternoon activities. We had daycare classes for kids and a playground. A news crew was meeting me there for an interview. There were hundreds and hundreds of flyers literally covering the playground with pictures of MLK in the crosshairs of a rifle. They said "Slappy dun be haffin a burfday but look who's celebrating now." The Aryan Woman's League. I had been on the job for maybe six weeks.

My husband is biracial. He and I met in Spokane while I was serving as executive director. He was a manager at the Spokane Arena. When we met, he was not in the Guard, hadn't been in for a couple of years. He had done around fifteen or sixteen years. He's helped out with big forest fires and floods in Washington State. A few months before our engagement, in May 2000, he told me the Guard had called him out of the blue and asked him to re-enlist. He said he had maybe five years before he qualified for retirement benefits. They said he could pick his unit to serve with.

Then he throws in this comment, "Maybe I can get more money and finish school." He asked me what I thought about it. I was surprised. He knew my position on institutionalized violence. But ultimately, it was his choice to make. I also recognized that the Guard does a lot of great stuff in our communities, and he missed being part of something that contributed to the community, and he was a little bit envious of the sense of mission that I obviously had in my job.

Then of course it was the old thing about the Guard: they never go to war. They'd only see combat if World War III broke out. That's what they told him, and that's what he told me.

So, we were still in Spokane, he did his Guard thing, one weekend a month, two weeks a year. He was happy to be back in it, part of that team. At MLK it was getting worse and worse. I was trying to introduce a program—desperately needed—to provide outreach and education about AIDS in the black community. They didn't want anything like it. There was a lot of push-back.

Increasingly, what was happening was, I was experiencing textbook discrimination at the hands of my board of directors. They hired me, but some weren't able to move past their own prejudices, unfortunately. I was told by the board that I couldn't hire someone that they had given preliminary approval to, when they found she was the minister of a church that accepted gays and lesbians. They told me I couldn't get her to speak. I resigned and was blackballed by the community.

Nobody had the courage and tenacity to speak up for me. I was left alone with no job or support. The MLK Center challenged my unemployment benefits. After hours of hearings, the state unemployment agency allowed me to receive benefits. The situation was that bad. Then I received from the MLK Center one of the first settlements for "reverse" racial discrimination. But I was still outcast, ostracized, even though behind closed doors people said, "What a lot of courage, you did the right thing."

Then my husband got offered a promotion, a new job as a food broker, so we were able to transfer to the Seattle, Washington area. I knew I'd never get another job in Spokane. I got an entry-level position as a front office person for a non-profit working with high school students, promoting the message of MLK. I was sitting at my desk one sunny afternoon in late October 2003, folding flyers for a workshop promoting non-violence, and Lorin walked in and said, "I got the call."

The call came out of the blue. Lorin was as surprised as I was. There hadn't even been gossip about it in the unit. Less than three weeks later he was full-time active duty. For about three months, he was training out of Fort Lewis, about thirty miles south of where we were at. They required the Guard to stay on base. He only came home on weekends. They don't require this of regular Army. Unlike regular active-duty troops, some Guard and Reserve units are put in lock-down while they train. They were prohibited from leaving the base in the evenings. Even though on paper the U.S. government guarantees that when the Guard are federalized, they'll get the same pay and benefits as regular troops, in reality they do not.

I was trying to figure out what was happening. He had already begun to withdraw emotionally, check out from our marriage. He acknowledged it, but said that it's part of the training, it is what they have to do. I asked why he was willing to do this, go to Iraq knowing what we knew even at that time. He said he had a commitment to his men. He said they were going to go build schools and things, do good stuff. And if he didn't go there, he'd go to jail.

His dad is a veteran. His grandpa served in World War II. Lorin wanted to know if he had what it takes.

Then at oh-dark-hundred on February 15, after his last weekend at home, I drove him to Fort Lewis so he could get on the bus with his guys that would take them to Fort Irwin, California for the last part of their pre-deployment training. I wouldn't see him until November of that year, when he came home for his two weeks.

We emailed several times a week. He called at least once a week. I got about a letter or two a month through the whole time. He was telling me what was going on as much as he was able, tempered by government orders and censors and his own internal censor. He didn't want me to worry. The longer he was there and the more he saw, the less able he was to discuss it.

We talked about my anti-war work, which started even before he was gone and then stepped up as MFSO grew. A few weeks after he got the call, I got hooked up with MFSO through a newspaper article. For the most part he was absolutely supportive. Lorin marched with me on MLK Day during the run-up to the war protesting the increasingly loud drum-beat to invade Iraq. He understood. He was not a soldier when we met. I was. There are many kinds of warriors. He knew who I was. My whole mission has always been to forward the message of MLK. No surprises there.

He was getting so frustrated over there; he had seen so many of his friends die. There was a vigil for the thousandth death. He said, "I don't know what the point is. You might as well buy a lot of candles, you're gonna need them. They are not doing any good." I'd tell him I was going to see a senator or a congressman and he'd feed me questions and stories to tell them.

The only times it tweaked for him was when he got some push-back. He'd always say, "If you are going to do this, make damn sure you have the facts." He's absolutely right. If I was wrong or uninformed, he'd correct me.

When I did *Hardball* with Chris Mathews, the segment aired at his base in Iraq. He didn't see me, but about five thousand of the soldiers at Camp Anaconda did. One of his COs [commissioned officers] was in the tent at the time and he saw it. They put Lorin's picture up on the screen. He asked me to be a little less forthcoming with his photo.

He got on the ground in early March 2004. He got two weeks R&R in November 2004. I was delighted to have him there of course. There was all the Thanksgiving stuff going on as well. Everybody wanted a piece of him. Part of him was always in Iraq. He went back, and came home for good on March 11, 2005.

In January 2005 there were already major reports from the GAO [General Accounting Office] and others about how the military was being broken by the war. At that point, he was saying, "When I come home, I am out, I am done."

He came home. It was an unbelievable relief to have him back. He got thirty days paid leave. He had a few weeks going to the base, processing, doing physical and brief mental health evaluations. Questions like, "Do you feel you are at risk of harming yourself or others?" Then that was done and he was home.

I encouraged him not to rush back to work, take another month to relax and regroup. He was very stoic, emotionally unavailable, distant. Little things would make him snap. For the most part, his affect was pretty flat. He used to be the most easy-going thing I'd ever seen. That's why I married him. I was thirty-five. I thought that ship had long past sailed. But he was unbelievable, so laid back.

Now, he's very distant. There are parts of him I just can't get to anymore. He's restless. In a way, he's callous. "Yeah, whatever. It sucks to be you." Or "It's your goat, you fuck it." That kind of stuff.

He stays up late, late, late, watches all kinds of videos of the war he got from the other guys in his unit. He tosses and turns when he is sleeping. He used to be able to fall asleep sitting up in a chair.

It's continuing. It's not getting better. At first, I just gave him his space, like it tells you in the little booklet. The military says give it time. It's not working so good. I still can't reach him.

I beg him to go to marriage counseling. We get five sessions. Lorin went to one. That was the end of that. I kept going. If you are the only one going to marriage counseling, doesn't that say something? He tells me he took the car in and a regular Army guy at the garage says, "You guys are so gypped. We go once a week for three months for group counseling. It's mandatory."

I wrote the book in pretty much real time. Started writing before he left. Some passages in there, I wasn't holding anything back. He was back in March, the manuscript was ready to go in June. He read it, but we didn't talk about it except where there was something inaccurate or that he didn't want in there.

When you have post-combat issues seven months after your service that they aren't really testing for and then you get the results ten months after that . . . What started out as a problem became kind of a pattern that defined the relationship. I ask him to reengage, point him toward resources, but you can't make anybody do anything. The gap in our relationship was never closed. My arms aren't long enough to make it all the way across.

So after a couple of years of this, living with this huge disconnect, I knew that PTSD was affecting me. It's contagious—anyone who has lived in a household where someone is struggling with mental health issues will attest to that. I was getting sucked in as well.

December 2006; I didn't have anywhere to go. I put everything into storage in February 2007 and flew to D.C. the next day. I have been in D.C. ever since, focusing on stopping the supplemental [budget for additional war funding], meeting with congressional staffers, doing media interviews, mostly regarding post-combat care for veterans, mental health issues and challenges. I am doing that because I raised enough money through donations and contributions.

Everything I have seen has shown me that the veterans' systems of mental health services are twentieth-century institutions that don't have the capacity to serve twenty-first-century soldiers. The system as it stands was designed for the single male soldier in his late teens, not today's soldiers. The average today is late twenties. The majority have family responsibilities. A hundred and sixty thousand women have served in the Iraq and Afghanistan theatres. Many have dual diagnoses: PTSD and military sexual trauma. Sixty to seventy percent of soldiers are married. So there are family issues. The wound-to-kill ratio is 16:1; in Vietnam it was 3:1. What that means is, this war—in Iraq as well as Afghanistan—is going to produce unprecedented numbers of soldiers with post-combat issues on a scale this country has never seen. The majority will have families and children. Virtually no programs are available for them.

A proposal I have now is to create sanctuaries for the veterans and families of the military, to provide respite, retreat, and services for families suffering the trauma of war: play therapy for kids; gender-specific programs. More and more wives and mothers are being prime caregivers for their loved ones with traumatic brain injury and other serious wounds. Who's caring for them?

Children are exhibiting more and more academic and behavioral issues. There are no programs for them. There are only two programs dealing with PTSD for women. Individual sessions are exceedingly hard to come by.

It's too late for Lorin and me and tens of thousands of others. But there are hundreds of thousands yet to come. Maybe it won't be too late for them.

# Chapter 9
# Michael Perkins

*Michael lives in Minnesota. His stepson Robert went to Iraq with the Army when he was nineteen. Robert now suffers from PTSD, for which he has so far refused treatment.*

I was born in England, and came here in 1963. I'm amazed what we have here. But you have to participate. It's amazing to me how little people know about what's going on.

I work for American Medical Systems. We design and build cryogenics for cancer therapies. It's rewarding. My little sister died of cancer, and I had it a few years ago. Chris, my wife, works at Target.

My son Robert joined the Army in June 2002. I'm Robert's stepfather. I've been his dad since he was four. Robert joined the Army right out of high school. He spent January 2004 to May 2005 in Iraq; he was nineteen when he went. He's having a tough time with PTSD. Some of the things that went on in Iraq really bother him.

On April 10, 2004, his friend Adolpho Carballo was killed by an RPG [rocket-propelled grenade]. Robert held him while he died. A month later, on May 5, another close friend, James Marshall, was killed while on patrol with Robert. He was with both young men when they died. Robert had their names tattooed on his forearms. He wanted to keep them with him.

When he called to tell us about Carballo, he was sitting there with Carballo's blood on him. He said he wasn't ready to wash it off yet. We had met Carballo when they graduated boot camp in Fort Sill, Oklahoma. My wife and I went to the graduation and spent a couple of hours with him. Carballo had a daughter born after he deployed. When Robert was holding him, the last thing he said before he died was for Robert to be sure to make it home so he could tell his wife and daughter that he loved them.

James Marshall was nineteen. Robert and he were on patrol in Baghdad when Marshall was shot and killed. Robert witnessed that. He called us when it happened. You can tell right away when your child is fragile; he was disillusioned. When they went over, the mission was to find WMD, but the mission kept changing. He kept asking me, "Why did these guys have to die?" He feels guilt that he made it out and they didn't.

While Robert was in Iraq, we talked regularly on the phone. He called me up one night, he was on patrol. I could hear mortar fire in the background. I asked, "Was that mortars?" He laughed and said, "They're always throwing those around." He was joking about sitting under the Humvee, the safest place to be. Then I heard machinegun fire. He said, "Oh my God, I have to go." We didn't hear from him for three weeks after that. I was a little upset!

When he got out of Iraq, he spent May 2005 to June 2006 in Fort Hood, Texas. When he first got back, communication was normal. We'd speak on the phone at length every week or two. While he was still at Fort Hood, he started drinking heavily.

He left the Army in June 2006 and moved back to San Diego. Things got bad quickly. He became irrational. He'd argue for no reason. He'd talk about things that never happened when he was a child. He has a job, but he works from three to eleven so he can sober up before he goes to work, basically.

We tried to tell him we needed to get him to the VA for treatment of PTSD. He started saying he didn't have a problem. Then he said we had taken money from him; then he said he didn't want anything to do with any of us. He broke off contact about four months ago. It's kind of like being tied up on the sidewalk and watching your little toddler play in traffic.

Most people say they support the troops, but they don't really know what it means to send your son or daughter to war. The year and a half that Robert was in Iraq, I don't think Chris or I had a full night's sleep the whole time.

My whole family is military. My dad is a combat vet, a lifelong Republican. He voted Democratic the last election because of Bush and the war. My two cousins, acting colonels, they emphatically say that what we do with MFSO is really supporting the troops—getting them better care, supplies and equipment. I feel, as a country, that we have an obligation to all the troops. We owe it to all the families and soldiers to speak up, so others don't get maimed or PTSD. Those people who say we don't support the troops, they have no idea what they're talking about.

My older brother Paul was in the English Army in the first Gulf War, a tank commander. He was in many fire fights. He had DU [depleted uranium] poisoning. They told him nothing was wrong. He killed himself four days before our mother's birthday. He had lost hope.

I have always been politically active. I started protesting in the Vietnam era. I have always written letters to politicians; but since this war, I've been very involved. We knew at the beginning of the war it was fake; there was no rationale behind it. Nobody believed this would escalate the way it did. As soon as we heard rumors of war, in late 2002, that's when we became active. You have to read, you have to participate in your government.

We're anti-war, but there are times the military is needed. Robert knew from the beginning we don't necessarily support wars. He feels the same way. Most people I know who've been in combat are not fans of war. Before we joined MFSO, we knew we'd be more public. I told Robert we were thinking about doing this. He said, "I know you, I know what you're going to do."

We're active in politics, working on PTSD and uranium testing issues. When Robert does ask us for information, we'll be much better equipped to help him. I'm working on the Minnesota legislature to do DU testing when the vets get home. Alliant Tech makes DU weapons. Minnesota makes money off DU, so they should test. I'm also working on legislation against predatory lenders to protect the troops. Military families are not getting paid very well; then they get hit by those huge interest rates.

MFSO has been very helpful to Chris and me. We started the Minnesota chapter in February 2005. I'd been communicating with Nancy Lessin for about a year and a half before that. When we came to Minnesota, we didn't socialize a lot. Now we go to meetings, and we've met some really nice people. It's nice to be able to talk to like-minded people, and people who have sons or daughters over there. Minnesota is a pretty good place for activists. The march we had for the fourth anniversary of the war had about four thousand people.

During the first 2005 march, we'd only been a group for a month. I jumped in as a speaker. I can't tell you how many people come up to me, after I talk about my son's and my brother's suffering, to say it's given them more strength. People take it to heart when they're told they're not supporting the troops unless they support the war. If I can do something to get people to help themselves, I'm successful.

It's good for Chris to speak, as a mother. As a mother, when your son goes to war . . . Robert wanted to be a soldier his whole life. We did help him do what he wanted. When you find it's detrimental to him—as a parent, it's hard to take.

We're going on a trip to San Diego. Chris called and made two appointments with the VA. Robert knows. He probably won't go. We'll go to his apartment and tell him it's time.

*[I speak with Michael again after his trip to San Diego in mid-April 2007.]* It was a very unproductive trip, as far as getting help for Robert. He's refused any attempts to get him to the VA. We've told him the clock is ticking; if he doesn't get to the VA by the end of May, his psychiatric benefits run out. The VA offers psychiatric care for up to two years after someone leaves the theater of combat. People are trying to change that. Robert left Iraq in late May 2005. When we called the VA to make those appointments, we wanted to make sure he could get help, and nobody contradicted us about that rule.

His girlfriend told us he has constant nightmares. It's really scary for me. My brother, who was in the first Gulf War, also went after terrorists in Northern Ireland. It's different in England. They don't walk around in uniforms and broadcast they're in the military, because they get killed. One of my brother's friends went home—his wife was having a baby—and at the train station he got kneecapped by the IRA, stabbed with an electric drill. My brother had trouble with that.

My son is now exhibiting the same type of behavior as my brother had. It just terrifies me because I see so many parallels. He's very paranoid, very quick-tempered, fights anybody who looks at him. Just like my brother, he was a very friendly guy until he served in the military. My brother lost his job because of what he did in Northern Ireland. When you're in the military, you do things you have to do, and then in private life we don't approve of them. I get real scared for Robert.

We called and told him we were in town. He told us he wasn't available. We found out he's not getting along with his roommate either; they're taking different shifts so they don't see each other. His girlfriend still plans to move to San Diego. She's giving up her job and her family in Texas. We're concerned for her welfare too. She talks to my wife and my daughter. When she saw Robert, he told her to go to see his sister Renée and her daughter in San Diego. Robert has no contact with them. He's trying to punish everyone, including himself, but deep down it seems like he wants somebody to keep trying. He's in so much pain, so hurt by what happened over there.

Most of the guys know that they were lied to. If we were protecting our country from people who attacked us, that would be different. But these people didn't do anything to us, and we're killing them anyway.

Robert did four years active duty, and now he has four years Ready Reserve. A while ago he talked about joining the Guard. They tell him if he does, they'll give him more money for college. But he already gets thirty thousand dollars. I tell him they're sending the Guard for indefinite service in Iraq now. His girlfriend is trying to talk him out of that.

We always have hope. But I'm so scared about Robert. We still cry all the time about it.

# Chapter 10
# Anne Sapp

*Anne and her husband Andy live near Boston, Massachusetts. Andy served for ten months in Iraq with the Army National Guard and suffers from PTSD. He is also active against the Iraq War.*

I'm a special education tutor and Andy, my husband, is a teacher in the same high school. We were in school on 9/11, and I noticed a big crowd at the school library. The second plane was hitting. I was just stunned. Right after that, Andy came looking for me. He said, "We're going to war." I knew with Bush in office, and Andy in the National Guard, he'd go. If it was to protect us, of course he'd do it; that's why you're in the military, to protect us. As it got sorted out and looked like Afghanistan, it seemed reasonable that something had to be done.

Andy knew even before 9/11 that we'd be going somewhere. His unit was being upgraded. They'd been using Vietnam-era equipment. They were getting new equipment and supplies; money was pouring in. Ordinarily that never happens. He said something was going down. Andy said before Bush was elected that if he got in, we'd go into Iraq so Bush could outdo his daddy. I knew when they started talking about Iraq that we would do it.

The night Andy came home and told me he was going, we were holding each other, and I looked over at my daughters watching TV. I thought, "They have no idea what's coming our way." So we talked about it. I wanted to make something good out of what's happening. I talked to them about being an American. In a democracy, if we see our leader abusing his power, we have an obligation to take that power away. The Bill of Rights says if the government isn't doing right, we should even go so far as to take up arms to take that government out of power. I told the girls we weren't going to do that, but we'd do a lot of things short of that. I talked to them about our freedom of speech, and that we needed to make use of that right.

My husband thought he'd be okay, because he's older and has formed his personality; he has security in who he is. But I said, "You're such a caring, intelligent, ethical person, so politically opinionated, you're not going to be unaffected." Our older daughter was sixteen when he left. Her biggest fear was that he would come back damaged as a person. A family friend told her, "Your dad's forty-seven, he'll be okay." But he's not okay.

Andy gave me his wedding ring before he went over. Shortly after he left, the car needed brake fluid, and I put it in a parking lot. Later I realized the ring was gone. I was almost hysterical. Late at night I went tearing back out to Concord. It was starting to snow. I was scouring the lot in tears, and didn't find it. I was driving home, crying, at eleven o'clock, and a policeman stopped me.

The car had been Andy's mother's. She died right before he left. Because he was in Iraq, his license had expired. The policeman saw that. He must have thought I was Andy, driving with an expired license. I told him what had happened. It was a weird thing: he said he just got back from Iraq. He told me he knew I was scared but it would be okay. It felt good to hear. I felt he was an angel sent by God.

Next day, I found the ring—at the bottom of the bathroom cupboard. I honestly don't know how it got there. I couldn't afford it, but I bought two gold chains to wear the ring around my neck.

Someone introduced me to the wife of an officer serving in Baghdad, in the Green Zone. She said, "Did he send you that gold from Iraq? Iraq gold is so good and so cheap." I thought, "I wouldn't wear Iraqi gold as war profit. Andy isn't over there to go shopping."

After her husband came back, I met her again. She looked awful. She told me he had not told her everything that he'd experienced because he didn't want to worry her. He'd jump out of the shower in two minutes. He said, "You don't understand, people get killed in showers." So even officers in the Green Zone, swimming in Saddam's pools, were in danger. I became afraid again of what would happen when Andy came home.

He was away from home seventeen months, in Iraq for ten months. What triggered the worst for him was that some Guardsmen had gone in a convoy and got blown up. There was nothing left. He had seen the survivors of the attack come into the chow hall. He couldn't eat, he was devastated. CNN was showing it afterwards: people dancing in the streets with pieces of exploded vehicles, a boy dancing with a piece of equipment with part of a guy's arm on it.

Part of his job was to travel from guard tower to tower and see what they needed. A couple of days later, there was a huge explosion that shook the tower. It turns out another Guard group had been blown up. Five killed in two incidents.

This hit Andy really hard. All he wanted to do was go out and level an Iraqi village. He wanted to kill them. He had never in his life felt like that before. This was existentially horrifying, to find this desire to kill a human being in himself. This is what triggered the PTSD. To me, this is a sign that human beings are ultimately good, not bad. PTSD happens because we can't handle hurting other human beings.

Andy sent me an email that said he wanted to kill Iraqis. I turned cold. My soul turned sick, totally ill. I knew something really bad had happened. I thought of what my daughter had said and that it had happened. I knew we'd have to deal with it at home. It was a horrible sense of frustration that there was nothing I could do.

That was about two months before he came home. He had the fear that he'd do something wrong that would result in someone he was responsible for being hurt. Plus he knew we shouldn't have been there at all, amid all the evidence that this was a money-making venture.

Halliburton is everywhere. Soldiers are not allowed to put up their own tents. They hire people from Pakistan or Iraq to do that. They're paid a couple of dollars an hour, three hundred dollars a month. Andy talked to a Halliburton worker. The guy said American procurement is paid three thousand dollars a month per worker. The company says they house the workers, but it's substandard, no hot water; they're allowed to go home for one or two weeks after three years. It's slavery, indentured servitude. The soldiers are told not to clean their own showers. There's so little privacy, they wanted to put up partitions, and scrounged some wood. Then someone came and yelled at them. You have to get contractors to do it.

Billions are going into construction but nothing is getting built except in pockets. Some soldiers are doing good work, but not as much as the administration says. On the 'net, soldiers said they were risking their lives to guard a truck full of shrimp and CDs for officers. The military is just another resource to be exploited, like the forests.

The National Guard is treated very poorly by the regular military. It's like being a racial minority. They'd get blamed for things they didn't do. They were outside, officially, twelve hours a day, in the towers, in 112 degree heat. Finally they brought in air-conditioning units, but it was a joke: there were no walls. They brought in Halliburton generators that were always breaking down; they weren't allowed to use anything else. The ones that worked probably went to the Green Zone.

When Andy came home, I knew I couldn't ask him anything. The military gives you cute little booklets to prepare for homecoming. The only honest thing they tell you is that it's more difficult than deployment. They say, "Don't ask; the soldier will tell you in his own time. Don't try to force it out of them."

The first two and a half weeks, he was so happy to be home. He always wrote he'd tell me what happened when he got home. But then they want to live life and forget about it. He started jumping at noises. He'd snap; he became more and more irritable. In his sleep, he'd twitch, moan, cry out like he was afraid. It was horrible. You're not supposed to wake them up; they might think you're the enemy and try to hurt you. He'd wake up and feel embarrassed and scared. I'd go to hug him, and he'd be stiff as a cement pillar.

He started driving really fast, coming behind vehicles close and fast and whipping around them. In Iraq, you don't stop and don't slow down. He doesn't want to have his back to a window or open space. He doesn't want to go out of the house. Waste cans scare him. There could be bombs in them.

It's gotten worse. At first, he'd cycle in and out, have good and bad days. My oldest daughter said she could tell when he's having a bad day: he holds his rifle arm close to him. Now he sees a psychiatrist and a social worker.

There's very little in the way of support groups for families of veterans. They can only do a VA group if the military person is there too. But they've already taken on so much guilt, families couldn't be honest about what they're suffering. Andy heard of a wife who killed herself while her husband was away. Dealing with it is hard enough, but trying to find help and not finding it is another injury.

I found myself on three meds for depression and anxiety from the stress of Andy coming home. I was feeling nothing. I slowly got off them, and I feel better. At least I feel.

My son was very angry. I worry about him. He would have gotten himself in jail, coming to demonstrate with us. He's been standing up for others since preschool. He's got a strong sense of right and wrong. I'm glad he's geographically insulated.

My older daughter closes up like a clam. She got no counseling or help. I fear it'll come back on her someday. She and I were so close with Andy gone. I worry about this adjustment on top of worrying about Andy.

Our youngest saw a social worker the whole time Andy was gone. Schools need to be prepared. Kids will come into their teens with baggage ready to blow up on them. *The Things They Carried* [title of a novel about the Vietnam War; by Tim O'Brien; Random House, 1998]: the extra duffel bag of guilt all soldiers bring home. Packing backpacks with it for kids to take to school.

Andy says PTSD is nothing compared to the suffering of the people who live in Iraq. He aches for the soldiers who don't have families with insight, who end up fighting about it, who don't know they need help.

When he speaks—he does an event once a week—he says he never saw action, never fired his weapon. He pooh-poohs his trauma. But even if someone hasn't been firing, driving down the streets of Baghdad, any minute they might have to. They were fired at every day. He found an unexploded mortar, with a flashlight, inside camp. He was standing right next to it in the dark.

I never thought I'd worry about Andy killing himself, but now I do. His driving scares the hell out of me. When he's gone, I think, "What if he doesn't come home?" A year after he came home, I thought he'd be in a better place. I'm still afraid I'm going to lose him. It doesn't end when they walk off the plane and they're in your arms. I don't know if I'll ever stop being afraid.

*[I ask about her activism, which began while Andy was away.]* There were times I didn't want to speak at events. People crave information but I wanted to say no, melt back into feeling numbness that would carry me to the end. Maybe if I wasn't involved, time would go faster. I wanted to keep as calm and positive an atmosphere as possible at home for my children. I don't want to get so angry that I hate people. But we shouldn't be letting this go on.

It's scary as hell to stand up in front of people. But it becomes very powerful, if I speak out and the person next to me speaks too. People think one person can't do anything. But when I get together with the wonderful, beautiful people in this movement . . . There's so much for us to do, who are involved.

I believe it's a good versus evil situation. I do believe good will win. But you can't sit back and depend on other people to do it.

*[Since our interview, Anne tells me, their family has continued to suffer repercussions both from Andy's PTSD and from their activism. After Anne called for the prosecution of former Secretary of Defense Donald Rumsfeld during an interview on a local TV station, Andy's unit received a phone call "from above" asking about their efforts to speak out, and*

*telling the unit that she and Andy were being watched. They have also received hate mail from military families who support the war. Andy retired from the military in April 2007.]*

# Chapter 11
# Claire André

*Claire's husband John is a chief petty officer in the Navy Reserves Construction Battalion. He spent seven months deployed to Iraq. They live in Boston, Massachusetts.*

I was born in California and mostly grew up outside Tacoma in Washington State. It was kind of a strange suburban area. Some of the neighbors had cattle and stuff. My family have never been activists. My dad is conservative. He doesn't have really consistent ideas, but he watches Fox News. He's patriotic in his way. I think my mom has kind of changed over the years from thinking similarly to the way he does to thinking closer to how I do, more liberal.

I went to school in North Carolina, Warren Wilson College, for two and a half years. I moved back with my folks for a few months, until I started Evergreen State College and got an apartment.

At Evergreen, we were reading Thoreau and Emily Dickenson. That's where I met John, in 2002. John was raised in California but settled in Washington State. Our class met three times a week and it was our only class, so we would go out with the group quite a bit. Then John and I started going out, just the two of us.

Initially I was pretty uncomfortable with him being in the military, because I was kind of anti-establishment. I didn't know what the military did that was positive. I had stereotypes about it. I had a really bad attitude about it until I got to know him. He's in the Navy Reserves Construction Battalion. He had been doing that for several years. He's a chief petty officer. He's actually been in the military altogether for twenty-one years. He's forty-one, I'm twenty-eight. He started when he was eighteen; he was Navy, on a ship. He was involved in the first Gulf War. Over the years, he's done Army Corps of Engineers and Coast Guard—that's what he really prefers, and what he'd recommend to young people.

He's very complicated. He reads *The Nation* and Noam Chomsky; he really has his eyes open about how the military is used for the wrong missions sometimes, and how it can be in defense of capitalism instead of democracy, and how when people sign up, they're trusting that they'll be asked to do noble things. He's still loyal to the Navy. I don't have it entirely sorted out and I don't think he does either.

We were both opposed to the invasion of Iraq. Actually, when he was being interviewed for the Sailor of the Year award, they asked him, "What do you think about the Iraq War?" and he said, "I've never heard a compelling reason why we should invade there, and I hope I wouldn't have to go." I think that interview question was kind of just about his poise. He still won.

We continued living in Olympia, near Evergreen, for a year while I finished. Then we moved to Pullman, Washington, near Idaho. He did a graduate degree in environmental science, an accelerated one-year master's program. He finished that, and then we moved to Boston for my master's in children's literature. We had been here about a year, and then he was deployed. It was July 19, 2006.

When he found out he'd be deployed, it was in May. He came back from the Reserves center—he'd gone to drop off a paper or something, not a big deal. But they had his orders in hard copy and they handed them to him. That was in Quincy, so he had maybe an hour to think about it on the way back to our Boston apartment. When he came in, he was like, "I have to show you this." He handed it to me and I said, "I can't read this"—it's hard to read, it has a lot of acronyms and numbers and things. He told me what it was, but we didn't know where he would be deployed. It said "up to two years" on there. So he was online looking to see what Seabees were doing around the world, to see what he might possibly be sent to do. It goes through a range of well-drilling in Fiji to Iraq. So we were like, it sounds like Iraq is the worst place to be sent right now.

We knew the date would be July 19. So we started looking at the technicalities of how we would get out of our lease. We wanted to move, but he was going to be gone when our lease was up.

So we got married. Here we'd been living together for four years. We'd talked a little bit about getting married but it didn't seem like something there was a reason to do. But then this was a huge reason. I had a feeling they wouldn't give me any information if we weren't married. He would also get paid more if we got married. The Reserves would give him a rent allotment. Otherwise I'd be on my own. I'd have to move in with a friend.

We got married June 2. It was all pretty quick. In Boston, you don't go to the courthouse. There was a real estate agent in the North End, and we went to her office. One of my friends came with us.

The deployment was more of a surprise than it should have been. His was the last Seabee Reserve battalion to be activated, out of twelve. The other eleven had gone, if I understand it correctly. But John had always minimized those risks, and I didn't really care to research it. I was interested, when he came back from schools or drills and told me what he'd been working on, but we didn't think that he would be deployed. We were heartbroken when it happened.

The decision to get married was about a lot of things. Once we had the actual ceremony, it was entirely romantic. But the decision was partly out of anger: "You're going to take him away? You're going to pay him as much as possible."

He was in Iraq from around September 1 until maybe April 1 of 2007. We would email every day or two. I would mail a lot of packages. I sent him magazines and snacks, and drawings, and cards and letters. After a while, I figured out that we needed to have a system of when he would email me, so I wouldn't worry until I had heard from him.

He served several places in Anbar Province. Most of the time it was in Rawah, near Syria. He did water-well drilling. Most of his projects were water-wells, but also roads. Other parts of his battalion were building barracks for the Marines and roads in their base. Mostly it was in support of American troops. The wells were for Marine bases mostly. The Marines or Army would be handling security, but they were still attacked while they were drilling wells. He would spend time on the huge air base, Al Asad, and that was safe, but everywhere else wasn't.

I was really amazed how little they helped me, the Navy, the ombudsman program and all that. They sent me a letter that was composed as if you were moving to the base. It was like, "Welcome to the base, here's the Reserves Center, here's the address, and we offer these services." They sent these letters all over America to different Reserve families of his battalion. That's the letter they have, whether you live in Alaska or Massachusetts or wherever.

They actually sent fourteen pamphlets in that one envelope. A lot of it's repetitive, and a lot of it's outdated. I didn't feel like they ever told me exactly what the rules were for operational security. John's battalion was more finicky about that than others. I didn't know if they would delete my emails if there was anything inappropriate, or if they were deleting his emails. I didn't know what the rules were. I asked the ombudsman who my detachment ombudsman was; I never knew who was in charge of me. She sent me an email saying it was one person, and a couple days later, she forgot and sent me an email saying it was somebody else. So I tried both of them and neither of them got back to me, because I was asking difficult questions about operational security. It doesn't feel like you ever get to figure out what the rules actually are.

It was horrible. I go to Simmons College for my master's, and that community supported me. They have a counseling center, and you get medication through the counseling center. My teachers and my fellow students were all supportive. But otherwise it wouldn't be possible. For a while, I was thinking that you would get more support if you lived on a base, and it would be better, somehow. But then I read some books about people who live on bases, and I was glad that I had my college community instead. It sounds like it's not as good as I was hoping, that the women don't take care of each other as well as they could. One book—*The Year of Absence* [Jessica Redmond; Elva Resa Publishing LLC, 2005], about people based in Germany, and their husbands are in Iraq—makes it sound like the worst possible thing, to be in a foreign country with no husband.

I didn't read very much about Iraq before he was deployed. I knew that I was opposed to the invasion, because there didn't seem to be a reason. I was always skeptical about anything the president said. It was like I feel about Darfur or anything else; I thought it was awful, but I wasn't crying about it the way I did after John left.

I was listening to NPR all day, every day. I cut and pasted news articles from the internet into gigantic Word documents. Because I'm a student, I think about things kind of academically, and I thought, "I'm going to research my way to the bottom of this, I'm going to find out what the point is." But there's not a point.

When I would cut and paste those articles and speeches and interviews and things, I would put responses in between. And I would try to figure out how much danger John was in. Like, he wasn't using ground transportation, he was helicoptered from site to site, so I would read about anti-helicopter weapons, and I would keep track of when Marines were killed in Anbar, because those were the people he was working next to. Only one person from his battalion was killed, I believe it was in October, really early. He'd only been there a month. So that made it seem more possible that other people from his battalion would be killed.

My hair fell out, and I couldn't eat. I don't mean that my hair all fell out, just that it was thinning. Every time I washed my hair, it was falling out. I couldn't eat, so I took a medicine through my health center. They had recommended an antidepressant that seems to help people have an appetite. So I was on several medications. I still couldn't sleep.

I think John would have already assumed that I was that bad off. That first day, when we were looking at his orders, he said he was more worried about me while he was gone than he was worried about him being there. And initially I agreed. I was like, "Yeah, I know you know how to do your job; I'm worried about how I'm going to be coping." And then after reading more, I was like, "Actually I'm worried about your physical safety." It was worse than I thought it was going to be.

I told him some. I was really torn about it. His sister was ill while he was gone, and I didn't know if we should tell him. We could never get to the bottom of things with email. We knew each other. We had the background of four years. But still, it's hard to figure out what an email means sometimes.

I carried my cellphone everywhere really religiously. He actually called on Christmas Eve, because they had a satellite phone and they each got a couple minutes. My impression is that lower-ranking people have down-time, but John—there's always more work for him to do. He didn't go wait in line to get on the phone. He had his laptop with him because he needed it for work.

John never told me about scary things. I would just read between the lines in newspaper articles. There's something—I still haven't heard the story from him—that happened in Hit, Iraq. It sounds like the American base is right next to the Iraqi military base that was bombed by mortars, and it says "mass casualty event" in the article. And it mentions by name people who were in John's water-well team of fifteen that were helping evacuate the hurt Iraqis. So I knew that he had been really near people being killed by mortars. I knew his boss said they were a great team, because they worked through mortar attacks and rocket attacks. But John wasn't telling me those things.

He came home before Easter, on the sixth of April. He's been back a couple of weeks, and he still hasn't told me too much. He went to Gulfport for about a week of debriefings. I didn't go to Gulfport to greet him. Only about forty family members flew down, for a battalion of five hundred service-people. It wasn't a big production. I greeted him at the Boston airport. It was just him.

It was in last October or November that I joined MFSO on email. That felt like a huge deal. It could have been a betrayal. I didn't know if he would be disappointed in my choice to do that. I don't know enough about the military. It wasn't a big part of our life. So I didn't know if he would get in trouble. But I felt better once I'd joined.

I'm also involved with my school; there were a few other students who wanted to do an anti-Iraq War group. And it turned out that I went to the January 27 protest in D.C. with them. A lot of them are from the International Socialists Organization, the ISO, and I felt like they were more theoretical. They didn't have a personal investment. Some of the people were excited about the prospect of being rebellious. They were really over-simplifying politics, down to the elite and the workers. One guy—he was really tired when he said it—but he said that we should be allied with the Iraqi insurgents. So I was like, "No, I'm not gonna hang out with you." I always wore a Navy shirt when I would do that stuff. I kind of don't give a shit about the Navy, but I am not going to go anywhere that John couldn't go. I don't want to be in a room where John wouldn't be welcome.

I guess I do kind of care about the Navy. I mean, I do searches online and find people's personal pictures of their Iraq deployment, and I'm like, "Oh, that guy's a Seabee like John, that's nice." So I do feel some connection. But it's all frustrating. I'm not sure how I feel.

I've been assuming that he would retire as soon as possible, but he wants to stay in. He could retire this September as chief petty officer; he doesn't want to do that. He's been saying he'd like to do several more years. He'd like to be promoted again. I think he knows he could do a better job than some people he sees in higher positions.

He says that they definitely can't deploy him for a year, that you get a year home safe. I'm always really skeptical about those rules. I told him it sounds like he might be mentally minimizing risks, like he did before he was deployed, like saying he's pretty sure he'll never be deployed, and we don't need to worry about it. Even once it was clear he was going to go to Iraq, he was saying, "Maybe I'll just go to Iraq for a little while, and then we'll drill wells in other countries." So I think it was partially to himself and partially to me that he was not facing the whole thing at once.

In January, I went to a candlelight vigil in Boston. That was the first time I ever went to a political thing. I guess I've done three events. I've been writing, but I haven't written to editors. I write about my feelings. I've written little statements for when I joined MFSO, and there was a letter to the Senate and Congress. I think I attached a signed statement to that. And I've called senators and representatives.

John says that he's not worried about his job at all, relative to my activism. It doesn't concern him. At one point, when I was leaving for that January march, in an email, he said, "Next time we'll both go." But he never said anything else about it. He definitely approves. I think we have the same read of the situation: that it's all a tragedy, and the American government is incompetent.

It's been strange. Since he's been back, I've felt more theoretical about the occupation of Iraq—a drastic difference in a couple of weeks. He's not there. When he was there, I was like, "They all need to come home immediately, even if it causes a catastrophe for Iraq." Now, I'm like, "I really don't know; let's think about it." And I recognize—I've heard about that before, other women feeling that way. Part of it is that he must have been doing a good job. He went and did seven months. Should we abandon that work?

In some ways we're the same, and entirely reconnected. But he hasn't processed things. It's like if he doesn't process things, we'll never be able to talk about them. It's hard. It's all kind of mysterious, in what ways he's been harmed by it. I read so many articles about people that are fucked up. I don't think he has PTSD. I think that he's the same person he was before. He's just working through things.

# Chapter 12
# Nan Beckwith

*Nan lives in Virginia. Her Marine son, Ryan, continues a family history of military service that goes back twenty generations.*

I used to be a Loudoun County Republican delegate. One reason why was because of the military. My dad survived Pearl Harbor. My mother was a Navy medic in the Pacific. My dad was conservative, but he believed in the separation of church and state. He worked for the Army Corps of Engineers. In later years, Mom became a Democrat; she believes in pro-choice.

My son Ryan is a Marine. In the spring of 2004, I got a call from him in Afghanistan. They were starving. They had one MRE [Meal Ready to Eat] and one small bottle of water each for twenty-four hours; that was it. After I hung up, I was shaky. They were near a military contractor's installation, Kellogg Brown and Root. I looked on Google, typed in KBR, and then I said, "Those dirty bastards." I started mailing food to "my kids." I thought I was feeding four Marines, but I found out later I was feeding a platoon of twelve. I had socks, food, and medical supplies in my back room, so my younger son could mail them out on a daily basis.

I live in Virginia. I don't want to hear BS that they couldn't send supplies because of rough terrain. My supplies got there. I believe Halliburton/KBR wanted to save a buck. It was an hour's flight by chopper from their big base.

The day after this happened, I spoke out about it. I have cut ties with family members and others because of this. I'm not the only one who has cut ties over this war.

My ancestors helped found Saybrook Colony in Connecticut. I'm a military buff, I go to re-enactments. One historian I've talked with helps with French and Indian War re-enactments. He says not since the Civil War has the U.S. been so divided.

We were in a Depression in the '30s and small companies got us out of it. Now it's filthy war contractors, Lockheed Martin, Boeing, and Halliburton. The money goes to states where senators and congresspeople have power.

Ryan joined up a year before 9/11, in high school, the summer after his junior year. It's our heritage. I can go back twenty generations, to the Battle of Hastings. My husband was a Marine. Both grandfathers and a grandmother served. My son is a military historian; he feels he can't be one unless he has lived it. The day before he disembarked for Pakistan, he wrote that he didn't want anyone to think he didn't do his part for his country.

When I signed those Marine papers, I was only worried about China. I had no idea the man I voted into office would do what he did, what a corrupt administration it was going to be.

I might be fooled once, but you're not gonna fool me again. I read the letters in *Stars and Stripes* every day; I read that we went to war for oil; there was a letter about the Project for a New American Century. The Republicans have lost a lot of military voters.

Ryan went to Parris Island for boot camp. When 9/11 happened, I knew within five minutes my son was going to be in a war. They graduated six days after 9/11. All the parents knew.

I have "adopted" soldiers and Marines. I write to encourage them. Two of Ryan's friends are first-generation Americans. I write to them about George Washington, John Hancock, I write them history. If George Bush and the neo-cons had read about the militias in the Revolutionary War, they would never have invaded Iraq. I think the whole failure of the Iraq War was that they didn't prepare.

After boot camp, Ryan went to the Pacific. He trained in Arizona, California deserts, Alabama. He was very highly trained. He was sent to Afghanistan in 2004. They were trained to help the Afghani people get the right to vote. Their platoon commander was fearless—he's Pakistani, but he was raised here. He saved their lives. But he was relieved of his command after the mission was over.

"My kids" got dysentery in Afghanistan. My son doesn't tell me anything. But I got a camera back from him and I developed the pictures. One was of a Marine that was so skinny, I didn't recognize it was my own son. He lost forty pounds the first month he was away. But they got rid of the Taliban; their mission was highly successful. My younger boy, two years younger than Ryan, was scared to death. My husband had a heart attack during that time.

I stopped believing in Christianity when my son was in a firefight. I woke up thinking, "If he dies, he'll be dead as a doornail; he'll be dust to dust."

We need to bring these kids home. Our military is drained. Our kids are exhausted over there. We have more than twenty thousand wounded, nine thousand seriously. Many are brain-dead. Where's the money to keep them going?

I'm for bringing back the draft. I want you, that supports this war, you, who says "They're fighting for our freedom," I want you to feel my pain. America needs help. We need every young American man and woman to serve two years, if not in the military, then in a civilian conservation corps. They all need to help out, with poor people, with civil rights, restoring wetlands.

My son is straight and narrow, very conservative. He'll have a few beers. If he goes into a bar, nobody will know he's a combat vet. He's decent, he has integrity. I see him getting a college degree, being a sheriff, maybe running for office. But when his grandkids ask what he's proudest of, he'll say, "I was a U.S. Marine."

I love the military. I love the U.S. Constitution; I'd take a bullet for it. I hate what they've done to our liberties. Don't you mess with our Constitution! That's where my outrage is. They betrayed my country.

# Chapter 13
# Anne Chay

*Anne is a teacher living in the Boston area. Her son John is an Army mortarman with the Second Infantry Division, the Third Brigade, First Battalion. His tour in Iraq was extended through October 2007.*

I grew up mainly in northern New Jersey. I have one older brother and everyone else was younger, so I did my fair share of caretaking as a kid. I was a tomboy. That was back in the days when you just got on your bike and you took off, and swam at the lake, and came home for dinner, and that was it. Not like today.

I always liked school. I did very well at math from a young age, and now I teach it. I worked in high tech for many years. I worked for Wang; they offered me great jobs, they moved me all over the world. I lived in Hawaii, San Francisco, Seattle. I toured Asia, Australia, New Zealand. I started working for them in '79. This was just in the early days of Wang. They were just getting big. I had a really good time. Everybody worked together. It wasn't like a big corporate thing.

When I was thirty-five, I was out in Seattle, and Wang was just starting their downfall. There were rumors that we weren't delivering products we were supposed to. Suddenly, I found myself pregnant. I decided I would have this child. His father didn't want to participate in childrearing. I didn't want to single-parent a kid and be doing the ten, twelve hours a day. You just can't do that. Even I knew that. So I took a cushy corporate job and transferred to the Boston area, and Wang eventually collapsed.

I met a guy who I was married to for a while, and had my daughters with him. John was two when he was adopted, so Campbell has been the only male in his life all along. John has always known about and did get to meet Tim, his biological dad, in Seattle. Even though he didn't need to be told, I didn't want it to be one of those stories that came out when he was eighteen—"Oh, you're not who you think you are." For all intents and purposes, John and his sisters are just brother and sisters. There's never been a distinction.

In four years, between thirty-five and thirty-nine, I had three kids. When they were little, it wasn't so bad. I did some consulting. I tried to keep my finger in the pie, even if I only worked three hours a day, to do something besides just child-rearing.

I shouldn't have married Campbell to begin with, but I wouldn't have my daughters without him, so it's okay. But things were not great, so we split up in '94. Then I did look at getting back into high tech, but oh my God. I had dabbled, I had never really left it, but this was during the take-off of the PC [personal computer], and I had never really done that much with the PC.

I didn't want to do that nine-to-five thing. I didn't want the kids hanging out by themselves all the time. As it is, they got into enough trouble, even with a policewoman living across the street. "Does your mother know you're doing that?" They were all on the roof. When I came home, "Yeah, Mom, she kicked us off the roof. . . ." Good thing!

My son, at this point, was diagnosed with a learning disability. One of the things we did for my son was to get him on the computer. There was remediation stuff: he could write better on the computer, it could help him spell-check and all this.

So I went back into education. I took out a student loan, at forty-whatever-I-was, and I got a master's in special needs. I wanted to use technology to help kids with learning disabilities.

We've always gone places and done things. We had a good time. I am the disciplinarian because their dad can't say no, so I am forever the bad guy, and you know what, that's just the way it is. Somebody's gotta do it.

John had his moments. He felt like stealing something when he was in eighth grade, a six-dollar item from the Andover gift shop. But he was always a very kind kid. He was a wonderful older brother, still is. He was never particularly jealous. Always independent, just couldn't wait to get out on his own. I remember when we'd come down to Boston to go to museums, he'd say, "Can I go for a half hour by myself?" Always independent, always busy, always up to something. I remember once I got mad at him. I said, "Just go outside, stay safe." He ends up on top of this potting shed that had a huge hole in the roof. This is his idea of staying safe. He broke his collarbone rollerblading. He was a climber and a mover, always.

Then we get into middle school. First he starts with the learning issues. For a couple of years he caught up in his reading. Writing, he would always struggle with. I was anxious to get him out of special education, because I think the stigma, all the secondary crap you get, affects you academically. There are gifted kids with learning disabilities. His abilities are either at this end of the spectrum or that end. He's a classic. Kids like that never feel good enough, ever, ever, ever.

But he got through school. His grades were okay. He started school with A's and B's; by middle school he got B's and C's. Then by high school they were falling off the edge. He's the kind that likes to get lost. He likes to be under the radar. He never acted out. He was never disrespectful. He would just fade away. They didn't call to say he was cutting class. They just flunked him.

By senior year, I was a wild woman. He almost didn't graduate. He needed two more courses, and he had quit going, totally and completely. But he managed to pull out the two courses to get his diploma. Then I thought I maybe shouldn't have pressed him, because two weeks after that he went to boot camp.

I found something he wrote as a freshman about what he wanted to do with his life. Even then, he said he wanted to join the Army, or go to school in Arizona. He did have a good friend, still does, whose dad was in the Army. He was in Vietnam. John loved hearing the war stories. They played war all the time. They would make their own guns, sand them and paint them and all that stuff. He was just fascinated with the military.

None of that came from encouragement from me. When I was growing up, we were all hippies. You know, "Make love not war." I did allow play guns in the house. One of my brothers didn't allow it, but I think you give it more power. I thought it was a fascination he'd outgrow.

The other thing that happened: as a junior, they start talking about college, college, college. In Andover, it's big. It stressed him out. I said, "John, low-key it. Let's go see one place. Don't make it a big to-do, don't pressure yourself." But he does, he's always put a lot of pressure on himself. I said, "Let's just check it out. You go and you try it. If you like it, you do some more, if not, you can do something else." I never even got him to look at a college.

In his senior year, he starts talking about, "I'm going to go in the Army." I thought, "Yeah, right." Well, he hung on to that. He went over to the recruiters in Haverhill on his own, but he was still seventeen. I did sign for him to have the physical, but that was it, I would not sign him in early. So they gave him his physical, said he had to lose some weight, which he did. He hadn't done much of physical anything for a long time.

Everybody who knew him encouraged him to look at another MOS besides infantry. I had him meet a friend of mine who was an Army Ranger, which was what John wanted to be in the beginning, but after doing the initial set of pushups . . . The Rangers had to do even more.

I had him talk to everybody I could think of to talk him out of it. All that did was, "If everybody doesn't want me to do it . . ." He's always enjoyed being different. This is a kid who couldn't stand to be told what to do. I said, "John, you can't stand if I ask you to take the trash out. They're going to tell you what to do 'round the clock."

I think part of it was a reaction to his panic over "What am I going to do with my life?" He answered that question without all the stress of applying to college. And he had difficulty with being organized, and procrastination, which is a real family issue—he is not alone. And he knew that they would organize it for him. I think in a weird sort of way, it answered a lot of problems that he had had over his life. I don't think in any way shape or form did he understand all the repercussions.

Finally, as we got closer and closer, I jumped on the bandwagon. Because I didn't want him going off . . . I mean, at eighteen, they can do what they want, unfortunately.

He did change MOS, for mortarman. They take the kids with the higher math scores, because you have to be able to figure coordinates. John says, "Mom, nobody likes being a mortarman, but this is where we are."

It still kind of astounds me, but he did it. He's funny. He has a great sense of humor. His mouth gets him into trouble once in a while, but in a fun way. He's never belligerent, he's never been confrontational, I don't know if he's ever had a fistfight. Since he's in there, he's had to learn to stick up for himself. They do some rough-housing he's not used to, just the physical nature of it. He's gotten into shape. The last PT test, he passed everything. He was so proud of himself. That was in, what, a year and a half.

He always was very responsible. He always had chores. He took over as the little man of the house, even though I went out of my way not to make him that; he had enough going on without feeling he had to be responsible. He felt very protective. When Sally and Stephie screw up, he gets on their case more than I do.

The independence is what got him into trouble. He saw a way to make some money, have his own money. I did tell him there's other ways to make money besides this. But in his eyes, this he could do without help, without counsel. You turn yourself over to them.

So we had talked about the fact that he would end up deployed. At this point, we really didn't talk the politics, whether you were for or against the war. As for me, I was still in that happy loyal American naïve mode. What I heard about it wasn't good. I think anything can be resolved without war; that's my own personal opinion. But I fell for the lies in the beginning: it's a necessary evil. Certainly 9/11 fired a lot of people up, not knowing that the people we were after weren't in Iraq, there were no terrorists in Iraq, it was all a big con job so Bush could go get the oil business. I didn't know that at that point.

All that was just coming out. And I thought, "Oh, sour grapes, complain, complain, complain." I didn't know how much it was costing. I had not a clue. I had not heard the horror stories from the young men and women who had gone over there. We had no real contact with anybody in the military.

I thought I was just going to have to endure this as the mother of a soldier, like this would be my cross to bear. It wasn't until last summer that I really started looking into what got us there, what's going on while we're there, and uncovering the lies, the deceit, the waste. But even if I had known, it wouldn't have mattered. He was gonna do this.

They killed him in boot camp. He could do zero pushups when he got there. He had to get to thirty-seven or whatever it was before they let him graduate, so he had to do a couple of extra weeks. It's too bad they didn't kick him out for doing no pushups. But he actually ended up where a couple of drill sergeants really commended him, because he showed that he could stick to it. He stuck to that like he had never stuck to anything in his life. He was gonna show them he could do it, and he did. A guy even said, towards the end, "If I had to deal with this other guy, I'd pick you, because I know you'd just do whatever it was until you were done."

He called me in tears the week before graduation. He said, "Oh Mom, I haven't done the pushups, I don't know if I'm going to graduate." I said, "I don't care, your sisters and I are coming anyway." So we went down. We hadn't seen him since he left in early July, and here it was October 20.

It was so exciting just to see him. Here he was in his uniform, and oh my gosh, he looks so grown up, and he's gotten muscular. He really looked good and was very happy to see us. He didn't do the pushups the next morning. They made him direct traffic. This is over three pushups, while all the rest of them are out there marching. So the girls and I hung out and talked to him while he was directing traffic.

They did give him a leave that afternoon. He had never left the building. He had never gotten any of the positive motivators because he never passed the pushups. So we went and saw a movie, and we went shopping, and we had a ball.

I'll never forget that he was so excited. They would retest them every other day. He worked at that so hard. Two weeks later, he passed the PT test. He's in the Second Infantry Division, the Third Brigade, First Battalion. He got his orders that he would be at Fort Lewis in Seattle with a mortar Stryker brigade.

Before he was deployed, we went out and stayed for a week in a local hotel and got to see Fort Lewis. I'm really glad we did. I think it was nice for him to have family there and make sure he had all his stuff. Everybody told me, "They need lots of baby wipes, take these baby wipes." So the standing joke is, "Don't ever send me another baby wipe." "Do you wear your sunscreen?" "No, Mom, sunscreen never works. Chapstick never works." All the things they're supposed to need and want, he didn't want. But we had that kid ready to go. You know, they're so limited in what they can take.

So he went over. He said, "We'll be in Kuwait for a month." Six days later, I get a call: "Guess where I am, Mom? I'm in Baghdad!" I'm like, "What!?" Six days later. He met the unit out of Alaska that was extended. Some of them got to Kuwait, some of them got home and they had to come back. So his introduction was meeting guys who had just been there for a year and were told they had to stay three more months. He said they were bullshit. He said, "Mom, can you blame them?"

Lately, sometimes I try to get him to admit that he regrets his decision. But now he's turned nineteen, June 21 last year, the day with the most sunshine. When he first got over there, he says, "Oh, fun and adventure," until they started running missions. He saw some things . . . They would have to tell the Iraqi police and military if they were going to go into any neighborhoods. Ever since the alleged raping and killing of the women and kids, that's the rule. We don't hear that over here. They would tell them where they were going, and he said half the Iraqi police are on the take, and they call their buddies, and by the time they get out there, there's no bad guys left. Or they round up the bad guys and bring them back, and they let them go. So why are they risking life and limb to round up the bad guys?

The worst thing he ever told me about was, they found a grandmother who'd been beaten and left in a ditch. This is a platoon of young men, cruising down the street in their tank. They do get the respect of the people in their tanks. He's a gunner, also. It's his claim to fame: although he's the youngest in the platoon, he's the best machine gunner. He's the fourth and last gunner. So when they're out tooling around, he's responsible for the one-eighty behind them also. It's a very responsible position.

In 2006, he got into Baghdad in early July, just a year from when he first went to boot camp. And then he came home for a week in November, and that's the last time we saw him. Between that time, email was not good. He'd call about once a week. They were in a thirty-person tent. It was 124 degrees. They wouldn't use the air conditioning. The buses would run out of gas, that would take them places. They were out touring the neighborhoods, trying to clean things up.

Sometime between July, when they got there, and November, when he came home, they found the beat-up grandmother, which he told me a little bit about on the phone, and talked some more about it when he got home. She was very badly injured. One arm was almost not functional. One eye was swollen shut. I said, "You just mean old like me?" He says, "No, Mom, a grandmother. An elderly woman." I said, "What happened?" There's always an interpreter. We treat the interpreters well. Whatever they want, we give them. According to John, she got caught with a cellphone, and they accused her of talking to the U.S. military. This is how we know it's not working. If we are the enemy, what are we accomplishing? Because she was doing the ultimate no-no, talking to the U.S. military, so they beat the crap out of her.

So they find her, and they did take her to the hospital, and they got her patched up. And she came out, and they had to find somewhere for her to go, because the insurgents killed her whole family. This is the kind of stuff that he would have flashbacks about. The whole platoon was really upset. This is not why they went off to war. It's not like they were standing facing the bad guys. This is what they were dealing with.

The things that touched him the most was that, and the kids—that they looked like waifs. He was talking with me once about soccer. So I went to the hockey shop and the guy donated a dozen soccer balls. We loaded them all and I sent them to him with a little pump. I said, "Pump them up and give them to the kids." He sent some great pictures of them running after the tank and playing with the soccer balls. At that point he said you never knew whether they were going to be friends that day or throw rocks at you.

It sounds like the regular Iraqi people have changed their attitudes toward the U.S. military. When he first got there, at least the kids—they'd throw candy and soccer balls and whatever other stuff they had—so that he felt good about. But some of the stuff he saw, this old woman in particular, struck a chord. I asked if he got a chance to talk about it. He said, "No, we've got to put that aside, because when we go on the mission the next day you can't be sitting there thinking about whatever you saw the day before." There's never time to debrief and deal with what they've seen, which is horrible.

When he came home in November, he got right in the car and went to see his friends. I bought him beer; I mean, if he's willing to die for the country, man, he can have a beer. He says he needs the beer to calm down and sleep at night. He says he doesn't sleep as well at home because he was worried about his unit. What would happen if they needed him and he wasn't there? When they're over there, it's all about taking care of each other.

He was having flashbacks about the kids and the old woman. He was worried about his people. When he was over there, he could think about home, and he really slept well. But when he was here, he'd be worried about them. So even though he enjoyed being home, he went back very willingly.

I said last November, "Do you want to go to Canada? I like Canada. Your girlfriend can stay with your dog and you and I can go to Canada until this war's over and then we'll come back." He goes, "Canada sends you back now, Mom." He also told me, "Real soldiers go back."

He had been very careful on the phone and in emails not to say anything negative, because there was one press person who was with their platoon. One sergeant said something that could be construed as negative: he said the entire Iraq War was bullshit. They made this guy's life miserable.

John's trying to stay under the radar. He doesn't want accolades. He doesn't want to be a general. He wants to do a good job. He wants to get paid what he deserves. Whatever job he's told to do, that's what he does, to the best of his ability. That's his job, whether he likes it or not. But he's a smart guy, he's seeing how wasteful and futile a lot of it is.

I hope that nothing I've done would impact the way they see him. I'd be all over them if I smelled that. Even though he's shared some things about what he's seen and done. The other day, last weekend, he called, and I said, "You think you're really getting anything done now?" And he goes, "Not really."

At first, when they set up the check points, he said, "You know, it is better, now that they leave people at the check points, because an area that was made safe, it keeps it safe." But now the suicide bombers are targeting the check points. They've moved back into some of the neighborhoods they'd been in before.

He sees all of Baghdad, not just one neighborhood. If somebody gets into trouble, they call the Strykers in. And I'm thinking, "Oh, dandy." At least he's back on base. They were working nights for a couple of months, and that was hard. I sent him a lot of food. The mess hall feeds them at midnight, and that's it. They're not open twenty-four/seven. I guess they give them some of that dried-out stuff in the tank, but I sent him a lot of snack food, so they'd have something else they could munch on when they were in the Stryker.

Over the holiday was when John spent five days off the base, in his tank, and they came back to a neighborhood they hadn't been in for a while, and he said they were throwing rocks at them. It wasn't really until that time that I got active. That was the kick in the rear end I needed to go do something.

I must have seen an article on MFSO last summer, as soon as John went. At first I was in support mode, you know, "What do you need, what can I send you?" In the fall at some point I joined MFSO and started getting all these emails, which I read. But with teaching, and now I have another daughter getting ready for college, I don't have a lot of spare time. I was still on the periphery. But over the Christmas holiday, I had a week vacation, and they put out an email that if anybody wanted to help in the office, to let them know. And since that was the free time I had, I emailed back that I'd come down and do something. So I did.

Nikki and Charley [of MFSO] told me the three-thousandth death was coming up. They told me there was going to be a rally down at Park Street in Boston. Charley made me up some posters. I gave him a photograph of my son and he printed them up and I glued them onto posterboard, and that was really the first action that I took to get involved.

I was so naïve. I thought once people found out that this war is wrong, we were just gonna leave. How stupid was that?! I'm a goal-oriented person, and trying to change a machine like the Bush machine is not an easy thing to do. Now I appreciate how hard it is.

You know, it's not just my son. Now that he's extended, it's another six months, every day wondering who is it going to be today. But even when it's not him, it's not much of a moral victory. It's twenty-two a week now. Twenty-two other families—brothers, sisters, mothers, fathers—are getting the news. Whether it's me or somebody else, what difference does it make?

And the Iraqis: my God, thousands and thousands. Two million have fled. Their lives are horrible. They were just saying on the news the other day, they had a better life when Saddam was in charge. After all this, to have it come to that. Given that we are now seen as the enemy, it's obvious that we are not helping the situation. So let's go, and if they want help, by all means. If when we leave, there's a specific need that we could help fill, by all means. I mean, look what we've done to their country.

My last phone call to Senator Kerry's [D-MA] office, I had a little chat with the aide, and this guy was saying, "Well, we don't want them to be without soap." And I said, "Trust me, soap doesn't come out of that budget, it comes out of a different budget, so if that's your argument . . ." He did say something interesting. He said it took eighteen bills to get us out of Vietnam. I didn't know if he was full of shit or not, but sure enough, I looked it up, and it was years.

My eighteen-year-old daughter and I went to the big demonstration on January 27 in D.C., which was awesome. I stood next to Jane Fonda. Oh my God, I turned around and it was Jane Fonda. We did get to stand on stage. I didn't have to say anything, thank goodness. I'm really not a public sort of person. But if we think it's going to help . . . And we went to one in Boston. Unfortunately, there's not a lot of MFSO people in the Merrimack Valley region. But there's a pretty good peace group, the Merrimack Valley People for Peace. So I vigil with them sometimes in downtown Andover. They like having someone from MFSO, and it gives me a group to be with.

*[I ask about the possible repercussions of her activism for John, now that his tour in Iraq has been extended.]* I do worry about that, but that can't be a reason not to do it. Somebody's got to do something. He did tell me, too, that he's proud of me for what I'm doing, and he's thinking about contacting Iraq Veterans Against the War when he gets home.

For him, the structured environment in the military, the well-laid-out consequences and rewards, all that kind of stuff, is a positive thing, and I think for a lot of the kids, that's true. And even having to go to war. But not a war so George Bush can go get the oil business.

In Michael Moore's book [*Will They Ever Trust Us Again?*; Simon & Schuster, 2004], he says that the military are willing to give their lives for this country, and the only thing they ask in return is not to take it lightly, not to put their lives at risk unless we absolutely positively have to. I think, for me, that just sums it all up. This was not a "have to" by any stretch of the imagination.

I'd love to have a little chat with George Bush. "Shame on you." I'd shake my finger at him. What has happened to vets' benefits? Somebody told me that now you need an advocate to get your vets' benefits. And they're now diagnosing some PTSD as personality disorders so they don't have to cover them. We have our young men and women putting themselves in harm's way, and it's, "Oh, by the way, we won't help you when you get out."

What do we do to get out? I write my letters and make my phone calls. They could give a rat's ass. I know one thing that makes this movement different from the one during the Vietnam War. At that point, almost everybody had a loved one involved, or knew directly of someone involved. With the draft, and fifty thousand guys dead, it was on a much greater scale. But here, it's just a handful of us. We don't get that visibility. It's not affecting most people at all. I don't know how we get people to see the harm it does for everyone, and the long-term effects. This will be a whole group of people with emotional issues.

*[I ask what she thinks about the Bush administration argument that you can't support the troops without supporting the war.]* That couldn't be further from the truth. This administration, which coined this phrase and has used it right along, they're the ones that sent soldiers off without correct protective gear, in Humvees that were deathtraps, they sent soldiers off totally unprepared, and yet they're the ones that use this line!

The one thing I have found that has warmed my heart since I got involved is the lengths the American people will go to, to take care of their soldiers. There's nothing they won't do. Which unfortunately enables Bush to say, "Pay for the war, or you're hurting your soldiers." It astounds me the way the Bush administration has been able to manipulate people to get them to believe that. What we need is a catch phrase like that.

I find that so many people say, "What can I do?" John just got a whole box of Girl Scout cookies from one friend. Another person made a quilt. I tell people now, "If you really want to help these guys, call your congressman." If we really cared for these guys, we'd get them out of the middle of a civil war, and bring them home.

# Chapter 14
# Melida Arredondo

*Melida works in public health in the Boston area. Her stepson, Alexander Arredondo, was killed in Iraq in 2004. Melida's husband Carlos often brings up the rear of anti-war marches in his pickup truck, which is covered with photographs of his son. Behind the truck he pulls a flag-draped coffin like the ones the mainstream U.S. media have agreed not to show arriving in the States.*

We're a blended family. Alex was eight and Brian was five in 1993 when I met Carlos. All three were very enchanting; I fell in love with them all together. Carlos was going through a nasty divorce. There was a lot of sadness at their separation. I married Carlos in 1997. Carlos and I were living in Roslindale, Massachusetts. The boys were with their mom in Randolph. We saw each other as much as we could.

In 2001, Alex turned seventeen, and he—apparently, we didn't know until much later—he had quite a relationship with a recruiter in his high school. The recruiter came to his mom's house and asked her to sign on the dotted line for early enlistment. Then Alex told Carlos and me. It was still peace-time.

Once 9/11 happened, things spun out of control. Carlos is a news junkie. I got on my knees and did a lot of praying. Alex went to boot camp in August of 2002. He managed to come home for Thanksgiving that year, and Christmas. After that was immediate deployment to his first tour of Iraq. He was in Kuwait in late January 2003, and entered Iraq with the first to go. He was there much longer than he anticipated. You could see from his emails how he was frustrated being in Iraq so long and he was unclear what his mission was.

He returned finally to the U.S. On September 25, we got a call from Alex. He said, "What are you doing?" Carlos was getting ready for bed, wearing a towel. Then the doorbell rang. Alex said, "Someone's at your door." Carlos looks out the window; there's Alex on his cellphone at the door. It was a very joyous moment.

Alex went back to Camp Pendleton in San Diego. He called a lot. I'd tease him about being a ladies' man. He had a girlfriend, Sheila, back home I really liked. His mother was living in Maine then.

He came home for Christmas. Alex didn't sleep at all, and he was a kid who liked to sleep. I hoped it was just due to his wanting to spend time with his friends. Now I think he had this feeling of anxiety, to live each moment of life to the fullest.

The boys were going to Maine to see their mother, so we had Christmas a few days early. I got from Alex a gold ring that says "Amor." I never take it off. I would joke around about looking forward to green-eyed babies; Sheila and Alex both had green eyes. Things were the best they've been.

Alex, Brian, Carlos, and I made a family decision. When Alex went back to Pendleton, Carlos and I would move back to Florida. My mother was getting older and needed more care. Alex supported the idea. Two of his closest Marine buddies lived near the neighborhood.

The plan was supposed to go: we would leave May 10 or so in 2004 for Florida. Alex had leave from the Marines. He was going to Massachusetts, then to Maine, then to Florida. But he didn't make it to Florida. Brian saw him; he was staying with his mom. We didn't get to see him that last time.

There were a lot of calls. The relationship between his mom, dad, and me was improved. Then on August 25, Carlos's birthday, he was walking around with his cellphone, expecting the boys to call. Instead, the Marines came to the house. Carlos was outside painting the fence. He was looking at the van, thinking Alex was in it. Then they said that Lance Corporal Alexander Arredondo had died in the service of his country, six hours earlier.

A habit we all have is to check the news. When I woke up that morning, NPR said three Marines had been killed in Najaf. I turned off the radio and decided not to tell Carlos. I just gave him his card and kissed him goodbye. When I got to work—I was the director of an assisted-living program—I went to see my favorite elder. This elder and his girlfriend asked me what I thought of the war. I said I'd heard about casualties that morning, and I had a boy there. Then I got a call from Carlos about 2:00 p.m. on my cell, which is very unusual. I always say, "Don't call on the cell unless it's life or death."

In Spanish, he said, "They killed Alex." I just went to pieces, started screaming and wailing, on my knees. I scared the elders out of their minds. My mother was visiting the assisted-living place that day. We drove home, three miles; I didn't drop her off. As I was about to turn the corner, my mom said, "That boy dying is going to kill Carlos."

That's when I saw the fire in front of the house. *[Carlos had jumped into the Marines' van and set it on fire.]* I saw my husband, and a Marine on top of him. Carlos was burnt. He was fighting the Marine. They said, "Don't park your car there, the van will explode."

I left the car at the corner with my eighty-two-year-old mother, and ran back. I saw Carlos was still freaking out, resisting. I said in Spanish, "Relax, calm down, you're not making it any better." Then the pain hit him. He was shaking.

I was saying, "He'll pay for the damages. . . . Are you sure it was Alex?" They kept saying, "Yes." I was wailing. A cop came up and said, "If you don't stop it, we'll arrest you too." I said, "Go ahead. My son has been killed." The cops didn't know why the Marines were there. Afterward he came up and apologized.

I have no idea when the media came. I heard copters overhead. They were filming.

Carlos's cellphone rang. My mother picked it up and gave it to me. It was Brian. He already knew Alex had been killed. The Marines tried to tell his mom and dad at the same time. I said, "Brian, my God, your father tried to kill himself." CNN was showing it live; he saw it on TV in Bangor.

Carlos first went to Hollywood Memorial Hospital, then Ryder Trauma Center in Miami. He was there one week. The press was all over us. I kept going without eating or sleeping. Seven days later we managed to get some money together. One of Alex's friends—his father was an Air Force paramedic—he and his mom came to us. They wouldn't let us go on a flight without medical personnel, so they came with us. The one and only time Carlos flew first class.

The whole family went: two dogs, Nana, Carlos, and me. In Boston, Carlos was transferred to Brigham and Women's burn unit. Carlos was on a gurney; that's how he went to Alex's wake, funeral mass, funeral, and gravesite. The procession was miles long, about two hundred cars. Alex was laid to rest in Walpole. The funeral mass was at St. Thomas's church in Jamaica Plain, where Carlos used to take the boys when they were little.

Carlos couldn't walk. So I stayed in the hotel, then slept in his room, being with him. We stayed in Boston for Carlos's medical treatment. They wanted to do skin grafts immediately; he had second and third degree burns. There was a delay over Labor Day weekend. Then they prepped him for anesthesia while they got the operating room ready. They all donned the hats, the gloves, etc.; they wanted to peek at him again. His skin had gone from gray to pink. In that time, the skin healed itself. Though he had scars, he didn't have to have surgery. The doctors said it was a miracle.

Sleeping with Carlos in his room, I thought he was playing with me or something. He would move his arms under the sheet like he was a ghost. He had dreams that people were watching him and touching him. On September 7, they decided to do physical therapy and see if he could walk. His burns turned purple as eggplant. I thought his legs would explode. By the next day, he was walking.

They said he just needed home care. But home was in Florida. We stayed with a friend and got short-term treatment and help from Upham's Corner Health Center, where I used to work in public health. We were in Boston until December. Then we went to Florida. Before that, we got to see Brian. He'd been staying with his mom in Maine, concerned she was all alone.

It was hard on all of us. It was really sad. We'd been going to Alex's gravesite once or twice a day. Carlos carved a cross as a marker until the monument was ready. We put flowers there. Friends put holiday ornaments. It was just a shock to everybody. I made sure there were a six-month and a one-year mass. His friends were invited.

We ended up relocating back to Boston in February 2005. I started working at Upham's Corner again. Carlos was seeing bereavement counselors through the VA, a psychiatrist through our medical plan. He was trying to get himself together. Brian's mom moved to Norwood. Brian's been living with us. He's nineteen now. He's still having a hard time. He hasn't finished high school, he isn't working. He's had a rough go of it. The code the kids use these days is, "bored" means depressed. At one point, the psychiatrist hospitalized him.

Alex was always there for Brian. Even when his mom and dad split up, got back together, split up again, they always had each other. Sometimes he looks fine, other times . . . At this age they're trying to find themselves; I don't see that going on. He plays a lot of video games.

We were opposed to the war from the beginning. I was arrested protesting the first Gulf War. We were ambivalent about how to support Alex in the first adult decision of his life, not take that away from him, not cause a rift. We didn't hit the street protesting. I would write some things. Our efforts to speak out were low key.

It wasn't until we were forced into the limelight by Carlos's actions that we decided to use it for good. We met Nancy and Charley [of

MFSO] through a mutual friend in October 2004. Carlos began to speak out in earnest at the one-year anniversary of Alex's death.

Carlos couldn't believe the charges were all dropped. Back in the day, you'd get hanged or shot for burning a military van. The thing that saved his butt, we found out afterward from the Hollywood police department, was that so many people called and wrote in, "You can't charge this man." In the police report, they told Carlos the Marines had stayed half an hour, waiting for me. He asked them to leave three times. The Marines said they wouldn't press charges, but the City of Hollywood was thinking about it.

During the week Carlos was in the hospital in Miami, people dropped off food and gave us cards with money in them. A radio station in California gave out our information and we got hundreds of condolence cards from all over the world. That's what aided me. My husband wasn't in the best of spirits, to say the least. His mom also was falling to pieces. All of that outpouring of love really helped.

I could tell speaking out was helping Carlos heal. It's a very important means of therapy. He says, "On the day I speak out, I sleep better that night." Speaking out doesn't come naturally in his family. The speaking out, the visual display, was all new to him after Alex was killed.

The reason we do this? People say sometimes, "You're disrespecting Alex." But Alex wanted peace in Iraq. All Marines say they don't leave their friends behind. That's what we're doing. We're not leaving them behind.

# Chapter 15
# Bob Watada

*Bob and his wife Rosa live in Oregon. His son, First Lieutenant Ehren Watada, was the first commissioned officer to publicly refuse deployment to Iraq.*

I'm a second-generation Japanese-American, born and raised in Colorado. I went to college and the Peace Corps to avoid the draft for Vietnam. When I came back they still wanted me to go to war. So I got a doctorate. I tried academia for a year, and then I went to work for state government. I wound up doing it in Hawaii for thirty-two years.

Ehren was born here and grew up in Hawaii. He played soccer, little league baseball. He was a good student. He was an Eagle Scout; I was an assistant scoutmaster. Ehren went on to college in Spokane, Washington. It was a little cold. He finished up at Hawaii Pacific University in 2003. Then he went into the Army.

I was very much against the Vietnam War. There was absolutely no way we should have gone over there. I felt the same about Iraq. I told my son I didn't think it was a good idea to go into the Army. But there was a lot of fear-mongering, telling young people to be afraid of terrorism. Ehren felt he should do his part for his country; he was patriotic. He went to basic training in South Carolina, then to officer school in Georgia, then artillery school in Oklahoma. He was deployed to Korea for one year, up to mid-June 2005. Then he was asked to go to Fort Lewis in Washington.

His commanders said he was going to lead his men into battle, so he should learn about the consequences of war. He was going to have to explain to his men why they might have to die for their country. He began to study.

He was shocked to learn about the lies by the president, in particular the lies in the 2003 State of the Union speech about weapons of mass destruction, saying Saddam had them and we knew where they were, and that we knew there was a connection between Saddam and Osama bin Laden, when in fact they hated each other. All this was coming out in 2005.

He was very disheartened to see that the president ignored the Constitution, which says we don't invade other countries. He saw we'd been bombing Iraq for six or seven years, enforcing the no-fly zone, destroying their electric grids, medical facilities, water systems. It's shameful. Thousands of kids were dying because of the lack of potable water. He was finding this out, telling me, getting me to learn what was happening.

At this time Ehren realized, not only do we have gross violations of the Geneva Conventions, the U.N. Charter, and the Nuremberg Principles—he explained we were violating Article Six of the Constitution. When we sign an international treaty, it becomes the law of the country. In 1996 we passed laws outlawing torture, but he found we were still allowing it.

He's being trained in Washington to order the shooting of homes where there may be civilians. Murder is what it is. He hears about the horrors and atrocities going on in Iraq, massacring the civilian population under the guise that we can't tell the difference. There are a lot of racial and religious undertones in the training, the idea that Muslims need to be vanquished.

My son is reading all this, and comes to the point where he says he cannot participate in this massacre of innocent people. He's finding it very troubling to put his own men at risk when the whole purpose of our government is to dominate the Middle East, not for us but for Halliburton, Bechtel, Chevron—the multinationals taking huge chunks; we're privatizing Iraq. We're doing this for oil. He doesn't say this publicly, but I do.

It's sad that almost everything this administration says is a lie. The U.S. has taxpayer-paid death squads over there, training them to go and foment this kind of so-called sectarian violence. I've talked to one young Iraqi man, a scholar in the U.S., who is half Sunni, half Shiia. He says, "Why should I want to kill a part of myself?"

In January 2006, Ehren writes to the Command saying he can no longer participate in this war. I told him to just go quietly; I don't want him to go to jail. But he says, "You always told me to do the right thing, and the right thing is not to participate in this war, not to participate in these war crimes."

Many soldiers are brainwashed very early, taught not to question. We brought him up to make decisions for himself. To resist was his decision. I support him. It's not easy for me and my wife. We'll do anything to try to keep him out of the brig.

There are two major charges: one, resisting a movement; and two, conduct unbecoming an officer and a gentleman, for criticizing the administration. He could get a total of six years. The court martial trial started in February 2007.

Ehren is confined to the state of Washington. Rosa—his stepmother—and I have been traveling around the country. My wife is from Peru. She gave interviews in Spanish on the west coast. Now Ehren's mother is touring the east coast. We've found tremendous support throughout the country, just about everywhere we've gone.

We're very proud of him. There have been several other resisters, not officers but enlisted men. At the base at Fort Lewis, he thought he'd be very unpopular, but he says all the time people on the base come up to thank him. They know he's doing it for them.

# Chapter 16
# Denise Thomas

*Denise lives in Georgia. She is both an Army wife and an Army mother.*
*Her husband Theartis has retired from his career in the Army and Army*
*National Guard. Her daughter Shanell was deployed to Iraq in spite of*
*severe scoliosis. Denise tried to kill herself during Shanell's deployment,*
*believing that would force the Army to send her daughter home.*

I was born Ritha Denise Camp in Alabama. I was the middle girl. It was
girl, boy, girl, boy, girl, boy, so everybody had somebody to fight with.

My parents divorced when I was eight, in 1964. My mom raised us
on a teacher's salary. My dad's financial mind was stuck in the '30s
about how much it cost to raise a child. She didn't get a lot of help from
him, and she seldom asked. When I got to college and she asked him to
help, he gave her fifteen dollars.

I did great in school until I got to the ninth grade. I had a black
teacher telling us that white people worked together and were always
progressing, and black people were always pulling apart and retrogress-
ing. He said that any white child could beat us academically at any time.
I made A's and B's until then. I think it set a tone for the rest of my life.
There was always his voice in the back of my head telling me I couldn't
do it.

When I started high school, there wasn't much integration. Then
there was forced integration. I went on so many marches, when I was
around thirteen to fifteen. I felt better doing something than nothing. My
mother told me she was proud of me for taking an interest. She was always swamped with paperwork at home. During the school year, she
worked twelve hours a day. When we got old enough, we helped her
grade papers. She always took a second job during the summer.

I went to college and started substitute teaching. When I was eighteen, I met a man and married him three months later. He was violent. I

found out I was pregnant when I left him. He was stalking me at school. I was hiding from him and missed a lot of classes. I had to drop out.

Before the baby was born, Mom talked me into moving back home. Shanell was born in December 1975, and when she was four months old, Mom got married and moved a hundred miles away to Dublin, Georgia. My older sister Angie bought the house, and I was living with her and her husband. I knew my sister loved me, and I knew I was in the way.

I was working in an all-night hamburger place. My sister thought I had a ride home every night but I was walking, five or six miles. At first I was sitting there at three in the morning waiting for a city bus at seven, but the manager threatened to fire me for that, so I began to walk home. I let myself get picked up one night. I was raped and I got pregnant.

A few weeks later Dad bought me a car; he died a few weeks after that. I put my daughter in the car and drove to Mama's house. My intent was to visit Mom, then go to a larger town and find an unwed mother's home, but I ended up telling her what was going on. Her husband wasn't keen on me staying, so Mama made arrangements for me to stay with his niece. That's where I met my husband Theartis. He and my new cousin worked together. I was making everybody think I had a bad marriage I was running away from; that's the story I told my husband when we met. But a few weeks later I had a miscarriage and told him the whole story. I was five months along.

He came to see me. It seemed like he was really concerned. He started making me laugh and told me things wouldn't look so bad even in a few days, and he was right.

We dated around nine months and decided to sneak and get married. This was before my daughter's second birthday. She called him "Daddy"; he was the only daddy she ever knew. He bought her a baby carrier for his bicycle and rode her around town on his bicycle all the time. They were inseparable.

I'd told my daughter where babies came from, as far as you could tell a three-year-old. She put her broken crayons in a scarf and brought them to me and said, "Here, Mama, this is for your baby son." "I don't have a baby son, I only have a baby daughter." "Well, call Daddy and you could be working on it!"

My husband was in the process of getting the house rented out and moving to Valdosta. I decided to go back to college at Valdosta State. I think the first day I was back in college was when I got pregnant with our son. Shanell was five. We didn't have any health insurance. It was really rough. My mother suggested Artis join the military, so that's what he did, in July 1981. My son was born at the end of September. People don't know what kind of hardships military families face. There was a lot of being separated and not being able to communicate, especially before cellphones.

Artis was able to be there when our son was born. This was while he was in AIT, Advanced Individual Training, after basic training. He drove close to two hundred miles from Augusta to Albany when I was in labor. I was overjoyed to see him. My mom was glad to see him too; by the time he got there, I'd been in labor twenty hours. By the next day, they decided to give me a C-section, after nearly forty-two hours. He had to go back after Jeron was born. I went into an emotional nosedive when he left.

Artis was always ready to go, but he was never deployed to a combat zone. He was gone more than he was home, working fourteen or sixteen hours a day regularly. The kids were used to him not being there. We usually lived in family housing on base, and we moved every twelve to eighteen months. We were in Georgia until mid-1982. Then we went to Kansas. By the time we got there we were only with him for seven months. We had to move again with a twenty-five-day notice. My daughter was still in school, and it really shocked me about the military that they don't care about young kids in school. We just had to do the best we could.

The first time my daughter showed behavior problems was in Kansas, in first grade. I know that came from a lot of moving. She was diagnosed as hyperactive. I had to watch her diet, sugar and everything.

Then we went to Fort Benning, in Columbus, Georgia. We saw our families in Dublin and Albany every chance we got then. We were there a year and a half. During that time, I was involved in a singing group at church. We ended up on TV a couple of times and traveled to other cities. That was the time I loved the most.

Then Artis was deployed to Darmstadt, Germany. He had been deployed earlier to Trier for a year and a half, but we didn't go with him. This time we went with him and stayed for three years. I liked the country and loved the Germans, but couldn't get along with the Americans over there.

I was kind of miserable. I couldn't even sing gospel songs in my own apartment. The walls were paper thin, and they'd yell for me to shut up. During that time, if it had not been for the church group, I think I could have committed homicide. I was never so angry in my life as I was when I was there.

In Germany, my husband started telling our daughter constantly to stand up straight, but she couldn't. Her back started curving really fast. It would pop so loud, I'd hear her yell "Ah!" in pain. She was diagnosed as having severe scoliosis. The doctor said to get her in a back brace immediately. We didn't find out she was taller than me until they put her in that back brace. She wore the brace for five years. It was a hard plastic brace. She would sneak and take it off whenever she could get away with it. Until she got the brace, I had back pain so bad until I could hardly function. It was all in my head. When she got the brace, my back stopped hurting. Her behavior changed after she got the brace, though; she was a little antisocial, and she cried and complained a lot.

We left Germany in '89. We came back to Georgia for about six months. My husband was on recruiter duty in Dublin as a compassionate reassignment. I was ill and needed surgery. After six months we had to relocate to Fort Bragg, North Carolina. When the Gulf War started, the rest of my husband's unit was deployed, but they put him on casualty duty. He didn't want that. His duty was to guide family members through the process after the death of their loved one. I knew he'd rather be with his own company. He tried to volunteer to go in some of the guys' places who had pregnant wives, but they wouldn't let him. That affected him a lot. He wanted to be out there with his men.

After the Gulf War was over, some of his men had gotten kind of cocky. They said he couldn't tell them anything, because they had gone to war and he hadn't. My husband figured if he had lost control of his men, he had no business in the Army. He got out and went into the Army National Guard. He started an automotive shop and I was selling real estate. Our daughter graduated from high school. She had gotten out of her back brace the year before. She could wear clothes she wanted to wear instead of those loose tops all the time. She didn't get any more treatment after my husband left the military.

My medical bills started to eat up our income. I kept getting chronic bronchitis, turning into pneumonia; then I developed high blood pressure. I was volunteering for Habitat for Humanity, but we lost our own home to foreclosure. We moved back home to Georgia, into my mom's house. She and my stepdad were living together in his house.

I think we were all kind of lost at this time. Shanell had gone to business school in North Carolina and got a license in cosmetology, but we ran out of money so she never finished business school. In Dublin we had four people in the house, six jobs, and one car. My son found a job in high school. I worked long hours as a manager in the mall. My husband worked as a mechanic and sold hardware. The kids tried their best to help us, but we were knee-deep in debt and had a lot of medical bills. But we were together, and I was happy for that.

My daughter got engaged at nineteen, to a straight thug with a capital T. I suspected he was hitting her. She broke the engagement and had to get a restraining order. The thug had run up bills and bad debt. He made a large purchase at Wal-Mart, and Wal-Mart sent the police after Shanell. By the time we got the identity theft resolved, we were several thousand dollars in debt. Shanell's job and mine were ruined. That's when Shanell decided to go into the Army. That stupid guy she almost married is the main reason she ended up in Iraq.

Shanell found out the Army was giving a twelve thousand dollar bonus if you went into the Intelligence MOS. She told them about the scoliosis. She was held back to be re-evaluated. By that time, the sign-up for the intelligence job had passed. Instead of waiting, she asked the recruiter what else she could do. He said with MP [Military Police], she'd still get the bonus. So she went in as an MP. Less than a year later when some of the intelligence people were getting their bonuses, she found out that it wasn't true.

She enlisted in '99, and left home with Uncle Sam in January 2000. I was trying to let her make her own decisions. I had to let her go. My husband, like me, was apprehensive, but proud of her for trying to get her life back together. I tried to quiet my own fears, because I knew she was not a warrior at heart.

She went into basic training in Fort Leonard Wood, Missouri. She had problems from the start. She fractured a hip in basic, finished it on crutches. I was proud of her determination.

Shanell was stationed next at Fort Lee, Virginia. She ended up working with the Richmond police, in narcotics. She loved that. I was really worried about her. But that was nothing compared to how I worried when she was in Iraq.

She got orders for Germany. That's when I found out her back was bothering her again. I could hear it pop from across the room. When she got to Germany, two Army doctors declared her undeployable. She should have gotten a medical discharge or reassignment. Instead, she was sent into a war zone. She was in Kuwait before the war started. I fully believed that the war would never start. I believed it was no more than a bluff. We were already in Afghanistan. There was no troop build-up. I thought we had a group of Iraqi dissidents ready to take Saddam out because he had killed their families, and our forces were there to back them up if needed. Starting the Iraq War under such circumstances did not make sense to me. Then came "Shock and Awe." It may not have shocked or awed the Iraqis, but it shocked and awed me.

Shanell got to Baghdad after a march across the desert. During the march, they had hardships. Food blew away in a sandstorm. She didn't have napkins for her feminine needs. Her jeep went down a few times. When they got to Baghdad, they ended up living in one of Saddam's bombed-out castles. When Bush was saying his "Mission Accomplished" speech, Shanell was seeing dead bodies lying in the streets for days, Iraqi women being raped, because there was no local law enforcement. Everything was total chaos and there weren't enough of them to do anything.

By now we'd moved to Atlanta. When I saw that speech, I went crazy. I started throwing things at the TV. I said, "I hope the soldiers don't believe him and think it's over!" A sinking feeling told me it was just getting started. Any respect I may have had for Bush was totally lost with that speech. By the time he made that "Bring it on" comment, I was sure he'd lost his mind.

By that time, my life was in total disarray. They were telling my husband he was going to Iraq, then not, then he was, then he wasn't. This went on for three years until he decided to retire in 2006. He was eleven and a half years active duty; the rest of his twenty-four years was Guard. I was going crazy. He kept his emotions under control; he's a soldier.

Our daughter stayed in touch as much as she could. We didn't have a computer then, and her unit didn't have email. Letters took three or four weeks to reach her. I couldn't help but follow the news on Iraq. I had even higher blood pressure by now, plus heart trouble. My new doctor wanted to place me in the hospital to get me stabilized, but I told him I had things I had to do. The medication he put me on didn't wipe me out and it got my blood pressure down, but I knew that when I ran out I'd be out for a while. I took the medicine every two or three days. I didn't tell my husband because he would try to work himself to death to get it for me and he was already working long hours.

I didn't smile a lot. I had a huge weight gain. I aged about ten or fifteen years while Shanell was gone. By the time she was in Iraq three months, people who didn't know me well thought I was my own mother.

I knew Shanell wasn't doing as well as she was saying. She told me she was guarding a large hole in the palace wall and in the darkness, someone came up onto the grounds. She yelled for them to stop, give their name, and state their business. It was an American lieutenant walking toward her. He dropped to the ground and yelled his name and rank, and the soldiers behind him ran forward and drew their guns. The soldiers behind Shanell had drawn their guns. They were ready to shoot each other. Shanell says they all laugh about it now, but I can't.

Shanell told us that part of her job was training Iraqi police. She called us, excited. "More than ten bombs dropped in the parking lot and nobody got hurt!" Another time, a rocket landed in front of her jeep and she hardly had time to stop. She thought all the prayers I asked church members to pray for her had stopped working, but I said, "You didn't get hurt, so they're working." I sounded more confident than I felt.

I was shaky the whole time. At one point, anything anybody said to me, I'd cry. One time at church, someone asked how my daughter was doing, and I just turned around and went back home. My husband couldn't even talk to me. It was just uncontrollable crying. I later found out from Shanell that she was close to death from dehydration and other problems during that same time, which lasted about three weeks. She was rapidly losing weight and would faint. They would hook her to an IV and pump her up with fluids, then send her back to work. That kept up until she was incoherent and had lost thirty-eight pounds in two weeks. Then she was air-lifted to a medical facility where a young medic took good care of her. I learned most of this much later from that young medic, after they both came home. Back then he'd seen what shape Shanell was in and tried to steal her medical records and get them to me, so I could get her out of there. I believe he got in trouble, but he won't discuss it. I only learn the real story when I hear Shanell talking to another soldier. Especially if they think I'm not listening.

I started going to the doctor again. My pressure had gotten alarmingly high. My heart was enlarged. I was totally depressed. I didn't tell my daughter any of this.

About two months after I got back on the medication, my husband wanted me to go see my mom. I think I had him at his wits' end. I felt I had failed Shanell because nothing I did could get her out. I started thinking the Army wanted her dead so no one would know what condition she was forced to fight in.

I went to see Mama; then my thinking really took a dark turn. The doctor said that if I got off my medication I'd have a stroke or a heart attack and I'd die. So I got off my medications to get my daughter home. I thought the only way to get her home was for my funeral. That made logical sense to me at the time.

My mother figured out what I was doing. She asked how I'd feel if she did that to me. That snapped me out of it. My mom is smart. She figures out everything without anybody telling her. My daughter later learned about this in a speech; I wrote the speech before I knew she would be there. She said, "If you did that, I'd have never forgiven you." I

said, "I know that now, but that was just my state of mind." She hugged
me.

That's what life was like before I heard about MFSO. Someone had
told me about it on an internet forum, but I didn't know enough about the
internet to search and find them. I wanted to get my daughter out of Iraq.
I wanted to tell people how medically-unfit soldiers are treated. I was
going to politicians' offices and being shooed away. I sent letters through
the mail that went unanswered. I learned to send emails, but they were
just ignored.

That January was when I met members of the Georgia Peace and
Justice Coalition. The first time they met me, I was marching on my own
in the Martin Luther King march in Atlanta in January '04. I was tired of
getting called the N word and a liar, on the internet and in person. I was
happy to see friendly faces. Sometimes I'd say, "You're middle-class
white people. Why are you protesting the war?" They just laughed.

Shanell was in Iraq for eleven months, three weeks, and two days.
She went to Germany after Iraq, stayed there thirty days, and came back
on the first anniversary of the beginning of the war, in March '04. The
next evening, March 20, she and Jeron were with me at a candlelight
vigil in Decatur to stop the war. There we met Cynthia McKinney [for-
mer U.S. Representative, D-GA].

About June of '04, Cynthia asked me to speak for her congressional
campaign. That's when I discovered that I really liked to speak. I've been
speaking ever since. Many times I even sing, and I've been writing songs
about my experiences. I got the Georgia Chapter of MFSO started and
became an extremely active member of the Georgia Peace and Justice
Coalition. It made a big difference in how I felt. I could network with
people and get ideas from them.

I also started a website, Peoples Rights Organization (org-
sites.com/ga/save-our-soldiers). I'd learned to network on the internet. I
wrote an article, *A Soldier's Mother Speaks Out!*, and sent it to the national organization of MFSO. They sent it to an internet magazine called
*Intervention*. Before I knew it, fifteen thousand people had read it, and I
got about three thousand emails. Most were totally supportive. The ugly
ones were really ugly. It was the first time I knew that anybody cared.

My daughter says, "Mom, you've really met some protesting people!" She talks about how much I have changed; I can surf the internet,
build a website, organize an anti-war group, I can actually fight with
people. She had never heard me get in a war of words before she went to
Iraq. She thinks I'm pretty weird, but she's proud of me.

Shanell was with us nearly thirty days, then took off five days early to see some of her buddies before driving on to West Point in New York. She was stationed there for one year, then she was technically out of the military. But the military has "counselors." They knocked on her door and threatened her with Iraq until she agreed to sign up for the Reserves. This is one reason I can't call it an "all volunteer" Army. It's a "partially stop-lossed, partially coerced, and partially volunteer" Army.

The first day Shanell got back from West Point, I was at a meeting in St. Louis. When I came home, she was in the house asleep, about one a.m. My husband said she went to sleep twenty minutes earlier. I walked into the room and she jumped up and screamed. I told her it was me and held her real tight.

A few months later, she called me. She was living across town. It was four a.m., and she was agitated. She said the insurgents were trying to burn down her grandmother's house. She was having flashbacks. Her fiancé was with her. He didn't know what to do. Shanell would not rest until I called Mama and made sure she was okay.

Shanell is married now, and they have some obstacles to overcome. She has PTSD; he's working and going to school. He's an African, and now he's a U.S. citizen. It's a lot of stress on them. He's so focused on getting his degree, a lot of what's going on with her goes over his head. But he'll call and ask me or Artis what to do because Shanell is so agitated sometimes.

Her back is the same. Last time I was in Atlanta, I spent two nights in the emergency room with her. She's waiting tables, and she was in excruciating pain from lifting those heavy trays. She won't admit this, but she has memory problems. Before she went to Iraq, she had almost a photographic memory. Now she has trouble remembering details. It's hard for her to keep any job that she really wants. She still has her bubbly personality, her get-up-and-go spirit. She looks like a happy young woman to everybody except me and her dad, her brother, and her husband.

They told her to "suck it up" so much when she was in combat, now she won't get any help. I can't get her to get help for PTSD or to push them to do something about her back. I know that the heavy equipment she had to carry while in the military caused the recurrence of her problems with scoliosis.

She's still in Army Reserves. If they threaten to send her back, that'll give me a platform to tell everyone how medically-unfit soldiers are treated. It doesn't frighten me anymore. I've learned how to fight back.

# Chapter 17
# Larry Syverson

*Larry is a scientist who works for the Virginia Department of Environmental Quality. He has four sons, all of whom have served in the U.S. military. Branden, a sergeant first class in the Army, expects to be deployed for a second Iraq tour in 2007. Brent is in the Navy and has twice been deployed to Iraqi waters. Bryce was a staff sergeant on his second deployment to Iraq at the time of this interview. Brian has received a medical discharge from the Navy. Larry started protesting the war before it began. He told me his most recent protest was number 218.*

I'm not anti-war or anything. I've had a son in the military since 1989 and this is the first time I've been against their deployment.

We knew Branden was going to join the Army. He talked about it through high school. At the time, it was a good career, good benefits; we were very proud of him.

Brent was talking about college. We said, "You can live at home, go to a good state school." He just came home one day and told us he joined the Navy. It really surprised us; he's always been one to fight authority. He said it was kind of a fluke. He was talking with a friend, and thought it was something he might like.

Brian definitely wanted to go to college. He thought about military academy. We knew he could go from inside. For Bryce, all through middle school, all his brothers were in the military. Bryce wanted to be a "real soldier," frontline troops. He wants a career in the military.

I felt quite honored in 1998, all four of them in: Branden in Korea, Brent in Seattle, Brian in upstate New York, Bryce in Germany. The sun never set on my family.

I think the military is a great career. But I wouldn't recommend it to anyone now, especially the Army or Marines. Now they'll go to Iraq— based on lies, a trumped-up war.

*[I ask Larry to tell me about how having sons in this war has af-fected him and his wife.]* My wife, in December 2003, the beginning of the Christmas season—we had two sons in Iraq, Bryce in Baghdad, Branden in Tikrit, and I was out in the street, venting [at demonstra-tions]—it built up, she was in the hospital for three days with real bad abdominal pains from stress. She ended up being home for a full month. It was all stress-related.

In early April 2004, Bryce had left Iraq. He went to Kuwait, and he expected to go to Germany in a week. My wife was all excited after his call. Next day, Bryce's wife called. Bryce's tour was extended, he was getting sent back to Iraq. Within a week or two of that, my wife broke down at work, crying uncontrollably. She worked in a bank, in the mort-gage department. They sent her home. She was home for three weeks, had her antidepressant doubled, started seeing a psychiatrist, taking sleeping pills. She was not doing well. She retired in February 2006. Said she wasn't up for work and having another son in Iraq, she couldn't han-dle it. I've started taking blood pressure medication since our sons are over there.

My wife is also a member of MFSO but didn't feel comfortable speaking out while she was working for the bank. Now she's been to D.C. to protest. It was in May 2006, for the Eyes Wide Open exhibit on the National Mall [a project of the American Friends Service Commit-tee]. One thing about that protest was, it was military families. I've got-ten to know people over three years. She got to put faces to names. Ev-eryone was hugging and kissing. She fit right in.

*[I ask about their sons' experiences.]* We saw Bryce in Germany in late 2004, and he was fine. Then on New Year's Eve, he heard fireworks that reminded him of incoming mortars. In February of 2005, Bryce told me he was suffering from PTSD. He saw a psychiatrist in April. Then immediately he had to be out in the field for six weeks. He worried about self-medicating. When he got back to the base, he saw a psychiatrist once a month, a psychologist once a week. His marriage was having a hard time; they considered separating.

In August, he started yelling and screaming and crying at work, had a breakdown. They sent him to the Landstuhl Medical Facility for a week, ended up flying him to Walter Reed, put him in lockdown, on sui-cide watch for a few days. Then he had individual and group sessions for three and a half weeks. They put him on Zoloft. He got out of the hospi-tal in September.

They had taken his guns away from him in March or April 2005. They were afraid he'd hurt himself or other soldiers. He was considered nondeployable. He wasn't allowed to have guns again until March 2006. A week later he was in Kuwait. Then he served in Iraq from August to November 2006.

In the year without guns, he did office work and trainings. He talked about when he left in April or May 2005 for six weeks training, not allowed to have guns. He said, "I'm not allowed to have a gun, but I'm in the barracks with all the other soldiers and their guns. If I wanted to kill myself I could take one of their guns."

It's comical, but in a horrible, horrible way. It did worry Bryce. He told me that because he was concerned about his suicidal tendencies; it really bothered him, that's why he brought it up. Like, "Dad, can you believe it?" He was surprised, uncomfortable. We were like, "Oh my God."

Bryce was against the war before he went and the whole time he was there. I kind of guardedly asked him about it. He's going back and forth about re-enlisting. He's still against the war. He thinks the soldiers should come home now. In the polls, seventy percent of the soldiers say they should come home.

He was home on R&R three weeks ago. We had our longest conversation in a while, two hours one Sunday. He's very chipper, sounds good. He's a good soldier, he doesn't complain. It concerns his mom and me. He has been taking antidepressants since he was in Iraq. Now he's stopped taking them. We're concerned whether he feels good because the antidepressants were working.

Bryce was in Iraq when [the torture scandal at] Abu Ghraib broke. He said a few soldiers ruined all the good work that the others tried to do. He was really mad, very upset that a few ruined it.

Branden supported the war when he went to Iraq in April 2003. About half-way through his tour, he wrote us he was going to quit the Army and not go back. Something happened over there. In his first letter, he said he was looking over the Tigris River—it hadn't changed in four thousand years. He loved the people, they brought him flowers, and fruit, and bread. He wanted to bring his kids over and move there.

Then in August, out of the blue, when out on patrol—kids were throwing rocks at them. He said, "When men threw rocks at us, we fired over their heads. But kids, we couldn't do that; we threw rocks back at them." They were occupiers. They overstayed their welcome.

But Branden did re-enlist. I don't ask him about Iraq.

*I ask Larry if his sons still in the military support his efforts to end the war. In answer, he tells me that he regularly protests in front of the fed-*

*eral courthouse in Richmond, Virginia, taking with him two pairs of combat boots to represent the two soldiers who are getting killed, on average, every day in Iraq. The last time Larry was with Branden at Fort Knox, Branden drove him to a surplus store to buy those boots. Since the interview, Bryce has re-enlisted.*

# Chapter 18
# Pat Alviso

*Pat's son Beto is a career military man, a gunnery sergeant in the Ma-rines. He has been on two deployments to Iraq.*

I'm Latina. My parents are from New Mexico; I was born in California. My father worked for Weber Aircraft in Burbank as a machinist. My mother had seven children, three after me. My parents were not well off. There were nine of us in a two-bedroom home.

My dad served in World War II. He kept a picture up on his wall of him in the Navy, on a ship. The ship had stars on it for how many times they were hit and how many times they hit other ships or aircraft. He was proud of that picture.

My ex-husband and I went to Claremont College. He was a farm-workers' kid. This was in the '70s, when there was some interest in get-ting diversity in schools. He majored in math, I majored in history, and we wound up being teachers.

I had two boys, six years apart. They both played soccer and went to pretty nice schools. The oldest was very interested in war at a young age. He didn't get it from us. We were very active in the farmworkers move-ment and went on some peace marches during Vietnam.

My brother came to live with us. My older son was about eight, then. My brother served with the Marines. He's an alcoholic. He came out of the military changed, troubled; he was not the same. I don't know what happened to him. He still won't talk about it.

My brother and my older son, Beto, are close. He was home all day. My son used to play with his uniform. He'd say, "Look, I'm a Marine!" And I'd say, "No, you're not." We were thinking it was a phase. When he was fourteen, we went to a pizza place and he went next door to talk to a recruiter. I said to the recruiter, "What are you doing? He's four-teen!"

He hated school with a passion. He kept getting into trouble. He said the minute he turned eighteen he'd join the military. We were getting divorced at that time and didn't pay enough attention. We did everything we could, but we didn't think we could stop him. Those last two years, my oldest wanted to stay in his high school; he chose to stay with his dad. I moved out with my younger son.

Beto joined the day he graduated, in '94. He had his head shaved in his graduation picture. The best we could do was to give him a hug goodbye. I have mother's guilt: I think I should have done this, should have done that. My other son thought he was crazy. He's still mad at Beto for joining the military.

Beto got married after boot camp, about a year after he joined, to a beautiful girl, Danielle. They had two children right away. I guess because my kids were far apart, they wanted theirs close. The military sent him away for training. With all the stress, especially right before the war broke out, his wife left him.

He was a staff sergeant in the Marines. He was gung ho; he wanted to be deployed. There was a super-patriotic thing going on, on the base. Everybody thought Afghanistan would be a flash in the pan. Hate started to grow about the Iraqis before the invasion. They were talking trash about these people.

They didn't deploy him the first three years of the war. He was training Marines to go and they didn't want to move him. I was remarried; my husband works for the Air Force. I don't like war. Defense, okay. My husband was in Vietnam. He suffered from PTSD, and he hates this war.

I began protesting. On the day before the Iraq War started, my teacher friend and I went to a corner and held up signs. We had stuff thrown at us, and people called us names. Ten people came at us, yelled in our faces, pushed me. We called the police. It made the paper. We wound up the next day on another corner. People were throwing things from their cars. Kids were calling out, "Bomb 'em!" We didn't expect that. Our signs said, "Bring the U.N. in"; "An eye for an eye makes the whole world blind"; nice things.

My son by then was living on base, hanging around gung-ho guys. He was mad about 9/11. We couldn't talk; there was no getting through. His dad was angry about the war too, so he was getting it from both sides. The whole family is against the war. They weren't all on board from the beginning, but they're all liberals. Now they're all, like, "worst president ever."

Finally he got deployed, in September 2005. Leading up to it, he was really good; he knew I was scared. He was a combat engineer. Tell you the truth, I didn't know what he did when he was in Iraq. When he became a staff sergeant, we had a party for him. It was a big thing for him, and I was proud of him. He loves the Marine Corps.

He kept telling me they'd deploy him. I still didn't see it coming; I thought they needed him on base. Closer to deployment . . . It's embarrassing to admit; I should've stayed more with the anti-war movement. I was totally disconnected with the peace movement shortly after the war started.

He asked me to sign papers about how to reach me if he was killed, and I just lost it. He tried not to notice. I buckled up. He's the one in danger. He got remarried really fast right before he left. He met her at the Marine Corps Ball. Boy, did he get lucky. I was telling him, "You're crazy, you just met her." But she's so nice! I went over and took them out to dinner to say goodbye.

I was trying to hold myself together. We were trying to figure out where to go for dinner, and he said, "We can't go to that place, there's protesters out there." Then he started in on me: "You better not be protesting this war, because I'm in it." I didn't argue with him. I was kind of sad. I just said, "I've been that way my whole life. I'm not going to change. This war is wrong." And he said, "Just don't use any pictures of me as an adult." So everybody knows me as the one with a protest sign with a picture of an eight-year-old on it. I get the best comments: "They take them younger all the time!"

They gave him a week or two notice. He only wanted his wife to see him off. I was kind of freaking out, and I needed a place to go. I wanted to go to the Indian Market festival with my sister and my mom; that's in August and September in Santa Fe, New Mexico. I was on the street there, and I saw a lady with a T-shirt saying Crawford Peace House. It just hit me. It was one of those life-changing moments. I kind of chased her down. I lost the group I was with. I said, "Sorry to bother you, but were you in Texas with Cindy Sheehan?" She said yes. I asked her all these questions; she was doing what I wanted to do. She said, "Are you all right?" I started bawling. This stranger was holding me in her arms.

She told me how to get to the Peace House. I had it in my head to go, but I was scared, because I get lost easily. I told my husband what I planned to do. He didn't want to go with me, but he worried. Jeff decided he'd drive with me and we'd find it together, but he'd stay in a hotel nearby.

The next day, we went to the Peace House. He didn't want anything to do with it. He was afraid he'd get caught; he had an Air Force decal on the car. We got a map and drove out. They had the second encampment by then.

I thought there would be just a few people. It was the biggest tent you ever saw, the size of a circus tent. Jeff stayed at the end of where everybody parked. He saw the crosses and walked off and left me. He stayed in the car, crying. I thought he was pissed. He has a big pro-America, pro-soldiers thing; he's so protective of the military. He thinks, "Bush, what have you done to our soldiers?" But I thought he ditched me; I didn't understand.

There were different tables in the tents. It was hotter than hell. I signed in and told them my son was in the military, and they took me over to the MFSO group. I signed up for kitchen work. Jeff and I both did kitchen duty, washing pans, cutting up vegetables. It was all outside. We stayed until the last night and helped pack up. When we came out we were changed people.

I was comforted by seeing other people. I went in scared and came out angry. I was like, "No, this can't continue." I was shocked at how many people were against the war. This was no small operation.

Jeff was dealing with stuff he didn't want to deal with. He felt close to my son. Jeff couldn't talk about what he witnessed in Vietnam. He was able to talk on the way home about how he really felt about the war. That's when I understood: he wanted to protect the military from the Bush agenda.

To me, the cause of the war seemed like pride: if we don't get along, bomb 'em. I believed in the weapons of mass destruction. Jeff didn't. He knew there weren't any. He would just say that, couldn't say more. He heard things on base. That whole thing was a sham. It was nice to have him on my side.

Beto believed he was going to rebuild Iraq. He believed in the candy and flowers thing, that they'd be so glad they were coming to help them rebuild their homes. He felt really good about it. He was gonna rebuild homes. I believed that too. I just knew the war was wrong. By the time he was over there, I saw pictures of them raiding homes; I found out later he was one of them.

He didn't write, and you can't call them. Because of his position, he could get some kind of radio phone and you could hear from him every week. He was working seventeen hours a day, seven days a week. He'd call his wife. I got little pieces, like, "My Marines are breaking into homes, but if they break anything, I make them go back and fix it. There will be no disrespect to these people from my guys." That's when I got wind of the fact that he was one of those guys making people come out with their hands up. That was a nightmare for me. Obviously he knew other people were mistreating families when they took them out, abusing them, scaring them.

He said he was learning some words, language, and customs. He was proud of his ability. He wanted to communicate in a nice way.

That September was a big march on D.C. MFSO was looking for families willing to risk arrest. I'd been teaching for thirty years and didn't care. The union said, "Just don't chain yourself to any fences at the White House."

I was thinking this would be a little ragtag group of people who wanted to see President Bush. I thought it would be a solitary act. I got there in advance, and it was highly organized. There was a workshop on how to get arrested; there were over a hundred people there.

We were supposed to stand in front of the White House and refuse to leave. The police came out. There was a huge circus of people. They cordoned us off. People threw us water bottles, food, and candy. The police plucked Cindy Sheehan out of the crowd quick, put her in a paddy wagon. Then we waited five hours before they arrested us.

We older people had to go to the bathroom. These women from Code Pink had made a tent, and called it the Pee Circle. There were rose petals in it. They had a five-gallon evidence bag for people to pee in. It was hilarious. They had all these pink drapes and scarves so you had some privacy. Then I look up and see sharpshooters.

The police were very nice. They wanted to take us out of town though. We were on a bus for another five, six, seven hours. There was an eighty-year-old woman on the bus. We were kind of looking out for her. I asked her how many times she'd been arrested: "Fifteen times . . . by the '80s." At one a.m. we started getting processed. It took until dawn. It was some old ratty place, like the old *Barney Miller* show; they were using carbon paper. We were laughing at them.

We wound up getting out at five a.m. We called a number they gave us and people picked us up and drove us to where we could wait until we got a ride to the airport. There were people who applauded when we came out.

A group of us had decided not to pay the fine. We had enough people for three separate court dates. The charge was "protesting without a permit"; I think the fine was fifty dollars. I had to go to stupid D.C. in December. I got to testify with Michael Berg; his son was the contractor who got beheaded. We sat in a bar late into the night and rehearsed. Our attorney made us practice. Our defense was like the Nuremburg trial: if your government is doing evil, you have to protest.

We were all going to plead guilty. We were acting as our own attorneys, so we had to cross-examine each other. It was kind of scary when they said, "The U.S. against Pat Alviso." This guy sat up really high, like he's God or something. I was one of three to testify. You need to look at a judge, there's no jury. It was difficult but empowering to look that judge in the eye and tell him my story. That was heavy for me. I got out that night, but we were all convicted.

When I got back, I started a chapter of MFSO in Orange County. Now we have eight chapters in California. Jeff is on the board too. I got six of the eight chapters started. Now I try to keep them all going. I'm working at it full time. My last class is at one p.m., then I start this job.

I got arrested again. This one was easier. This time it was in Nancy Pelosi's office, right before the vote to de-fund the war. We had five moms. One brought four Vets For Peace and two Iraq Veterans Against the War. We all went to read the names of the soldiers killed in Iraq since the Democrats took over. We had to sneak a camera into the federal building. We thought we were slick. But they were there with handcuffs before we got to her office.

We walked in and I could see them coming up behind us. We said we were here to talk to Nancy Pelosi about the war, going to read the names of the dead. Her chief of staff wanted to talk to us. He asked us if we would come out of the office, and got us in the hallway. We'd been lobbying to meet with him for eight or nine months and he'd been putting us off. He thanked us and read a letter from Nancy Pelosi for us. It was pretty personal. I read this letter about why we were there. He left, and the police came right away. They said, "Your business is done here. If you stay, you'll be arrested."

They wound up arresting all of us. We started chanting. There were six or seven police officers. They asked us to be quiet. We got out in forty-five minutes. It was the nicest arrest you'd ever want to be in.

We joined the Eyes Wide Open exhibit in D.C., with all the boots. We went through the halls of Congress inviting everybody to come see it. In Orange County, our representative is Dana Rohrabacher. He's evil. He thinks rendition [the practice of flying prisoners to countries that allow torture] is necessary. We knew he was a bad guy, but he's my rep so he doesn't get a pass. He was there in his office. Jeff told him we all had family in the military. He said, "Your son is there?" He lit into us. He called one woman in our group a traitor. He made Dede, Cindy Sheehan's sister, cry. He just chewed us out. He said we should be ashamed of ourselves. It was outrageous. We were pretty mad.

Later, Congress was about to go in session. We went to Rohra-bacher's house with about sixty people and started chanting, "Bring them home." I said, "Let's put some boots on the sidewalk." Then he comes out without his shoes, says, "Get those boots off my lawn! You woke up my damn babies!" We weren't all that loud. One soldier's dad said, "My son doesn't get to sleep, why should yours?" Rohrabacher called the police.

We walked back to the park and the police came. A policeman said he saw us leave peacefully, so, "Have a good day!"

When Beto came home from deployment, he started showing pictures on his computer. They were awful. I didn't want to see them. Tanks, things blowing up. I was really upset. We couldn't talk about it. But he wouldn't leave it alone. He said, "Mom, you were right, we were there for oil." It turns out he had seen contractors doing work for big bucks. But I hadn't said anything about oil; I hadn't figured out the oil thing. Now I think there are a lot of factors, not just oil. But that was a big change for him.

He was told that he was not going to go back. But then they said he'd done such a great job—nobody had died in his unit—they needed his leadership. He wasn't wanting to go back. He hadn't had any time with his wife or his two kids from his first marriage. We knew they were having trouble getting enough people. They were shortening the time home from seven months to five.

They were going to give him a raise and a promotion. They sweetened the pot. So he went. He's a gunnery sergeant now. He's career military. He started talking more gung-ho. He was saying, "We're gonna win this war. You only see the bad stuff on TV." He said, "I'm gonna be fine, Mom." So we went through the whole thing again.

This time we heard a lot less from him. We heard he'd seen a lot of bad stuff, but he couldn't talk about it. I know he's feeling bad; he witnessed a lot of death. The first time, he was in Anbar. This time it was Fallujah. It was about the time of Haditha [site of the massacre of twenty-four Iraqi civilians by Marines in 2005]. I was afraid he was involved, but he wasn't. But he couldn't talk about it.

He was in charge of all the equipment that goes out. He had to make sure all the equipment was clean, ready, and distributed correctly. This time, they didn't have the gear. We sent him Kevlar gloves. You pay for your own supplies to work with concertina wire. He had to clean some of his men's equipment, armor and guns. They had to retrieve ammo and guns off dead bodies. He had to help clean blood and guts off them.

The pride of the Marines kind of went, there, for him. When he came home this time, he made it really clear, he didn't want anybody at the gate to greet him. "I'm really tired, I don't want to see anybody. I'll call."

We always check the latest deaths online. He says, "Right before you come home, that's when people get killed." We got the call; he said he was safe, he was going to take a shower. It took about a week to see him. He's not talking about Iraq. He told me that his hands are shaking. I'm sure he'll get some help. If they call him again, he'll go again.

The Marines are sending him to Hawaii now. His wife lost her dream job because of it. She has to go to Hawaii and start all over. It's creating problems for them. He won't be with his kids on weekends; that's another drama.

But who cares. He's home and alive. When he came home, I stepped on his flip-flop. He said, "Are you following me?"

It surprised me that he was already talking to somebody. He listens to his wife; she's an intake worker at the VA for soldiers that come back. She's really looking out for us, guiding us along. She can ask questions for us. He's on edge. He was edgy, grouchy, short-tempered after his first tour. This time, he knew he wasn't going to talk about it: "Iraq is Iraq. It's just there."

He feels a responsibility to look out for his soldiers. He has sent some of his men home who were suffering from PTSD. I'm kind of glad to hear he has that attitude: that they needed some help. He's totally sympathetic with them.

He probably did some really bad things; I don't know. I hope not. He hasn't told me, but I think he will. I'll understand if he did. But it will be hard to hear.

# Chapter 19
# Laura Kent

*Laura's only child, Phillip, a first lieutenant in the Army's 720th Military Police Battalion, committed suicide not long after his honorable discharge following his return from Iraq.*

I'm originally from Detroit. My parents moved to South Carolina in the early '70s. I attended college at the University of South Carolina, where I met Phillip's father, John Kent. Within a couple of years, we got married. He worked in the education field. I had my son, and then we relocated to Beaufort, South Carolina. That's where I raised my son. I was a stay-at-home mom for a long time. Eventually I got my degree and became a teacher. I teach special needs students; I've been doing it about twenty years.

His father and I divorced and I went on my own. I continued my education and got my master's degree, for economic reasons if nothing else.

I've changed my whole outlook since my son died. I'm a new person. I'm a politically active person now. I work with MFSO for better veterans' after-care.

Phillip was an inquisitive child. He just loved being involved with different things. He played basketball and soccer. We were a big swim team family. He won lots of awards in sports, had lots of friends. He played the guitar, self-taught. He was very interested in history. He was just a free spirit when he graduated.

He enrolled in the University of South Carolina and spent the first year living at home, then transferred to the main campus in Columbia. He'd come home on weekends. He was a lifeguard in the summer.

In his sophomore year, he started talking about military history. He was very interested in strategy. His father talked him into ROTC [Reserve Officers' Training Corps]. He was a scholarship student anyway, but he got some additional funding from ROTC.

During his junior year, he met his wife at the pool, lifeguarding. He fell in love head over heels. She was about five years younger than him. Then a couple weeks after graduation, in 2002, he got married and got his Army commission and became an officer. He did everything all the way. That's the way he liked to live.

He was a good boy. I was very lucky to have known him.

He went to training at Fort Leonard Wood, Missouri, from that summer until his next transfer to Fort Hood, Texas. He and his wife went together. That's when Mama caught up to him. I moved from Beaufort—where I lived for twenty-three years—to Dallas, Texas. I just packed it up and went out there.

Between Fort Hood and Dallas is about a two-and-a-half or three hour drive. It was very convenient to go back and forth on weekends. It was such a wise decision I made, to do that. Everyone else thought I was crazy, but I knew what I was doing. I knew I was going to get a job. I visualized the whole thing.

I was in Texas two years. Phillip was there about two and a half years. I got there in May, after the school year was over, and moved during summer break. In August or September, he got orders to deploy to Iraq. It was like someone just slapped me. So we spent as much time as we could together before he left in November 2003.

Fort Hood is the largest Army base in the world, one hundred miles across. It's like a city of tanks, barracks after barracks and tanks. His wife stayed there, "keeping the home fires burning." If she had really done that, he might've been alive today. But she didn't.

He was a platoon leader of the 720th Military Police Battalion, the largest Army MP battalion. They're called "The Soldiers of the Gauntlet." His unit was the one that got Saddam out of his foxhole. They're responsible for guarding prisoners of war. He had a rough job. He had men under him; their job was to keep security in the prison. They were overcrowded with detainees. The jail held 218 prisoners in a facility intended for eighty. He said, "Mom, I can't even tell you about it." He went as a second lieutenant and came back as a first lieutenant. There were Saddam-sightings, a lot of activity in that area, Tikrit.

They were on the move all the time. The prison wasn't the only thing he did, they were very mobile. He wasn't a computer type of person. He was old-fashioned. He'd write in this really nice handwriting, tiny little print, meticulous. He was a wonderful writer. He wrote his own songs, very poetic. He sang them to me.

It's been surreal. I thought I had lost all of his letters. Then on Mother's Day, I was cleaning out some drawers, and I came upon them.

In the letters, he talks about how, as platoon leader, he was like a father to a lot of these guys. Some were contemplating suicide. Their marriages were breaking up; he felt so bad for them. He felt he had to be strong. I read every one of those letters that morning.

Ilona Meagher [the author of *Moving a Nation to Care: Post-Traumatic Stress Disorder and America's Returning Troops*; Ig Publishing, May 2007] was the one who found the time capsule, a quote in the college newspaper. During our email interview, she asked, "Is this your son?" Some reporter saw him on campus in his fatigues and interviewed him after the bombing of the World Trade Center. I had never seen the article before. It happened to be my birthday. That was the most beautiful present.

He said something very noble. The quote from the book is: "Kent told the reporter from the student newspaper of the University of South Carolina, 'America has been pierced by terrorist forces. If the Pentagon is on fire, you can bet there's going to be war. We're the future leaders of America, so it's our duty first and foremost to serve our country.'" This was in his final year of the ROTC program.

He did his duty. He was good enough to serve, but not good enough to take care of once he got home.

People think we're in Iraq because of the bombing of the World Trade Center. It had nothing to do with the bombing of the WTC.

He wasn't excited about going to Iraq. He was very stressed out over leaving his wife. He was worried about his marriage. I didn't want him to get married in the first place, but we don't know anything, we're just parents. My suspicions came to fruition, unfortunately. He probably knew she'd be unfaithful, and sure enough, she was. He really wanted the marriage to work, he wanted a family. But she just wasn't the right girl.

In Iraq, he called at Christmas; it was the only time he called. He called his wife more. He'd write these beautiful letters to me. I was doing all the emailing, sending packages. He brought home some beautiful souvenirs. I got one. The rest are probably in a junkshop or something. She broke or destroyed everything.

He was in Iraq until March 2004. They did a rotation every six months. He was not in the same shape when he came home as when he left. When he got off the bus, I didn't even know it was him. He was under a hundred pounds. He had amoebic dysentery. He wasn't sleeping. He was strung out, a jittery mess. He had the weight of the world on him. His wife was screwing around while he was gone, and he knew it.

She spent forty-five thousand dollars of his bonus money while he was gone, on entertaining—she was a big drinker and drugger. She had these expectations of him as a man that he couldn't fulfill when he got home. He just wanted to take a bath, smoke a cigarette, eat some good food. She just didn't get it.

He got home in March. In April, they had their wedding anniversary. They got into a scuffle; they were always very physical with each other. He got arrested by the city police. She was calling the cops, and he slapped the cellphone out of her hand. That really messed up his life: "MP Arrested for Stopping 911 Call." I'm not saying he was justified, but her boyfriend was calling her on their anniversary. She was very manipulative; she knew what she was doing. So they separated.

I knew there was trouble, but he didn't tell me much. He was all over the place. He'd leave his assignment and come see me in Dallas. He started drinking. He'd be gone for days. He was bulimic.

I called the chaplain and said, "You have to talk to my son, he needs help." The first call, ignored; second call, ignored.

At this time, his wife had left him. She had moved to Austin and he showed up at her door. She checked him into a mental hospital, he was so strung out. He was diagnosed with bipolar disorder, but he had PTSD. He went in Friday, came out Sunday. Then he was harassed by his commanding officer when he got back to his unit.

On the NPR [National Public Radio] show about PTSD, they described the military philosophy about troublemakers: "You don't fit in, you're going to be punished." He just got back from Iraq. They were only debriefed a couple of days, then back on duty.

He didn't take his medication. He said it was making him sick. But he was ordered to therapy. I don't know how helpful that was. They gave him a hard time about that too. That was seen as being weak. He couldn't win for losing.

Then he started getting suicidal, in the summer of '04, I think. I've been so traumatized, I have trouble remembering dates. That summer, I saw him as much as I could. He was so erratic, couldn't sit still. He was having outbursts. He was so difficult to be around. He drove to see his dad, didn't get along with him. He drove off to God knows where. He said, with Jack Daniels and a gun, he'd take care of things himself.

I knew he was taking NoDoz, drinking those energy drinks with caffeine, living on that stuff. He wouldn't sleep in his bed. He slept on the floor, curled up in a ball.

Once he called me from his car, threatening to kill himself. I told him to call when he got home. I didn't know what to do. He came one night and said he was being chased by something. I kept him in my apartment for a day and a half that time. But things were getting worse and worse and worse. I was completely helpless.

I'm so glad I was in Texas. I needed to be there for him. I was like his home base.

In November '04 he got an honorable discharge. That's when he lost hope. He told me he had let everybody down.

He was still trying to reconcile with his wife. His dad got him to sign divorce papers, but he tore them up. He finally signed them when he moved back to Beaufort. He lived in the home where he was raised. His dad was going to help him get back on his feet. He got a job as a security guard. He had all day to think about all his problems. He drove himself to his death.

I moved back to South Carolina in June '05, to Columbia, where my family lived. Phillip was my first visitor. He didn't find his niche, after all that training. He was talking about re-enlisting. In August, I spent my birthday weekend with him. We had a good time together. Then school started, and I got busy with my job. Then Hurricane Katrina hit. He wanted to volunteer for that.

In September, I lost touch with him; he quit calling me. He wasn't answering his phone. I was sending cards, letters. I don't know why I didn't go down there. I wanted to give him some space. He saw my brother in Beaufort. They socialized in the evenings. They're like comrades, close in age—about ten years apart. I heard from people that he got a little puppy, he got a new girlfriend. I thought things were better.

My mother got very sick. She had an emergency: appendicitis. I called him and said, "Your grandmother is very sick." We had brisk words for each other. I said, "You need to stop feeling sorry for yourself." That was the last call we had.

People told me he wasn't calling anybody. He was coming home and drinking himself into a stupor. He didn't like living in that house; he was traumatized by our divorce, we had a very nasty divorce and he never got over it.

Then I got the call that he had shot himself. He had gone to work, came home, sat on the big porch in the wee hours of the morning. I don't know how many beer cans were scattered around. He was text-messaging some girl about what he was going to do. He shot himself, and he was there all night. The next morning, the trash man came and saw him on the porch.

I wanted my life to be over for a long time. Now I just thank God that I had him. He was a good son. I have such a hole in my heart right now.

But what I'm doing now is important for him. I've been asked to speak at two peace rallies and told everybody his story, how he loved his country and wanted to serve so badly, and how shabbily he was treated when he got home.

Whenever I hear about somebody else dying in Iraq, it just breaks my heart. But I've gotten to the point where I can help other families. It helps me to help others.

I like to be known as a peace activist instead of anti-war. I'm a Code Pink member. I participate as much as I can. A local TV station did a nice remembrance of him on September 11 last year. They also did a piece on the VA, with me, about PTSD and veterans' care and our returning troops. I've walked the halls of Congress. I've spent the day talking with Congressmen and their aides. Now they're turning into wimps.

I'm a member of Survivors of Suicide—SOS, ironically enough. They told us, "Always drink a lot of water when you're grieving." You do so much deep sighing, you lose a lot of water. I do a support group every month too. But sometimes I can't go. It's so draining for me. I have to be in the right frame of mind.

I'm trying to reclaim my life.

When I came back after my son's death, nobody talked to me at school. They don't know what to say. I had two weeks bereavement time. Not very long.

Now is the hard grief, the stuff that can take you down. You can make it through the first year, but they don't tell you that once it sinks in, that's the journey. Your mind never rests. It's like a video unwinding in front of your eyes. You still see that same thing. You never stop thinking about it. There's no room for anyone else. It consumes me; it takes all my emotional strength to deal with it. But I want to heal.

So many people have been very good to me. You have to be kind to yourself. I took myself out of therapy. I stopped taking antidepressants a year ago. I felt I had the tools to be active in my healing. When you're on antidepressants, you have no energy. That's not me. I'm very active. I'm getting back to that, finally.

I just quit my teaching job. I want to do something different. The events of that day, where I was: I have to get that behind me. The job was one of the pieces of that.

My son lived in Columbia. He wanted to get out of Beaufort; it's a beautiful place, right on the ocean, but you can get in a rut. He loved being in Columbia. I think about how much he loved it. I feel his spirit is here.

I don't have a husband to fall back on. Probably I would have left him by now, anyway. I have some really good supportive friends, but others never came through. They didn't know how to deal; I'm not blaming them. But the ones that were there are very dear to me.

Something traumatic like that, it just happens. You think your life is going on, and then suddenly, boom, it's like you're blown out of your chair.

*[I tell her I hope she gets back her joy in life some day.]* Joy doesn't just happen. You have to look for joy.

# Chapter 20
# JoAnn Gross

*JoAnn is a printer for the New York paper* The Daily News. *Her only child, Walter, a sergeant in the Army, served fourteen months in Iraq with the First Armored Division, and expects to be deployed again either there or in Afghanistan.*

I grew up in North Brunswick, New Jersey. I have a brother, four years older than me. My father died when I was nine years old. My mother raised us. I got married when I was around twenty-one. A year later, I had my only son, Walter.

Walter's father was an alcoholic. He drank heavily. We got divorced when Walter was around twelve. I decided to home-school Walter. He was having difficulty in school. The principal thought it would be a good idea. I had no teaching degree, but he was very happy. He got a home-school diploma.

At seventeen, before the war in Iraq, he wanted to join the military. I thought it would be a good thing. His friends were partying; it didn't seem like they were going anywhere. I thought maybe it would help him get an education.

I had taken him to the recruiter. He wanted to be a Marine. I said no. I was afraid of the Marines; you always hear they're the first ones in. I said, "Why don't you join the Air Force?" My father was in the Air Force. I thought that would be the safest branch. He said no. "Navy?" Didn't want to live on a ship. "What about the Army?" He needed my permission. It bothers me now that I signed those papers. He would have joined anyway when he was eighteen, but I still feel guilt.

When I took him to the recruiter, I asked about the rumors of war in Iraq. The recruiter said if it happened, it would be over in a few days. We'd be greeted with roses. I just couldn't believe we'd get into a big war—that it would happen again after Vietnam.

I thought there were around two hundred jobs he could choose from. I told him, "Anything but infantry; maybe a medic. Anything but combat." I didn't realize at the time, they're all combat. He finally came up with combat engineer. What I thought was that the job was like construction, for bridge crews. I said okay. I thought he'd learn a skill. I really did not believe we'd go to war. I said, "The president would never go to war."

He went to Fort Leonard Wood, Missouri, for basic training. He was put on a waiting list first because he wanted to be stationed in Germany and see the world. My father was German. He had to show up every weekend and do physical training. He took his ASVAB tests and did very well, scored high.

The war broke out during that period. He went to basic in February, did nine weeks plus five weeks AIT, Advanced Individual Training, combat engineer school—something to do with clearing bombs. Then he came home. We picked him up in June and went to Wisconsin to see my family. We were all so proud of him, and he was very proud of himself.

He went to Germany for more training. He was with the First Armored Division. His division was already deployed to Iraq. Then they came back, and stayed a year or fifteen months at the base in Germany. Christmas came and I went to Germany for ten days. That was nice. It was me and him. We had a great time. We visited castles, ruins, museums; we loved it. I asked if he wanted to party or go to a bar. He said, "Heck no, I'm enjoying this."

They kept telling him he'd deploy to Iraq, but wouldn't say when. I started getting very upset, started to write letters to magazines and papers saying we should get out of Iraq. I started to cry a lot. Watching the news depressed me. I'd cry every day. Most of the soldiers dying were so young; I felt sorry for their parents. That shouldn't happen.

My boyfriend wasn't understanding. Walter is my only child. We were very close. He was my joy ever since he was born.

Walter had orders to go to Iraq in January '06. He came home for two weeks and I didn't cry. I tried not to let him know how upset I was. He was strong. I let him know how proud I was of him. He looked so handsome in his uniform.

I took him to JFK Airport. As soon as he got out of the car, I started to cry. I gave him a hug, told him to come home to me. I gave him a lighter inscribed "Praying for my soldier. Love, Mom." When he got out of the car, it fell out of his pocket. He couldn't find it; he was so upset. I got him another one online. Later I found the original.

I cried the whole way home. I couldn't stop. It was uncontrollable. I cried every day after that; it was horrible. My boyfriend told me I was weak. I went into the bathroom and turned the water on so he wouldn't hear me cry. I went to a psychiatrist once; I had panic, anxiety attacks. He put me on Xanax to calm me down.

Every day, I'd go on the computer and see that a couple more soldiers had died. I'd try to find out where. They'd always say, "Names withheld pending notification of relatives." I had nightmares. My boyfriend started to tell me he was going to move out.

I found MFSO online and started going to vigils.

We sold our home when my son joined. I moved to a rented apartment in Palisades Park, New Jersey, with my boyfriend. In the beginning it was great, until I started getting upset about my son. He said I was obsessed with my son. I tried to explain. He didn't know what it's like to have children.

Everything that Walter felt, I could feel it. Once, Walter was in Germany, and I was sleeping. I had a horrible nightmare that he was very, very sick and he needed me. I tried to get to him in my car. It was so real. I told my boyfriend; he said it was just a dream. A couple of days later, my son called. He had a virus and was very sick for a few days.

Also, when he came home, I was waiting for him in Palisades. I heard a lot of car doors slamming. Then I heard one door slam and I said, "That's him!" I ran to meet him. It was him. He stayed with us for about a week. He's been in the Army for more than four years. He loved the Army, never complained. As long as he was happy, I was happy.

The next Christmas, he came to Palisades Park. We work nights—we print papers. We work seven days a week. I took off because my son was home. It was wonderful. He came home with a suitcase full of gifts for me: Army shirts and shorts—I work out; a pewter clip of Old Ironsides for my keychain. Before, I was lucky to get a card.

After the orders to go to Iraq, I cried for two weeks straight. I had hurt my hand at work around that time, crushed by machinery, and was on workman's comp for seven or eight months. I don't know if I could've worked. That whole time was a nightmare. When he was in Iraq, he'd call all different hours. I'd go to sleep and keep my cellphone on. I was very depressed.

I went to see a psychiatrist because I had nobody to talk to. It didn't help. I told him my situation with my boyfriend and how cold he was about my son in Iraq. He advised me to leave him.

I was going to a weekly vigil, went to a march in New Orleans, went to D.C. a few times. My boyfriend wouldn't go. He said it was coming between us, that I put MFSO first, my son first. I blew up. I said, "I have to put my son first." We lived close to the bridge. He worked over the bridge, for the *New York Post*. I worked in Liberty State Park, printing the *Daily News*. He complained about the bridge, traffic, said he wouldn't do this shit. I said, "What shit? You mean me?"

He wanted to move to the Bronx, but it would've been a two-hour commute for me. We started to fight. He wouldn't talk to me for sometimes two weeks. He says he hopes the old JoAnn would come back, the happy, optimistic JoAnn. Everybody liked me. When the war began, I changed. I started arguing with people about the war.

My boyfriend went to Texas for a whole week and didn't tell me he was going. I saw the printed itinerary in the bedroom while he was in the shower. I needed a vacation; I could have gone. He came out of the shower and said he was going away. "I'll call." I was just, like, in shock. How could he do this to me? This man was supposed to love me.

When he went to Texas, I decided to move out, and not live with someone who would torture me like that.

I find it peaceful where I live now. I couldn't move in until August. A couple days before I saw the psychiatrist in April, a young man from Walter's Camp Hit was killed; twelve or fifteen were killed. I called the Red Cross. I was panicking. I didn't know how to find out if my son was okay.

The Red Cross was very kind. They said the commander could not get through to confirm anything. I decided to go to work; this was before I went on comp, I got hurt in May. One of the guys put his arm around my shoulder, and asked, "How's your son?" I just fell on the floor and cried. My union shop chairman at work, a very kind man, is a Vietnam vet. They took me to his office. Friends sat with me all night, held my hand, tried to comfort me while I waited. About four or five a.m., one friend said, "Want to come home? My wife will take care of you." I said, "What am I, a kitten?" It kind of made me laugh.

I pretty much cried myself out. I still hadn't told my boyfriend what was going on. I lay in bed, took about four Ambien, still couldn't sleep. The phone rang. It was the Red Cross: "Haven't heard anything yet." "Please, don't call until you know something!" The Red Cross called a few hours later to tell me the commander told them my son was okay, thank God.

I thought, "I want to hear my son's voice." I didn't believe the commander. I wanted to go to Baghdad; I was so crazy and scared and angry. They said they'd notify the commander. Three days later, I got a call from Walter. He started to scream at me, "Mom, are you crazy? Do you know how much trouble I'll be in?" I started yelling, "You're my kid, I'm worried about you . . ." The line just dropped. He was mad at me. But that was okay. A week later he called again, like nothing happened.

He said the commander would call if anything happened to him, and it was more dangerous for them to bring him to a phone to call.

He was a machine-gunner, on a tank. They got hit by a roadside bomb. He got knocked unconscious. The lieutenant was so damaged, he couldn't stop laughing. It was shell shock. My son wrote that he had split his eardrum. He saw white and felt an eerie calmness. Heard people screaming his name. He woke up and couldn't walk. He was off-balance. They sent him to Tikrit for a week to relax and get over it.

He'd been in Masul. Then they sent his unit to Camp Hit, near Ramadi. That was worse, very hostile conditions. They were embedded with Iraqis. He was there for a year, extended six weeks. He spent fourteen months in Iraq.

I'd gone to Operation House Call in D.C. I had a printout from a young man named Ryan Kahlor in Camp Hit. You didn't hear about these little primitive camps. I was showing it to this man from MFSO. He says, "That's my son's letter!" We had this instant connection. Our sons were together. He's a sweetheart. One of the few men I know who isn't afraid to cry.

My son's in Germany now, calling me a lot lately. He was promoted to sergeant. He wanted to be a career soldier. He re-enlisted while he was in Iraq for another four years. He got angry when I tried to talk him out of it. I said, "If that's what you want to do, okay." I stopped trying to give him advice. Lately he says, when his four years are up, he'll get out.

He's never told me not to protest. He says, "Mom, I gave you that right to say what you want." When he came home on leave last September, I started to show him the articles about our protests. He said, "It's better if I don't look at this." He never once criticized me. And my son isn't shy. He'll come out and say what's on his mind.

I ask him sometimes why he thinks we're there. I get different answers. Once, "We can't leave the Iraqi people that way." Once, "Not sure."

He says his job is to kill the enemy. That's his job. I respect that. I just wish I'd never signed those papers.

He'll be twenty-two. I wish I could go back to when he was seventeen. I would have handcuffed him to a chair to keep him from going to Iraq. I've been through a lot in my life. Besides the death of a child, having a child in Iraq must be the worst. Every day of your life, you fear: is he being shot at? I'd try to convince myself he was safe. I'd visualize him being safe.

I sent two big boxes every week: food, DVDs, funny movies, WD-40 for the guns—he asked for that.

When he came home in September, he had lost thirty pounds. He's five foot ten, 135 pounds, very lean. He was a bag of bones. He had diarrhea, and didn't tell me; it upset me. He said a lot of people were sick in the camp. They took craps in a big barrel and burned them. A lot of times, they didn't have running water.

I also met a Sergeant Henk, writing a column for the *Chicago Courier News*. He wrote about Camp Hit. He replaced a man who refused to leave the gates of Camp Hit, too scared. I wrote to him and said, "My son calls me but doesn't say anything." He wrote back, "It's such bad conditions, he doesn't want to worry you." He met my son and said he's very polite and well-mannered. I thought my son would be mad at me, but he introduced himself to him. He wasn't mad. Said he was a nice guy.

He was due to come home in February. I couldn't wait. It was fourteen months of hell. I remember once I was in bed and the doorbell rang and I fell out of bed, I was so scared. I used to have nightmares that the doorbell was ringing. Or coming home and seeing a white van. It was a constant thing. When I left the house, on the way home I was afraid to turn the corner.

My son just called me today. He told me to get back with my ex-boyfriend. He says, "You're getting old." He scared me. He said, "I could get killed." He's trying to tell me not to be alone the rest of my life. He says he knows most guys are jerks; John was a nice guy.

He's coming home May 15. He will stay about three weeks, then go to North Carolina to join his new unit. After that, I don't know. He'll have to go to Iraq or Afghanistan. I'm upset that they extended the tours. They can do whatever they want.

I don't drink. If I was a drinker, I'd have been drunk the whole time he was in Iraq.

Now I feel better. But I stopped watching the news. My son said to stop watching it, it's bullshit. There was a big story, a while ago, when two soldiers were kidnapped. I was watching and got so upset. I asked Walter when he called about the missing troops. He said he didn't know what I was talking about. I started to cry; the first time I'd cried to him. He said, "I can't take this shit," and hung up. He didn't need to know his mom was having a nervous breakdown. He called a few minutes later and said, "Mom, are you done?"

He needs to concentrate on what he's doing.

I'll take him to Wisconsin again, see my family, maybe with my ex. When Walter comes home, he always comes to visit. Walter just got a cellphone and he called him.

*[I ask whether her activism makes a difference in how she feels.]* I feel like if I sit here and don't do anything, and God forbid something happens to my son, I'd have to live with that regret the rest of my life.

One day I was online. I thought, "I can't be the only person in the world who's against this war who has a kid fighting it." I found MFSO, people like me. We're proud of our kids. We're not anti-military, we're just against this war. We support our troops. We want them home now.

We have a bunch of peace coalitions that get together. I go to those meetings. It's support. I've met the kindest people I've met in my life. I always go to meetings with my congressman. But I don't like to watch the news too often. I was following politics a lot, but it upsets me, makes me depressed. I can't constantly be involved and let it consume me. I have a life.

At my first vigil, I held a photo of my son. Every week I would go. We get a lot of coverage. But occasionally I have to block it out. It's a mental thing. Some people do something every day. But I can't. My son's coming home, and I want to be happy for his sake.

# Chapter 21
# Stacy Hafley

*Stacy and her husband Joe live in Missouri and have three young sons. Joe is a former military policeman in the Army Reserves. Stacy developed serious health problems and she and the children became homeless while Joe was running convoys in Iraq.*

I was raised by my dad in Idaho Falls, Idaho. I had a peaceful middle-class upbringing. Then I moved in with my mom in my senior year of high school—probably not my smartest move. I hated my dad, hated the world; a typical teenager. The grass is always greener on the other side.

At my mom's house there were no rules, no structure of any kind. The only rule was, "Don't wake us up unless you are bleeding or dying." I have four brothers and three sisters, one biological. I am twenty-seven; my little sister is eighteen months younger; my brother Tyler is a Mormon missionary, twenty-one; twin brothers, almost eighteen; a sister, fourteen; and a sister, twelve.

Mom's house was an experience. I took full advantage—though it didn't always serve me well. I graduated high school, started college in journalism, and got pregnant in my sophomore year. My family wasn't thrilled. I moved into a maternity home in Texas. I knew no one there. It was tough. It was a very conservative maternity home; no radio or TV.

After I had my son, I was nineteen. I moved to Missouri to a fabulous program, a maternity transitional home. They let you stay through pregnancy until your child is two. There were a lot of parenting and budgeting classes. After six or eight months I moved out on my own. I graduated college with a four-year degree in graphic and web design.

I met my husband online the week I graduated. At the time I was planning on doing freelance graphic design work. I was bored with my project, went online, and we met in a chat room. We talked all night.

We eloped two months later. My mom knew about it. His family
didn't. We went to Gatlinburg, Tennessee, and got married in the Great
Smoky Mountains National Park, next to a waterfall.

His infant daughter had died at birth. He had been with his fiancée
for three years, and then it fell apart after his daughter died. He and I
weren't in the greatest places.

It was really what we both needed. It was this amazing life force. He
was madly in love with my son from day one. We just instantly clicked.
It was instant family. He was in the Active Reserves in the military. His
commander put him on inactive duty to get over his daughter's death.

We moved into his childhood home. Eventually we bought it from
his parents. It was a tiny house, but we worked on it. We went on day
trips, to the zoo and all that. Happy, happy, happy.

Not too long after we married, I got pregnant with my middle son,
Garrett. My oldest son is Kobe. We were overwhelmed, but it was fun.
Not too long after, when Garrett was four months old, I got pregnant
with Jack. So we were banging our heads against the wall: "Holy crap,
what are we going to do?" Jack was sick when he was born. His lungs
collapsed. It was a rough patch.

We'd been getting by. My husband has a degree in criminal justice
and he worked for a security company. Then one day—I was barefoot
and pregnant—he quit and decided to work at a different company. He
was loading tractor-trailer trucks. I was doing graphic design off and on.

The following spring, in May or June of 2004, Joe got a letter from
the Army: he had ten days to report to the Reserve Command Center in
St. Louis. Then they told him they'd be preparing him for deployment to
Iraq.

They were pretty honest with us. When you don't hear from the
Army for four years and then they come looking for you . . . We kinda
knew. There was a desperate need for MPs at that time. They called everyone up.

We hadn't really thought about him and deployment. We thought
that the Soviets would have to invade Kansas before the Inactive Reserves would get called up. We weren't keen supporters of the war from
the beginning, but never thought that we'd actually be involved.

Joe was so angry. They told him he'd be a tractor-trailer driver running convoys. In August, they sent him to school in Alabama for a month
for military truck driving training. That month was just hideous. It was
the hardest month of my life. We'd never been apart. I had a really hard
time emotionally with it. The kids had never seen their dad gone. They

went completely out of control. I was not the primary disciplinarian in our home. They just went crazy.

He came home in September. He left in October to train for Iraq. The unit he was deployed with was ragtag. They compiled guys from twenty-five or thirty states. The unit was from Belleville, Illinois. We'd never met any of these people. We went in for the family briefing, and I am thinking—these were young guys fresh off the farm—I thought, "These are the guys that will be defending us?" It was very chaotic. Nobody knew each other. There were families from Virginia and Washington State. It was not comforting. There was no unit cohesiveness.

He left from Camp Attenbury, Indiana, and trained for about four months. It was not so fun. We started a routine. We saw him at Thanksgiving and Christmas; that was very fortunate.

There was a lot of conversation among the wives. They never told us exactly when they were leaving. We had to keep saying good-bye. Several wives were saying, "Just leave already, get it over with and get home."

They left after New Year's. I went down myself to Indiana to see him off. It was the most sickening thing. We had a lot of young wives and pregnant wives. The wives were a wreck. The mothers were hysterical. Some guys were crying when they boarded the bus for the airport. Some guys were throwing up, they were so stressed. One little boy held on to his mom's leg—she was being deployed . He had to be physically pulled off, screaming and crying.

We were not thrilled about a lot of this. I tried to keep it to myself in the beginning. I wasn't sure how the other wives felt. FRG, the Family Readiness Group, was basically defunct. Usually an officer's wife is the mother hen, a liaison between the Army and the families. Sometimes they are really good, but ours didn't work well.

I didn't know a lot of families. My best friend Bobbie's husband was deployed at the same time. We were each other's support system. She was two hours away. My family kept saying, "It will be okay." I didn't want to hear that. My mom would say, "He's statistically more likely to die in a car accident than in the war."

It was frustrating. Not a lot of people understood what I was going through. My friends had moved away to different places. My family was supportive but far away. My husband's parents were older, not able to help or give me a break from the kids. It was a very isolating time.

We got to talk when he was in Kuwait. When he got to Iraq, his unit was running convoys. He was the commander's driver, so he didn't have to leave the base much. That helped a little. This was March.

We had been fixing up our home. We visited my little brother at my dad's house for a couple of weeks before he went on a mission. I'd been saving money and putting it into our house. The contractor came in to work on the basement while I was gone. They found several hundred feet of black mold in the basement. I wasn't allowed back in the house. That stuff is lethal.

So I left my little house with my kids and my car and my cellphone, and we were basically homeless.

When we were in Idaho, my husband told me he'd be leaving the base. He would be a member of the military transition team (MIT)—a small group of soldiers to complete a special task. They'd be going to an Iraqi base and be responsible for training Iraqi soldiers as transportation specialists. There were twenty-four Americans and nine hundred Iraqis. The base was called An Nu Maniyah.

The commander left with him to be the head of the MIT. He hand-picked Joe for his MP experience. I was not thrilled to say the least.

When he found out that I had left the house, he had just gotten to An Nu Maniyah. There wasn't a lot of communication. I told him online that we'd lost the house, and we'd try to find something else to do.

That is where the problem started, where the deployment went from being just stressful to a living hell. I didn't ask for my husband to come home. At that point, my plan was: "I am a strong Army wife. I can do this."

I called the FRG leader. She said, "I can't help you." The military said it couldn't help. I called the local VFW [Veterans of Foreign Wars]. They were very nice. They pointed me to the Red Cross, who gave us some minor help. We got a hotel as a temporary home for awhile until my husband got paid and we could afford first and last month's rent.

They gave me a Wal-Mart gift card for two hundred dollars so I could buy the kids some clothes. That got us by for a week in the hotel. The hotel was awful. One room, two beds, three kids, and me. And there was a Rottweiler convention in town and the whole hotel was full of Rottweilers and their owners. It was a worst-case scenario. I had a mini-fridge. The hotel had a continental breakfast, but it was moldy. We had oatmeal for breakfast, peanut butter and jelly sandwiches for lunch. Fun!

I found an apartment. It was very expensive but in town. I wanted to keep my son in his preschool. The complex was a gated community, so it was safe. But the apartment was incredibly tiny. There was no yard, no place for the kids to play. It was a pretty rough summer.

May came around. My husband came home for leave. I didn't want him to have to worry about us as well as about being shot. We still couldn't retrieve anything from our home. The house had to sit dormant for four more months before they could even enter it. The mold was in the ventilation system throughout the house. It was as if the house had burnt down.

I had to buy everything—a couch, kitchen stuff. It was frustrating. I remember walking through Sam's Club. What do I buy first? Towels? I was so overwhelmed. My mother-in-law was very generous. She bought the kids bunk beds.

I bought this huge round glass lemonade pitcher. It looked so beautiful to me. It cost twenty-five dollars. I was so irrational at this point. I was so lost, I didn't know what to do. I could have bought a lot of things for that twenty-five dollars, but my mother-in-law said, "If you like this, buy it." When I brought it back to the apartment, I put it in the perfect spot on the counter. I had this wonderful glass thing reflecting sunlight.

I tried to make the house a home before he got there. We got some furniture. My family bought the kids some clothes. Very low budget, but I decorated. When my husband came home, the first thing I remember him saying—I had stayed up two days straight, scrubbing and cleaning—he said it looked beautiful, but like we didn't have a past. We had no photos, no knick-knacks. I burst out crying. But I got over it.

My in-laws kept the kids awhile so that we could have some adult time to ourselves. But in the pit of my stomach, I had an uneasy feeling, because I knew he was going back. We tried to settle back into normality, but it is that much harder when they leave. It is a huge disruption, especially with kids. Not that I didn't want him home!

It was nauseating taking him back to the airport. Bobbie had to drive. We came home and the apartment looked so yucky, so empty. A week before it had looked like heaven.

I was complaining a lot to my friends at this point. I'd gotten to know one of the other wives online. Neither of us was sleeping well. We were complaining partners, safety people for each other. She was going through the same thing. We became very close very quickly.

Not even a week after he left, I was in the kitchen talking on the phone, and the room started to spin. I grabbed the counter. I thought I had to eat something. I lay down and it went away, but a couple of days later it happened again.

I ended up having intermittent nauseous spells. I'd be exhausted for hours afterwards. The spells became more frequent, several times a day, hours at a time. I couldn't figure out what was wrong with me.

Finally I went to my ear, nose, and throat doctor. He immediately sent me to a neurologist. At this point, my mother-in-law had to drive me, I couldn't drive. She had to take care of the kids a lot; I was in bed almost full-time. I had snacks in a cooler, toys and a TV in my bedroom. I let the kids play in the room and locked the door so they couldn't get out.

I was diagnosed with Meniere's Disease, a central nervous system disorder, primarily involving the inner ear and balance. It causes dizzy spells and hearing loss. It was like riding a roller coaster for a long time and then having someone beat the crap out of you.

It was summertime. I had no help besides my in-laws, couldn't take the kids swimming. I said, "Enough is enough. My husband has to come home." I started on his chain of command at home. No help at all. I called every military installation, lawyers, family services. I called congresspeople. I was on the phone twenty-four/seven. My doctors wrote letters on my behalf. The Red Cross wrote that it was an unsafe situation: "She can't take care of the kids." I was denied four times.

I knew the military had programs on bases, but there was nothing for reservists. I didn't live anywhere near a base. The nearest one was Scott Air Force Base in Illinois, an hour and a half away. The outreach coordinator tried to provide support, but I was so far away. She started making provisions for us to move closer.

They let Joe come home ten days for emergency leave at the end of July—I got sick in May. The problem was with his command. My husband's new commander told him to shut his wife up, stop the letters. He didn't know my husband or work with him but he had the final say. We tried to get him compassionate reassignment but we were turned down.

I was still in bad shape, had to walk holding on to walls or with a cane. They were still tweaking my meds. Dizziness was constant. My husband's command said, "You need to get back to Iraq." They were watching him like a hawk.

When he came home for ten days, we moved to Columbia City. We found a house, rented it, dropped the boxes in the middle of the house, and the next day he went back to Iraq.

The Missouri Veterans Commission got me some in-home help using solicited donations. She'd come help with meals. It became unsafe for my kids, I couldn't care for them. My hearing was so bad, I couldn't hear them in the middle of the night if they cried out. I had fallen several times. The military has a Family Care Plan [FCP], a legal document. It states who will care for your dependents while you're absent. If the plan is broken, then legally you can't be deployed.

So the military started focusing on trying to make us find someone to care for the kids. They kept asking, "Your parents, his parents, your brothers or sisters, why can't they do it?"

My family still has kids at home. My dad is a fireman, on call. He couldn't care for them. My husband's brothers and sisters weren't financially able. Their cars weren't big enough for their kids plus ours. His parents were in their seventies. I had to get documentation on all that. I'm calling every place, saying, "Here's the deal, my FCP is broken, my husband has to come home."

Finally they told me I had ten days to find twenty-four-hour childcare for my children or else they'd have to go into foster care. I went hysterical when they told me that. My husband was freaking out. I was talking with him on the computer every day. He was running convoys between Baghdad, Fallujah and Ramadi, pretty much the most dangerous work out there—they made big targets. He couldn't focus on his job. He was sure the kids would go into foster care and we'd never get them back.

I ended up calling the local university, the early childhood education program. I asked if any students were looking for work. I hired four girls. I put Kobe in kindergarten full time, the other two in daycare. I hated that. These girls would pick them up, bring them home. They'd rotate. They'd cook dinner, take the kids out to play, help them work on homework. It was really hard emotionally, watching strangers take care of my kids. That started in August. I loved the girls. Well, some I liked better than others. It was frustrating to get them all paid. It cost a hundred dollars a day. I had to let my home health lady go. We couldn't afford this. We were going into major debt. The money for childcare in my home was basically what my husband was making per month in Iraq. I had applied for disability, and got five hundred dollars a month from that. All I could do was sit in bed and worry about my husband being killed.

At this point, we were asking for a hardship discharge. His commander was threatening him with a dishonorable discharge. My husband said, "Fine, do that. My wife will be on *Good Morning America* tomorrow."

I finally got so angry, I couldn't take it. I called 411 and said, "I want to talk to the Pentagon." He must have thought I was the biggest nut on the planet. He said, "The Pentagon Hotel?" "No, the Pentagon." I didn't want to hear "suck it up" any more.

I called the Pentagon and unloaded on the poor woman who answered the phone. She finally transferred me to another person, and I did the same thing. They were pretty freaked. I was out of my mind. I continued to be transferred higher up until I got someone who said they'd do something. I felt a little better.

I had a few people in the military who were unofficially guiding me. But the Pentagon thing was all my idea. This was the end of September, early October. Finally I got word my husband was coming home on REFRAD, Relief from Active Duty. When his deployment ends, he goes back to the Reserves. He came home in December, a month before his unit. He was home for Christmas. That was nice.

When we moved to Columbia, I'd called my husband's employer about his job. They said they'd preserve it for him, he'd keep his seniority. He was home for a week or two, then he called them and asked for a transfer to their job site in Columbia, and they denied it. So now he had no job.

He couldn't commute three hours to work part-time at his old job. His contract with the military was up, but they didn't want to let him go. They were trying to work out his travel pay. There was a problem with the per diem. I feel like the problems happened because of all those letters.

He got his job back eight months later. Meanwhile he worked at temp agencies. It took that long for him to get discharged from the military.

When his unit came home—those twenty-four guys became their own unit, they separated early from the rest—they no longer seemed part of the original unit. We wanted to go to the homecoming ceremony. They had a T-shirt made up with all the guys' names. They didn't include my husband's name on the T-shirt or give him one of the little crystal eagles because he didn't complete his deployment. He was really upset. Even though he didn't believe in what they were doing, he still regrets not staying for the full deployment.

I called MFSO last May, saw them online. I said, "What can I do? I don't want other families to go through what I did." The first day I joined, I started the Missouri chapter. I called families in the area and we hit the ground running. We met other families that are now pretty much my family, we got so close. We expanded to different states, and became regional.

This idea that the military takes care of their own . . . I started explaining what the war has done to families, how detrimental it's been, how poorly planned it was. I dove headfirst into the organization. It's the best therapy ever. It gave me a goal to work towards, helping other families. I learned so much about how to manipulate the system to get things done. I can use my experience to help others.

I deal with a lot of crisis cases now: disabled soldiers being sent back; female soldiers who were sexually abused; family crisis situations; how to get the best care from the VA. I've made a lot of connections that can help them. It shouldn't be that way. The average Joe can't do it, because he doesn't know how to work the system.

I have made wonderful friends. It's a great bunch of people. Now I'm on the board of directors. I'm in the minority as a younger woman and a spouse. Wives are so afraid that the military will take it out on their spouse [if they speak out against the war]. I keep telling them, "You're a civilian. You're not the property of the military." I refuse to let the military intimidate me or tell me what to do or how to run my family.

Other wives refer to me as the crazy lady who called the Pentagon. I don't care. We've screamed at senators. They know I'm willing to go that far, have gone on other people's behalf. I'm on talk radio all the time, talking about the VA system. They know I'm not kidding.

I've cried all I can cry. I've been angry all I can. I've had to let it go. That's the only thing that helps me stop being bitter, or being a victim. I have to keep moving forward. Sometimes it gets ripped wide open though.

War is always in our home. We lost our entire life while he was deployed. Everything is defined: before the war, after the war. I went through so many things he doesn't know about. He went through things I'll never understand.

Eventually we started to recover financially. But we have a new fight. My husband has been diagnosed with severe depression and PTSD. He lost everything: lost his home, his job, has a disabled wife who was okay when he left, on top of the dangerous deployment. He was having rage outbursts. I was the catch-all for his screaming fits. We were walking on eggshells around him.

He was so angry, so depressed, so much in a funk. His social anxiety has gotten out of control. We can't even go into a store. Places like Wal-Mart just enrage him. He doesn't want to leave the house. It makes it difficult because I can't drive.

Memories from Iraq trigger my husband's anxiety. My oldest child is multiracial and he looks very much like Iraqi kids. The things that my husband saw happen to Iraqi children reminded him of our son, and they still haunt him today.

For a long time, I fought with him to go to the VA. He wouldn't go. I was telling other families they have to go, but he wouldn't. I told him if he didn't get help, the kids and I would leave until he did get help. I didn't really mean it. He needed to get help. He's gained a lot of weight since he's been home. He's said, "You guys would have been better off if I'd died in Iraq." I don't think he'll do anything, but I'm hyper-vigilant.

The other day we almost got sideswiped. He has road rage and anxieties about driving. He says, "It wouldn't be the worst thing if I died in a car crash."

It took a year to get him to an appointment with the VA. Then they said his PTSD was not combat-related; it was a childhood problem. But now he's getting excellent care. He was very honest with the counselor. He's on antidepressant medications.

I have a feeling this is going to go much better. He's getting ready to start a new job. He got a promotion at work. He will be driving a company truck; he's been working toward it for five years. Now he's very nervous because of his situation mentally. But the counselor thinks it's a good idea.

From part-time to full-time at his company—he'll quadruple his pay. It will definitely lead to our recovery financially. We're looking to buy a new house. We're tired of throwing money away on rent. We loved being homeowners. We're really excited. We'll buy a fixer-upper, do the work ourselves, and start over.

We'll be married six years in July. We're lucky, in a way. It's put us in a position to really look at ourselves. We got a chance to get some perspective. We don't take a lot for granted, and our kids don't. Our kids have learned to speak out and question things.

There are days I wish I could go back to being ignorant of the world situation, not be so involved, like ninety-nine percent of Americans. But I'm really glad. We wouldn't have met so many great people. Soldiers with PTSD come to stay with us. People say, "Don't you worry about them with your children?" But these people are heroes to me. They're fighting to make something good of their lives, as opposed to people just floating around in space, living in their selfish little worlds.

Most people I've met who are working towards ending the war have so much compassion; they really care about what happens to other people. I'd rather my kids have them as heroes than sports stars and celebrities.

Nothing gives me more pleasure than going into a senator's office and telling them how some of the legislation they're voting on has direct impact on military families and veterans. It's such good therapy. I'm really glad I got to that point. I feel in some small way that I'm making a difference.

I believe in having a military for protection. I'm not a total pacifist. Sometimes, violence has been for the greater good. I'm not against all war. My husband would have gone to Afghanistan in a heartbeat.

We're doing really good. Our kids are happy, doing well in school, they've made wonderful friends. We're back to normal things, going for nature walks and playing baseball. I refuse to let my family, my marriage, be casualties of this war. I refuse to let it happen to others. It can make or break you. We didn't let it break us.

# Chapter 22
# Linda Waste

*Linda and her husband Phil live on a boat in Tennessee. They have three sons and two grandchildren who are veterans of the Iraq War. When Linda spoke with me in October 2006, her family had given a total of eighty-four months of service in all, with more to come.*

My husband was in the Navy, not career. We met in San Francisco and headed to Oregon. We have a "yours, mine, and ours" family; he has two older sons. We raised five boys together. We were always anti-war, but the boys loved history and the military. They spent their allowance at the Army surplus store.

My oldest, Tony, screwed around in college. We told him we wouldn't pay for it any more. In retaliation, a week later he told us he was joining the Army. We thought it would be positive for him, teach him discipline, help him to grow up. Tony was going to a liberal arts college, it cost a fortune.

Tony's been in the Army fifteen years in February. He's enjoyed it, it's a good life for him; he loves to travel. His two younger brothers—ten and eight years younger than him—he was a recruiter, and recruited them out of high school, during Clinton, before it all went crazy. They got great sign-up bonuses and scored high.

Tony's thirty-four. He's married to a woman with older kids, and he has a step-daughter who also went into the Army. Phil's oldest son was in the Navy. His oldest son, our grandson, is in the Navy now. We had five family members in the military; then 9/11, and everything went nuts.

We knew they'd be sent somewhere eventually. Then Afghanistan went down. None of them went there. When Iraq started, we bought into the rhetoric, and I don't know why we ever did, because we never did before. When Tony was sent to Turkey in February of 2003, he had only been home from Kosovo for three months; he was supposed to go into Iraq from the north.

Wesley was in North Carolina on March 19, when the war started. He's twenty-six; he's out now. He'd been disgusted with the Eighty-second Airborne; he's an excellent soldier but he hates taking orders. We're amazed he went in the Army, he said it was a dog and pony show. He went out, then back in, to Georgia, Third Infantry Division, left Fort Bragg, went to Fort Stewart. At the time, the Third Infantry was already deployed in Kuwait, moving into Iraq in January of 2003. He was going to work on the post. For three months they were told they were going, then told they were not going. On March 18, he called and told us that they said to put their desert combat uniforms away, get their BDUs [battle dress uniforms] instead; they weren't going over. So he shows up to work on March 19 on post, and they're told to get their desert uniforms and pack, they were going today. So on March 19, we're listening to the radio, hearing the first bombs fall on Baghdad, and he was preparing to leave.

He gets sent to Kuwait, waiting for orders. They have good communications now, but in the beginning they didn't. We didn't know where he was or what was going on. We heard every day about soldiers from the Third ID getting killed. Physically, it started eating me up. They thought I had a brain tumor; I had migraines.

Finally, he called, after at least three weeks. Then they sent him to Fallujah. We didn't know they were usually kept in Kuwait for two weeks.

What really turned our thinking? All kinds of little things. Were there WMDs? Why were they really sent over? What really hit me was the day Bush flew to the Abraham Lincoln [a Navy destroyer] with that big "Mission Accomplished" sign behind him, saying it was all over.

I've never in my life been as angry as I was at that moment, because I knew what was going on over there. I was getting the information.

To backtrack: Wesley went over March 19; his younger brother went in April; our granddaughter, Shon, also went in April. She and Dustin, my son, are both with the First Armored Division out of Germany. So we had all four over there. Wesley was in the Third Infantry Division from Georgia; also Tony, in the First Armored Division. We heard from them occasionally online. Later on during deployment, Dustin was in Baghdad, Shon was driving trucks in Baghdad, and Wesley was in Fallujah. It's been hard.

Phil and I are real positive people. To feel like we've felt for four years is just unbelievable. If I'm quiet, I'm as guilty as those other people who say nothing. I have to talk about it. To think that so much of our nation doesn't really understand, doesn't even think about what's going on, is very disturbing. It blows me away, some of people's attitudes.

Tony came home in late July 2003 and Wesley came home in August with the Third ID. Dustin and Shon were extended. They were there for sixteen months. Dustin came home July 2004. Our grandson has been there two times with the Navy. He's just home from his second tour, three months ago. People don't understand, Navy is boots on the ground. They're doing things they don't normally do. They were rescuing people from a fire at an oil well. The four killed this week were three Marines, one sailor. The military can do whatever they want with people.

Kyle, our grandson, was over there then; Wes went back for his second deployment in January 2005. All overlapping. We didn't think Tony would go back. Dustin went back November 2005, his brother went in January . . . I'm losing track. Wes is out now, got out of the military in April 2005. He still has a year of inactive duty. Now we're worried he'll be sent again. Dustin's been home the past seven months. Tony's going back today, with the Fourth Brigade, First Cavalry, out of Fort Bliss, Texas. He told me last night that our granddaughter will go to Afghanistan in January for her second deployment. They have both been extended to fifteen months.

We've run the gamut. This is one thing people don't think about, what we go through as parents, spouses, siblings. You hear about a death in your son's unit, wait for seventy-two hours to hear. Then you're so grateful it's not yours. Then you cry from gratitude and grief—gratitude it's not yours, grief for the families who lost theirs.

A year ago last August—August 9, 2005—I was reading about Cindy Sheehan going to Crawford. I sent an email to MFSO saying we supported her, our hearts were with her, we were sorry we wouldn't be there. We were in Georgia, living on a boat. Within twenty minutes we had a response to our email from Nancy and Charley. They said, "Call us." It took us an hour to decide to call. We knew if we called, we'd go to Crawford. Phil and I talked for an hour, and then called. Sure enough, we were in Texas the next day.

We sent an email to all our kids letting them know what we were doing. Tony said, "That's great, go for it; just make sure Dad cuts his hair and wears a clean T-shirt." The kids' sentiments were all that way. We don't speak for our kids, but they support us. They think the same way: we need to be out of there.

Originally, the kids supported the war too. They still feel they're helping the Iraqis while over there, helping directly, but now they know we shouldn't be there. A lady said to me, "If your son Tony (a sergeant first class)—if he was a true leader, he'd tell his men not to go." But my son cares about his men; he feels he'd be putting their lives on the line.

Unless people are there, they don't know how the soldiers bond. Their motivation becomes staying alive and keeping each other alive. If he did tell his troops not to go, they'd be court-martialed. Tony has put fifteen years in the Army: this is his career. Lots of people are getting out now. They're fed up. The day Wes got out, in April of 2006, he said there were over six hundred people getting out that day. He said it was like that every week. The military has dropped their quota and added high-pressure recruiting in the field—you need to sign within twenty-four hours or you don't get a bonus. In Iraq, Shon signed for bonus pay of ten thousand dollars for six more years. Even Wes—he was on stop/loss; Dustin was going to be stop/lossed so he signed up for another year so he'd get a bonus. If you're stop/lossed, you get nothing.

When we went to Crawford that August, they had a rally, and Phil and I spoke. We did one interview after another. We did radio and newspaper interviews. When we were leaving Camp Casey [named after Sheehan's son, killed in Iraq], we were asked to join four buses in the Bring Them Home Now tour, from Texas to Shreveport, Montgomery, Gainesville, Atlanta, Tallahassee, Savannah, Richmond, Norfolk, then D.C. on September 21. That tour was gut-wrenching. We spoke every day, drove to the next city, told our stories, shared the stage with Veterans For Peace and Gold Star Mothers. It was grueling. It was an important time for us. Phil and I met with John Kerry along with several others. We spoke on the Mall.

The last time we had all our kids under one roof was Christmas 2000. They haven't seen each other since then, except Wes and Dustin, briefly. It's been very difficult for them.

What it's done to us . . . Wes is doing very well. He came back the first time, and it was four or five months until he was himself. Until then, he was extremely tense, kind of grumpy, stressed. Loud noises made him jumpy. They tell them they'll get psychiatric help, but that's baloney. They get "reorientated" for two weeks; Wes said it was baloney. No follow-up. I heard on the news last year, they've upped that; but there's nothing. A so-called "review."

Our youngest son had a really hard time. The first time back, his wife said he had nightmares. His wife was there for him if he wanted to talk. He opened up about some things. About other things he hasn't. I think he had health and emotional problems; he shouldn't have gone back. Some of his friends didn't go back because of their constant complaining. It used to be, when Phil was in the Navy, you went to sick bay. Now you have to go to your NCO [non-commissioned officer], say you don't feel well, and get permission to go to sick call. If you go to the NCO and say you don't feel well, you're told to suck it up and get out there. Nobody wants to go.

It's tearing families apart. Phil and I have had a really hard time emotionally with this, knowing our kids were in danger and being unable to do anything about it. I went to Operation House Call in August and I told the women I was such a mess, I couldn't do anything. I went to the doctor's office, said I needed to see somebody; I fell apart, went on anti-depressants. I've been on them for almost a year. The women on tour said, "Oh my God, me too."

You feel helpless, hopeless. How do I make a change? Phil kept me away from it for a while. But if I'm not speaking, not acting, I feel guilty.

People need to wake up in this country. I'm so ashamed and as-tounded that people don't even think about it. If it's not affecting them directly, they just don't worry about it. Americans are just so comfort-able.

I had a congresswoman say to me last August, "Don't you believe the world is a safer place with Saddam Hussein out of power?" I just looked at her. How can you say such a thing?

"Better fight them there than here"—I think, how can you possibly believe that an Iraqi woman's life is any less important than mine, that her son's or husband's life is any less important than my son's or hus-band's?

Being with MFSO—it gives me hope, that there are sane people who know how wrong this is, willing to put it all on the line to get the truth out there. I'm so proud to be associated with these people. There's a lot that's positive coming from it, but it's very difficult to do. We talk with some people who get all their news from right-wing talk shows. That's scary. The frustration is that there aren't enough people protesting out there.

We listen to talk shows about us being "radical communists," like we're all these freaky people. I look around at the other people in MFSO. We're middle-aged, overweight, from all walks of life. Yeah, we're pretty dangerous!

It's so hard for me to talk about it, but people who've lost people, out there doing it for the human race . . . Thank goodness for all the families doing this. I'm lucky, I have an exceptional marriage. Phil is my rock. I cry. I can tell when he's dealing with it and I baby him. He's hurting right now too. We really didn't think Tony would go back. We hoped the war would be over by now.

I'm fifty-five. Phil is sixty-six. We lived in San Francisco; we were both in the streets over Vietnam. The movement now is moms, dads, grandparents. I'm amazed not to see more young people out there. They come up to us, saying, "We didn't know," but they're too busy to get involved.

They've learned not to show the flag-draped coffins. You're burying young men and women who gave everything, and bringing them back in shame and darkness. They learned what not to do in Vietnam.

Phil and I live on a boat. We were in a motor-home for nine years; we traveled to Germany to see Dustin, who's married a German woman and had a baby. We try to keep relaxed. We're not the same people we were. Our sons are not the way they were. I look at pictures of us from before this all started, and the pictures of us now . . . I hate to think what this war has done. Our friends in Europe fear us. Our governments pull this crap, but people are people everywhere.

I'm very proud of my sons. I just don't agree with this war. Why are we not in Darfur?

# Chapter 23
# Joyce and Kevin Lucey

*Joyce and Kevin's son, Lance Corporal Jeffrey Lucey, killed himself on June 22, 2004, after serving in Iraq with the Marine Reserves, Sixth Motor Transport Battalion.*

*Kevin:* We live in Belchertown, Massachusetts. We have three kids: Kelly; two years later, Jeffrey; two years later, Debbie. This is a rural area, tremendously wooded and green. Jeffrey loved to play sports, the girls were involved too. They were in Scouts and gymnastics.

*Joyce:* We'd go up to Maine, have campfires, toast marshmallows. I'm a nurse, but I stayed home with the children. I remember thinking that we had it all: a dog, a cat, a gerbil, and three kids. So fast, everything changes . . . Jeff put in a letter we found that he had a happy childhood. He wanted us to remember him like that.

*Kevin:* Jeffrey did a year at Holyoke Community College. When he died, he'd been accepted in UMass Amherst School of Business. Jeffrey lived with us until he died, at twenty-three. His girlfriend lived about ten minutes away. If he wasn't here, he was at Julie's family's home. We saw him every day, so we felt the loss that much more. We never lost contact with him.

*Joyce:* He was a charmer, very social. Girls would call here all the time. They'd say to him, "You're like my psychologist." He was a good listener. He wasn't perfect; he got into mischief and hassles. But he learned from it. In his core he was a really good kid.

*[I ask about when they knew he was interested in the military.]*

*Joyce:* I didn't want to acknowledge it was happening. The recruiter was very aggressive. Jeffrey bent to authority. If he didn't want to disappoint someone, he was embarrassed to say no.

*Kevin:* Jeffrey always wanted to be helpful. In '99, there were no war drums beating. On TV you saw the Reserves helping people. You got the idea that the military is about noble causes and honor. Marines are the toughest branch. Jeff felt he'd be proving something to himself.

*Joyce:* Jeff did boot camp on Parris Island in 2000. At first, he felt it was a large mistake; he wanted to come home. By the end, he felt good about himself.

*Kevin:* Jeff was really looking forward to the brotherhood that would follow. He came home and was supposed to start the Reserves in December. He was stationed in New Haven, Connecticut, at Fort Nathan Hale, in the Sixth Motor Transport Battalion. They didn't need an administrative assistant, which was his MOS, so his assignment was changed to truck driver. That's how he became a convoy driver.

*Joyce:* I was a little ignorant. I said, "Thank God he's driving trucks; he won't be on the front lines." I didn't realize all of Iraq would be a battlefield. He went back to HCC in January; he took off the fall before the war. He felt it was coming.

*Kevin:* The apprehension started September 11. He wanted to go to help with the recovery in New York City. Then, he could understand going to Afghanistan. But Iraq—he questioned that. He'd watch the debates in late '02; he said, "This doesn't make sense."

*Joyce:* He wanted no part of that. On Family Day, before they left, there were television crews around. They were told if they didn't have a positive feeling, don't be interviewed. He didn't, so he steered clear of the cameras. I thought, "We're all free, except the military who are fighting to keep us free." Jeff said, "They own me now."

*Kevin:* On January 14, 2003, they received orders. In February he went to Camp Pendleton and then to Kuwait. That's when he started writing a journal. The journal ended the first day of the war, one day after he turned twenty-two. His birthday is March 18. He put down his thoughts about where he was, the purpose of them being there. He was sure he had to conceal it.

*Joyce:* He also wrote about his fear of coming back a different person.

*Kevin:* His last entry was that a Scud missile went overhead, so they knew the war had begun. It crashed within a mile of the camp. They were in a panic. A friend of his looked at a picture of his three-month-old baby and wondered if he would ever see the baby again.

*Joyce:* He wrote, "The reality of the war has hit us." He crossed into Iraq very early on. We didn't hear for the first two weeks, then we got two quick letters in April. He wrote his girlfriend in mid-April that he felt he had done immoral things; he wanted to erase the last month of his life.

*Kevin:* His letters to us were really sanitized. He'd say, "Don't watch the news." Little did he know, Joyce had three TVs and watched all the news programs. She paid the price. She had a stroke three weeks before Jeffrey came home.

*Joyce:* I couldn't run and get him and bring him home.

*Kevin:* Jeffrey wanted continual contact with the family. His sisters would send him care packages, and he'd share them with other Marines. You could tell he was exhausted.

*Joyce:* His letters to us kept a good tone. We didn't know about his letters to his girlfriend until after he died. We also didn't know he was writing to Kevin's brother, a Vietnam vet. We have a letter Kevin's brother wrote, promising Jeff, "I won't tell your parents the fucked-up stuff." He was in Basra, Nasiriyah, up and down the river Euphrates. Their unit was scattered all over.

*Kevin:* He came back early July '03 to the States. He was very tan, had lost weight, not that he had much to lose, and he looked fantastic. The Marines told us to expect a lot of re-adjustment. They never mentioned PTSD. But they said, "If your Marine doesn't want to do something, don't push."

After he died, we found out that when he and his girlfriend went to the Cape for a weekend, Julie said he didn't want to walk on the beach; he said he'd had enough sand to last him a lifetime.

*Joyce:* Nobody was sharing things they noticed. We thought they were insignificant. He was drinking a lot. I was not happy with that.

He was vomiting every day. We took that as, he must have caught something. I wanted to send him to the doctor but he put it off. Before Iraq, breakfast was a must. After Iraq, he didn't eat breakfast. If we'd picked up on that . . .

*Kevin:* On Christmas Eve, 2003, Jeff declined for the first time ever to go to Julie's parents' house. I said, "Look, he's only been back a few months, let's not push." Debbie came back home around 9:30. Jeff was drunk and crying in the kitchen. Suddenly he took off the dogtags he always wore—that was so significant, but none of us knew back then—and he threw them at Debbie. He said he was nothing more than a murderer. She said, "No, you're my brother." But she didn't know what to do. On Christmas Day, he woke up and seemed fine. I rationalized it. I thought it had to be the alcohol.

*Joyce:* He had nightmares. He'd yell out. I heard him say, "They were coming after me in an alleyway." I could kick myself now. Why didn't I ask him more about it? What was I thinking? I should have noticed this. Part of why we come out to talk now, is, maybe now someone will do that for their kid.

*Kevin:* We were going through a transition, from blaming drinking. Do you open a can of worms you can't close? Do you have him remember things that will drive him over the edge? We were afraid if we pushed him too far he'd get to a breaking point.

*Joyce:* The real crash came the week of spring break. He just sat in the living room, in melancholy. He talked low-key, a hopeless tone in his voice. We encouraged him to see our internist. We were starting to think of PTSD. He begged us not to tell his unit. He was afraid he'd get Section Eight [medical discharge]; he didn't want it to follow him through life. He was interested in the state police, he had taken the exam. He figured he wouldn't be able to get a job. We got a letter after he died: he was accepted into the state police. He scored above ninety-five percent. If he only knew . . .

*Kevin:* The stigma, and our ignorance, started him falling, crashing. The stigma still thrives in the military.

From mid-March, things changed drastically. There was sleep deprivation for Jeff and for us. The atmosphere at home changed. I found a trauma institution in Connecticut. They were willing to talk to him, but when he found out no one there was a veteran, he wouldn't go.

*Joyce:* We found out he wasn't attending his classes at college. He said he got panicky, felt people were looking at him; he had to get out of class. Our family doctor put him on Clonapin and Prozac. Jeff was also having a problem with dizziness.

*Kevin:* Back to March '04. Things became very strained. Jeffrey never got mad at us personally. He watched political shows; he got very angry at the administration over the conduct of the war. When Reagan died, he said it was too bad they lowered the flag to half-staff for one guy—why not for the guys who die every day? His drinking increased. When I got home, he'd say, "Let's go for a ride, let's talk." I had so much work, sometimes I couldn't. He'd say, "Let's have a beer." He said the beer was so he'd pass out; he couldn't sleep. He experienced visual and audial hallucinations. He heard camel spiders . . .

*Joyce:* He didn't tell us this. We learned after. Had I known he was looking for camel spiders in his room with a flashlight, we'd have been in his bedroom. He was deathly afraid of spiders, from a little child. He spoke to different people. None of us seemed to connect it all to get the full picture. Julie was trying to get him to take off the dogtags. We didn't know it.

*Kevin:* We know he took them off twice. Christmas, when he threw them, and the day he died. He laid them on the bed.

*Joyce:* The military say things Jeffrey talked about didn't happen. One reporter went to his captain and he said he wasn't with prisoners of war. But he and Paul transported them together. The reporter went back to the captain, and he said, "I might have spoken in haste."
 In April, right after the Marines were in Nasiriyah, he wrote to Julie that he'd done things he'd only seen in movie theaters. It wasn't bravado. He said he'd never want to fight in a war again.

*Kevin:* The Marines investigated themselves. We believe Jeffrey. They have a vested interest in making certain findings.

*Joyce*: Jeffrey said an older family trying to get back into their house were shot down. And he talked about bumps in the road, referring to children getting run over by trucks. Only after he died, talking to other military families, did we realize this could have happened. If someone doesn't get out of the way of the convoy, they'll get run over. Jeffrey said the things he had to do, he never expected to do.

*Kevin:* Joyce and I believed in our government. Even though we'd disagree with the administration, we'd never believe they'd be as bad as all the other regimes in the world.

His drinking and anger got worse. The first two weeks in May we thought he was still going to school. The week before finals, Jeffrey didn't get out of his room. He'd just started seeing a private therapist on May 10. Mark believed Jeffrey was suffering from PTSD; he tried to encourage him to go to the VA. We were naïve enough to believe the VA would care. Jeffrey drove to the appointment intoxicated.

In April, we were all hurting. We were very tense, focused on Jeff and Jeff's needs. I think families can have a form of PTSD. I'm not saying we suffer anything like what the soldiers suffer. But dealing with the changed essence of a person, the whole family suffers the impact tremendously. We were worn down, isolating ourselves.

*Joyce:* It happens slowly. You adapt. Were we that crazy? Kids go through panic attacks; we didn't always put it down to the military. When he went downhill, I don't think anybody realized it would be so fast.

*Kevin:* The family develops a masking system. We put forth an image that everything is okay. We were trying to respect Jeff, who was begging us not to go to the VA, "You'll destroy my future." Finally, in mid-May, I called the VA, anonymously, and gave them the symptomology. They said it was classic PTSD. They said, "We're not the military. Bring him in as soon as possible." Every day he'd say, "Not today. Maybe tomorrow."

I think Jeff felt he was a failure because he didn't take his finals. Mark called HCC; they were angels. They immediately said to tell Jeffrey not to worry, he could participate in graduation, he could walk with Debbie, who was also graduating; they'll work with him.

*Joyce:* The professors gave him until September, even December, to continue the program. Jeffrey had days when he'd say he was on the right track. But that would only last that day, or that moment. I think he always thought he would overcome this. I told him he'd get better, and he gave me this sad smirk.

He had social anxiety that kept him from going to work at the Career Center. They invited him to a pizza party, and he said, "Wow, they remembered me." A lot of people cared about him.

*Kevin:* An integral part of all this is shame. Guilt is about what you did. Shame is about what you are. It's deadlier. He was convinced he was letting us down. He felt he was nothing but a screw-up.

We were in a twilight zone of chaos. Every day I'd get up and be scared of what today would hold. Finally, May 28, we got him to the VA. Jeff had been pretty well, not drunk all the time. But I came home and he was really drunk, and drove out for beer.

*Joyce:* I said, "Where are you going with that beer?" He said he'd drink it after the VA.

*Kevin:* We later found out that it was EKU, a powerful German beer with a very high alcohol content. Julie was there. I came in and said, "Jeff, it's time to go." Jeff resisted initially, then said, "Okay, I'll go, I'll just get ready." Julie and I left the room. We heard a crack like a crack of thunder. Jeff had slammed his fist into his dresser in total frustration. I went back, and he was sitting on his bed. I said, "Okay, now we have a perfect excuse to go to the hospital." His hand was already red and swollen. He fell, right outside of the car.

Jeffrey brought beer into the car with him. I slipped the bottle away from him, put it between the door and the seat. He asked for it, and I said, "You drank it." He laid his head against Julie. Their relationship was floundering.

We drove one hour to Leeds, Massachusetts, to the VA. Jeff seemed to have sobered up a little. He was functioning okay, but he was very angry. A female nurse started the intake process. He wasn't himself. He was usually very polite, respectful. A male nurse overheard him talking sharply to the female nurse, and said, "We're not going to put up with this shit." Jeff and he connected. His whole attitude changed; now he was talking to a Marine.

At seven p.m., he took the breathalyzer test: it was .328, four hours after he stopped drinking. The psychiatrist tried to get him to go in voluntarily, but he wanted to go home. Julie and I were sitting in the hospital foyer. The doctor said, "Your son should stay, but he won't." We decided to do involuntary commitment. This is where we heard about the hallucinations, and him finding a rope in a tree to hang himself. Jeff went in to see the psychologist, and came out with a smirk, and went out the front door. They dragged him back. We went home.

People in the VA . . . I have serious issues with the system, but they were good. Jeff was there until June 1, over the four-day weekend. We arranged to go every day, even though we shouldn't have with their policies. Unfortunately, Jeff was the only Iraqi vet on the floor. Most of the others were Vietnam vets.

Tuesday morning, Jeffrey called his mom and said he'd been discharged, "Come pick me up." Joyce and Julie brought him home. He went to Julie's house. It turned out to be the last time.

Jeff started drinking again. The issues seemed worse. On June 3rd, Jeff went to Dunkin' Donuts for coffee for him and his mom. He asked his mom if he could drive the family car. Suddenly he's back, with a police officer. He totaled the family car. He saved the two coffees, his and his mom's. He wasn't drunk. He did tell the police officer that he'd taken four Clonapin; you're supposed to take one a day and one at night.

*Joyce:* He was having a terrible time with his balance, and dizziness. The effect of the drinking was worse with the Clonapin. He didn't understand what was happening to him.

*Kevin:* We met a doctor later who said he would never have prescribed those drugs for someone with PTSD who was drinking. Jeff had never been diagnosed with PTSD except by Mark, his private therapist.

*Joyce:* The VA told us they wouldn't assess Jeffrey for PTSD if he was drinking. They wanted him to go into an alcohol day program.

*Kevin:* He was going to have to maintain sobriety before they'd assess him for PTSD.

*Joyce:* He could barely make it through the day; he couldn't give up that crutch. Jeff was not cooperating. The advice was, we might have to throw him out of our house, so he'll realize he's reached rock bottom. Or we might have to say our son hit us and call the police, and they'd take him to a psych unit and then the VA. We'd have to lie. We didn't want to compromise our relationship.

*Kevin:* When you hear advice like that—give him a criminal record to get him through the system—it makes no sense.

June 5 was graduation. We got down there, and finally saw Jeff after the graduation started, being walked on the arm of a Holyoke fire department lieutenant; he was intoxicated. He was clean-shaven usually, concerned about his appearance. He had stubble, his eyes were glazed. He drove thirty miles; I don't know how he survived it. I was so worn down, I got angry. I was frustrated. Oh God. I took him and said, "What the hell are you doing?" Jeff said, "Oh, Dad, come on, this is nothing serious, I made it." It was time to get the diplomas. As Debbie went up the aisle to get her diploma, Jeff runs up and hugs her; he held up the whole ceremony. It was Debbie's last hug.

He was sort of okay afterwards. He did what he came to do.

*Joyce:* It was his mission. Our son-in-law Don took him back to our house. His car was in the lot. We found some beer bottles and got rid of them, and took his car back. We were going to have a cookout. There's a brook behind the house, a pathway there. Don helped him up it but he fell in the road. He tried to get Don to have a drink with him. My parents saw him like that for the first time. Nobody felt like eating. My mother said, "I can't believe Jeff is like this."

Prior to this, Jeff had taken me down to the brook and played the song *45* by Shinedown. The words alluded to suicide, looking down the barrel of a 45 gun. "Whatever happened to a young man's heart, swallowed by pain as he slowly fell apart." He said, "Don't take it the wrong way, I won't do that." I was so terrified, I didn't know what to say. We talked about a lot of things, but not that.

I was in some kind of la-la land. We took the dog up through the brush and climbed up to the house. We were loaded with ticks. I'll always treasure that last walk, the last time we connected. We were always very close. We were just talking.

*Kevin:* The phrase from that song is on his tombstone. We felt totally powerless, helpless. We called the VA, and they said, "Get him over here." His sister got him to agree to go if she hit ten whiffleballs. He said okay, but she hadn't hit ten. She felt weird that he didn't notice.

Jeff got into the car after I promised I wouldn't go. His sisters and Kelly's husband got in the car with Jeff's grandfather. I called the hospital and said, "They're on the way." Then I got panicky calls from our daughters. They said the VA wouldn't take him. Jeff wouldn't go in voluntarily; he wouldn't enter the building.

*Joyce:* His grandfather pleaded with them to help his grandson. Debbie said he wouldn't say he was suicidal or homicidal, so they wouldn't take him in.

*Kevin:* We expect people to make rational decisions about their care when they're suffering PTSD. They have to serve the system's needs. Joyce and I went through the house, clearing it of bottles of liquor and knives. Debbie's boyfriend disabled his car. We purged the house of everything we could. I never felt so furious as at the VA not taking him then.

After we found out the VA wouldn't help, we called Massachusetts emergency services. I explained my son was a veteran and the VA wouldn't help, and we needed someone to come evaluate him. As soon as I said he'd been drinking, they said they wouldn't come. So what do you do then? I felt everyone had just deserted us. I didn't know what to do with my anger.

We were beaten down. We were desolate. Jeff came back. We just stayed home with him.

The next significant event was six days later, on Friday evening. We had watched a Red Sox game. The Sox won; he felt good, and said good night. We knew he couldn't sleep. We couldn't sleep either. We got a call at midnight. My daughter Debbie was on the phone. She said, "Jeff's not home." I said, "Yes he is." Turns out he snuck out his window and asked our neighbors to take him to the package store.

If I could go back . . . I was so exhausted, so angry. He was getting out of the VW, dressed in camies, had knives on each hip, and a .38 revolver—it had been changed to a pellet gun—and he was holding a six-pack of beer. It took all I had to smile at the girls and thank them.

I grabbed the beers. Jeff said he needed two. I smashed them against some pine trees. It was one of the most pathetic sights. Joyce was terrified. Jeff followed her like a little puppy, and he said, "Give me one, I just need one beer." I told Joyce to go in with Kelly. I thought Jeff would be furious, but he just sat in a chair while I ranted. Afterwards, I apologized, and he hugged me.

On June 14, we thought we had a major breakthrough. He started to cry. "What's wrong with me? I know all this doesn't exist, but I feel it." We asked him to go for help and he agreed. The next day, Joyce called the VA and said he'd stopped drinking. "We're watching our son slowly die. We need help immediately." They mentioned the Vet Center. Jeff called and made an appointment for Friday at 3:30. From that moment, Jeff didn't drink. He had all sorts of emotions, but they seemed manageable.

On June 18, he was in the Vet Center for three hours. They were going to come to the house to meet with him three times a week. The next
day, we went to Camp Sunshine in Maine, for children with life-
threatening diseases and their families, where we all volunteered. Regret-
fully, they had an open bar. Jeff started drinking. It was Father's Day.
Jeff was passed out in the car. I left with him. He came in the house later.
Joyce and Debbie were still up there volunteering.

*Joyce:* We didn't want to stay, but we couldn't find the keys for Jeff's
car. Debbie was kind of hysterical. We should have been home.

*Kevin:* Joyce called and spoke to Jeff. Sunday evening, Jeff just wanted
to talk. He would go to bed around one or two, then float around the
house. I went to work on Monday, June 21. When I came home, Jeff was
in a rage. Not against me; he hated the Bush administration, the war. He
started talking about suicide. I called the Vet Center. The woman got me
calmed down, and talked with Jeff for about half an hour. He was in a
much better place. I was working on progress notes; I type with one finger, so it takes forever. Joyce called again. It was around 11:30 or 12.
    A week beforehand, Debbie had been here, and she was leaving. Jeff
turned and asked if he could sit on my lap. It took me by surprise. When
he was a small boy, up until he was ten or eleven, he did that a lot. I said,
"Of course." We'd just rock back and forth. Monday night, he did that
again. We rocked in total silence for about forty-five minutes. We
hugged and went to bed.
    June 22, I was on the cellphone to Joyce, coming home from work. I
drove into the yard, and said Jeff must be watching TV. I was walking
through the house to his room. I noticed that the dogtags were on his bed.
I saw the cellar door open. The light was on. There were pictures on the
floor. I went down, and focused on the pictures. He had his platoon picture right in the middle. On either side, he had a picture of his sisters. In
a half-moon crescent, there were pictures of the family. There was a picture of the crazy psychotic epileptic beagle we had; Jeff would always
rush him outside and stay with him when he had a seizure.
    Beyond the pictures . . . At first, I thought Jeff was standing there.
But he wasn't. I went over, lifted him on my knees. That was the last
time I held him on my lap. Too late. He was gone. He was very cold and
clammy. But he looked at peace, finally. I got the hose from around his
neck and laid him down. I went upstairs and called the police, came
down, kept him company. The police came here, they were all over.
Joyce called.

*Joyce:* Kevin was supposed to call me. Debbie was taking a nap. It was around 7:15. I knew something was wrong. He could barely speak. "Is it Jeff?" "Yes." "Is he okay?" "No." "Is he dead?" Debbie heard us . . . I just knew. Debbie jumped up and grabbed the phone.

*Kevin:* I told her Jeff was being taken to the hospital. I didn't tell her . . .

*Joyce:* We ran through the rain, barefoot. It was so crazy. You're in a world that doesn't exist. All these little kids are coming in their little costumes for their party . . . I went to the office. They brought in the camp social worker to help us reach the hospital. We couldn't get any information. I knew he was dead. Kevin would have called to say he was okay.

*Kevin:* In the interim, my brother came. He told police I wanted to go to the hospital.
    Jeff did a lot of writing. He had three letters downstairs, and a poem. "It's near 4:35 p.m. and I'm near completing my death." We didn't know for a year. The state police didn't want to give them up.
    The last person Jeff spoke to was the therapist from the Vet Center, approximately at four. He needed directions. Jeff gave them to him, but he got lost, and never made it.
    I called my older daughter. I said to Don, she had to go to the hospital. My brother and I left here, got to the hospital grounds, and saw Kelly. She was sitting on the side of a hill, sobbing hysterically. She had demanded to see her brother. The doctors said, "Sorry, there's nothing we could do."
    She literally ran and collapsed. I had my brother stop and we went to her. Then the phone rang. It was the social worker from Camp Sunshine. She didn't know. She said, "Talk to your daughter Debbie." I remember saying, "Your brother is not feeling any more pain. He just passed away."

*Joyce:* Debbie started screaming, "It's all my fault." He had told her about the rope at the brook. She called Jeff's girlfriend. Julie started screaming, I could hear her. I could hear her father screaming, "It's not your fault." I was looking at the sky, saying, "Where are you? Why?"
    They took Julie to the hospital. She was in bad shape. They put her on Atavan. We were in a state of shock. People packed our stuff, drove us three and a half hours back to our place. It was the longest ride, in the dark, with people we didn't really know. Debbie was talking to people on the phone. Jeff was pretty well known; he did all the sports in high

school. He had friends at every level. He mingled with everybody. For his pallbearers, we had kids with the highest academic ranking in their class, jocks, Marines, a kid with problems who didn't graduate.

*Kevin:* The day after Jeff died, the whole family were out in the driveway. I wanted to find out how the whole family wanted to react. They all said nobody was ashamed. They wanted to be forthright and blunt about it.

We stumbled into activism. Two weeks later, we told Jeff's therapist we wanted to do something so nobody else would have to go through what we went through. Mark got us the number of the Veterans Education Project. I called and a woman answered; her name was Sue Leary. I told her the story about Jeff. She said they were an organization where they send veterans into schools and talk about the reality of the experience. We wanted them to give us the names of families who had experience with PTSD, so we could be a resource.

The director, Rob Wilson, asked if we'd come have a cup of coffee. He said he was interested; he'd heard Jeff's story. Our next contact was when Eyes Wide Open, the boots exhibit, came to Amherst. Rob called. He had told the organizers of the exhibit—the American Friends Service Committee—about Jeffrey; he said they would like us to participate. We donated Jeff's boots, his uniform, and placards telling his story. The Friends invited us to come to the Amherst town common.

In the interim, Rob wanted us to go to the Veterans For Peace convention, in Boston at the same time as the Democratic National Convention, to meet Nancy Lessin and Charley Richardson. They brought us to the national meeting of MFSO.

*Joyce:* They had a circle, and we all introduced ourselves and gave the reason we were part of the group. We were eighth or ninth to speak. I was the first one to say our son was gone. Everyone else had a son over there or at home. I couldn't get the words out; I couldn't say he was dead. Kevin took over. They were all supportive.

*Kevin:* From that moment, Nancy and Charley took us under their wing. They asked us to go to Cambridge and talk on a radio show. We said we'd do whatever we could. They had us sit in with Amy Goodman on *Democracy Now.*

*Joyce:* I was like, "I don't want to be on anything;" I was still reeling. Then we found the program aired nationwide. Somebody called from

Japan, crying over Jeffrey's death, a publisher. She's published Jeff's story in Japanese.

*Kevin:* Through Nancy, we met a very nice woman who was trying to produce a documentary about the war. She had heard us talk with Amy. We were rushed into a room with her and a cameraman. They asked us questions. Joyce and I were—it's hard to describe . . .

*Joyce:* . . . in a daze. We were just functioning; we were going through the motions. I remember the producer of *Ground Truth*. She met us at Fayetteville, North Carolina, where we spoke on the anniversary of the war. She interviewed us there, and also at Central Park in New York. She said later, my eyes were a lot better then than at the first interview.

*Kevin:* During that time, we went to New York to see Jeff's boots at Central Park. Whenever the exhibit came around in the northeast, we felt compelled to go. Nancy and Charley introduced us to Sue Niederer, who confronted Laura Bush; she said, "Your husband murdered my son."

*Joyce:* Sue grabbed Debbie and us. She said, "You're not going home. You're going to march with us, protesting the war." We were already out of the hotel with all our stuff. So we marched. That was our first introduction to activism, in New York City during the Republican National Convention.

Debbie had the little card from Jeff's wake. She was holding it up on the side of the march, telling everybody the story. CNN stopped her.

*Kevin:* We tried to walk away. Nancy grabbed two women; they turned out to be from PBS *Frontline*.

*Joyce:* They came to our house in September. They asked us to come to New York in December to complete the interview. It was shown in March. They asked us not to do more interviews until the segment aired.

*Kevin:* We got calls from Matt Lauer, CNN; we declined. After the show, on March 1, 2005, then we had a call from a regional TV station, New England Cable News. Joyce told her, "You don't really want Jeff's story; we had a documentary, so many people had already interviewed us; do you really want him again? You don't want to overexpose this story." But Iris did three people; Jeff was one. She did an excellent job, very sensitive, about PTSD. One of the men is back in Iraq, though he was totally destroyed; but he was like, "If my country calls me, I'll go."

There was a film producer from California, Bedford Falls—they produced *I Am Sam*. The woman was very interested in Jeff's story, but I declined at the time. They wanted to buy the rights to Jeff's story. That seemed foreboding. They'd have to approve everything we did.

*Joyce:* It wasn't even that, for me. I spoke to her the night of *Frontline*. It made me feel uncomfortable, like we were going too fast. Where are we going with all this? We want to help, but not have Jeff being used. You don't know how it's going to come out. I was nervous about that.

The first Christmas without Jeff, Nancy mentioned that Cindy Sheehan, who'd lost her son, was also having a tough time. I emailed her. She'd just formed Gold Star Families for Peace. She asked if I would join. I said I didn't know if we belonged; Jeff didn't die the same way. She said she thought we belonged. So we became members. She was very down-to-earth. I remember her holding my stuff the first time I went on stage to talk to more than one or two people. My knees used to shake in high school when I had to give a talk. But we have a mission now.

*Kevin:* With suicide, it'll always be—he won't be counted or acknowledged as a casualty of the war.

A man read a paragraph in *Newsweek* about Jeff, an interview with Debbie, and wrote a play. It was going in a different direction, and then he heard Jeff's story. Now it's about PTSD. Before we knew it, we were on a plane to Kansas to see *Army of One*.

*Joyce:* A woman from California wrote a three-act play about Jeffrey; she changed all the names. It was strange. Because of my son, she wrote this.

People have sent us poems and songs. I forget all the things that have come about because we went public. Jeff would be amazed—he was very unassuming—that his story has been in *Rolling Stone, Maxim, The New York Times*; he wouldn't have believed it.

*Kevin:* We once said to an audience of veterans, "Because of the loss of our son, we have adopted all of you."

We have nothing to gain. We have lost our veteran. We have to portray the truth: Bush has not supported the troops. They abandon the troops and leave them behind in the battlefield of their ravaged minds.

*Joyce:* People still don't understand that kids are coming back hurting inside. We're not doing enough to help them.

Once, Jeff was sitting on the deck, and he said to me, "I just want to help, now." So now we feel, maybe Jeff is helping, through us saying what happened to him. Our message is, what happened to Jeff was because of the rush to war and the inability of this administration to take care of our veterans when they come home.

*Kevin:* Bush is reducing the reimbursement for the therapists providing treatment for PTSD. Last summer, a hundred million dollars was earmarked for PTSD, and it mysteriously disappeared from the supplemental budget. The press didn't make it an issue.

In a couple of weeks, a lawsuit will be filed on behalf of Jeffrey.

*Joyce:* We didn't go looking for this lawsuit. John Bonifaz was running for Massachusetts Secretary of State. John's dad, Cristobal Bonifaz, came looking for us. John had asked us to present Jeff's story with him and state rep Jim McGovern. As I was leaving, this burly elderly gentleman got me in a bear hug, crying. It was Cristobal. We wanted people to find out how dysfunctional the VA was. We offered to pay for the suit out of our own pockets. Nobody would take us. A week later, Cristobal contacted us, very interested in making sure that what happened to Jeff wouldn't happen to anyone again.

Cristobal thinks that the system in the VA has become very arrogant and complacent; they need to be challenged so they'll upgrade their system. *[The medical malpractice lawsuit was filed in federal court on July 26, 2007; it accuses the government and VA Secretary Jim Nicholson of negligence in Jeffrey's death.]*

*Kevin:* Joyce has been teaching me about the computer. We spend hours and hours. We found a site that really did it. In 1980, the VA created a Special Committee on PTSD. In '86 it issued findings, twenty-four recommendations that would make them effective. In February '05, Representative Lane Evans asked the General Accounting Office to investigate the status of the recommendations. Not one had been implemented.

*Joyce:* One of the recommendations was to do dual-diagnosis, for substance abuse and PTSD. They wouldn't do it for Jeffrey. He had to give up alcohol to get treatment. Since then, they have implemented that here.

*Kevin:* They also found out that you must deal with the family. That's still never been implemented.

When this administration and Congress decided to go to war, they didn't care about the troops. They love to shout from the rooftops about their support of the troops. But we have such a horrible scandal of hypocrisy and manipulation, especially the Republicans.

*Joyce:* The Democrats aren't perfect but their voting is better.

Our oldest daughter has trouble with all this. She'd prefer us to just live our own lives. For our youngest, it's about anger. We've met so many nice people, and veterans, who encourage us to keep going. It's a mission. If we just help one person, his death meant something. I think his life meant something if we can help.

We have anger issues about the war. We feel it should never have happened; not then, anyway. My son felt the same way.

Some people say we're desecrating our son's memory. But this is the way Jeff felt. He was so opposed to George Bush. He said, "If Bush wins again, I won't be able to handle it, I'll go to Canada." But he was torn in both directions; he would go with his unit if they were sent back.

*Kevin:* We want Jeff to have a legacy, to realize his hope of helping.

It bothers me when people say we're so brave. No, we're not. You should be here late in the evening when the raw emotions are flowing. But we've got to try to do something to make people understand what this is all about.

*Joyce:* We started doing work on PTSD to help others in the same situation. We thought there were probably other people having trouble with their loved one, and they might recognize their loved one in Jeff. You see on the news, three were killed, seven were injured. What happened psychologically, physically? How were they injured? They don't say; you don't know.

*Kevin:* They say twenty-seven thousand are wounded. They don't talk about the hidden wounds they'll carry the rest of their lives. Or veterans reacting in a maladjusted way, charged with crimes and sent to prison. They should go to the mental health wards; they go to a cell block instead. I hope the country will wake up.

*Joyce:* Jeff's boots were the first to represent the emotional cost of the war. His was one of the first stories to come out; he's almost like the poster-boy of PTSD for this war.

*Kevin:* We don't focus just on Jeff. It's more than just Jeffrey. That's what people must understand. If there's another war, we'll be condemning our grandchildren to the same horrors.

I have a very selfish motive. I let Jeff die once. I can't let him die again. If we stop talking about him, it seems like he'll die again.

*Joyce:* We don't really have a choice. It's not bravery. It's for our survival.

# Chapter 24
# Brenda Hervey

*Brenda lives in Iowa. Her son Michael was seriously injured in Iraq while serving as a specialist with the Army's First Armored Division, First Battalion, Sixth Infantry Alpha Company. His military service ended in May 2007.*

I'm a single mom. I work in the nonprofit community. I have two step-children, four kids altogether. Rachel just turned twenty-four; Michael is twenty-one; Sarah, sixteen; Meg, thirteen. Rachel and Michael have been in my life since Rachel was four and Michael was two, when I married their dad. We shared custody with their mom in New York State. We had them in summers and occasionally on holidays.

Bill was a professor at Colorado State University. He taught political science and constitutional law. He was a brilliant, brilliant man. The kids are biracial; Bill was African-American, I'm Caucasian, so our kids have beautiful brown skin. We lived in Fort Collins, Colorado, for around fourteen years.

When he died, five years ago, I moved back to Iowa where I'm from, to be near family. I have a sister in Sioux City. Bill had brain cancer. It was very awful. He was diagnosed in August, died in December. He went from diagnosis to hospice care.

The most difficult thing was preparing the kids in a short time for losing their dad. Also watching him—a man who spent his entire life in pursuit of knowledge, not just political science but history, religion, sports—watching cancer take that capacity away. That was a real hard thing.

Michael was with us shortly after his dad was diagnosed. Then he went back to New York, but he made several trips during that time to be with us. He came back for the funeral.

That probably had an effect on his plans for the future. Education was very important to Bill, so the kids knew college was an expectation.

But Michael didn't feel ready. Michael and I talked after Bill died. He told me he didn't tell his dad he was thinking about going into the Army, afraid he wouldn't approve. I laughed and said, "We talked about you, and we thought the military might be a good option for you." Michael felt good that his dad would have supported his decision and wouldn't have been shocked.

After Michael was hurt and couldn't believe he wasn't sent to Germany, he knew I'd be the person to try to help him. His biological mother, Laura, and I talked almost every day, sharing updates. She wanted to help him too, but at one point she said, "You have to be able to live with what you do." She's not an activist. She did make frequent calls to find out his health status, but calls and letters to papers, congresspeople—I did that.

When Bill died in December 2001, Michael was sixteen. He graduated at seventeen and joined a delayed enlistment program in his senior year. Laura didn't feel comfortable signing, but he was very determined.

I think Michael looked at the military as a job, something to do instead of college that might help pay for college eventually. He picked Germany as his first choice; it was exciting to him, to travel. He went to basic training and then realized, it's not just a job. He's often said he should have gone to college first, gone into the military as an officer instead of a grunt.

Michael's first MOS was as mechanic in a Bradley tank. He hated it. He asked to be changed to regular infantry, as a gunner. He started basic in October 2003. He got some credit for delayed enlistment. He was supposed to serve for three years but he was extended.

When the war started, I felt dread. Depending on how things went, I knew it would impact Michael in some way. I felt incredibly afraid for Michael—and also every ounce of me believes in diplomacy and statesmanship instead of military occupation and might. I was pretty amazed that the war escalated to the point it did.

Michael got to Germany in January. He was sent within twelve weeks to Iraq to catch up to his unit, which had already deployed. That first time, he was in Iraq less than eight weeks before they came back. That was fine with me!

The war raged on, and little by little we were finding out that all the justifications Bush used for this war were not true. When Michael was deployed the second time, it was January 2006. He was hurt in November.

Until then, Michael was hanging in there. With his family, he had a good attitude. Michael is not one to complain or worry. Occasionally I could tell he was frustrated. It was hot there; they had no ice or way to cool things.

Our routine was, the girls and I sent him a box each week. We had a box on the table, Michael's station. Once, Megan wrote him a poem. We mailed him a giant Easter bunny. We teased about putting camo on it. We'd send extra things for guys who might not have family.

Some things we did for us as well as Michael, contributing to making his time more bearable. We sent lots of pictures. Michael's not much of a letter writer. I got about two letters from him. He called as often as he could. But sometimes we'd hear a couple of times a week. Then he'd say they were going on a mission, and I'd really worry.

When I'd show up at work and show the latest picture of Michael, it was like—"Oh yeah, that's still happening." I wanted to scream, "Wake up! It's happening!" What is it about this war, where the average American seems so divorced from what's going on over there? But even for me, a person who's an insider, who had Michael to tell me, it was really difficult for me to comprehend it.

A year ago, if you'd asked me if I was an anti-war activist, I'd have said, "Probably not." Even having Michael, and having strong views on the war—I wrote letters, voiced my concerns, but not at the level I am now. When Michael was hurt, that was the turning point for me, when it all came crashing in. I thought, "My gosh, almost three thousand soldiers have died; Michael was within a hairsbreadth of being one of them." I had to do something more.

I was at a conference meeting in Omaha, Nebraska. I'd stayed over the night before. Friday was supposed to be a full conference day. At five a.m. my cellphone rang. Rachel calling. My stomach just dropped. No way she'd have called that early unless it was Michael. I didn't answer. I couldn't pick the phone up. In about ten seconds it rang again, and Rachel told me, "Michael is okay, alive, but he was severely hurt. They didn't know details, but he'd been in an IED explosion, he was in surgery." I said, "Call back as soon as you hear any news." I called his mom. That's all she knew. She heard the explosion had impacted his leg.

I called my sister, said, "I need to go home." I called my boss, and told him, "I need to go, Michael is hurt." My sister Yvonne came to get me. I was on the phone calling all the way home, trying to piece together everything we could. That evening, Michael called me after his second surgery. He was kind of groggy. He said he was okay. He was in a Bradley on a mission to help out some Marines. An explosion ripped through the turret gun door, and the door ripped into his leg. He asked me, did I want the good news or the bad news. I said, "Bad." He said, "That's what happened." The good news was that he'd probably get to leave Iraq.

They airlifted him to Al Asad airport for surgery. When he woke up from the surgery, an officer said, "Son, you've earned a Purple Heart." He said, "Yeah, but do I still have my leg?"

I called the Red Cross. The military liaison for the local chapter was wonderful. She called D.C., got all the information she could, and said he'd probably be airlifted to Walter Reed within twenty-four hours. "When he gets there, we'll apply for family orders, we'll be able to bring you to him."

The next day, Michael called again. He said his leg was open. He had developed compartment syndrome: the pressure was too much, it would compromise the vascular flow. It was very serious. They had to leave the incision open from the knee to the ankle to relieve the pressure. It was open for more than three days. Then he had a third surgery to close it. I kept asking, "When will they move you?" His mom said there were no orders yet.

Next day, Michael said, "You're not gonna believe this. They're going to keep me here until I can go back to my unit." He also had surgery on his elbow, where he lost some bone. I said, "How can they do that?" I said, "Don't worry, let me figure out what they're doing." His mom called, and said, "Yes, they're keeping him."

I don't think I was off the phone for the next week after he was hurt. Michael has such a deep sense of faith; I thought a chaplain would be helpful to him. They said chaplains were few and far between, and so many kids were getting hurt. Then I said, "You'll have to dig deep, and look to each other for support." I kept trying to reassure him that he was at least safe, and we'd get him out of there.

At that point, I came across an article in *The New York Times* about Michael's unit, by Michael Gordon. I got names from that of two soldiers who were quoted. Later I found out they got reprimanded for speaking out. I was so desperate, I even called Michael Gordon. He gave me the boys' fathers' numbers. That led me to Ryan's dad, Tim Kahlor. He certainly helped me.

I was talking to anybody who would listen to me: Hillary Clinton and Charles Schumer, Michael's senators; Harkin and Grassley, my senators. I thought somebody should be able to help. Hillary's office said, "Have Michael send something in writing. That's the process." Schumer—at least I got to talk to his military affairs person. They also wanted something in writing, but from me. I spent the longest time with Harkin's military case worker. Grassley's office was a waste of my time.

I connected with Nancy Lessin of MFSO. This was right after the elections. Nancy Pelosi was the new Speaker. MFSO met with her chief of staff. They said they'd bring Michael's situation to her. When I became connected with MFSO, that gave me an added avenue for expression. I felt I could do more to help. When I got connected to other people in my situation, it empowered me and helped me find my voice, gave me support on a level I didn't have before.

I hope that parents realize they can be powerful advocates for their kids. It's so tempting to feel isolated and helpless when your kid is in the military, like you have no power. Even if it didn't help bring Michael home, at least I felt people were listening to me.

I explored all these avenues. I told Michael to hang in there, told him about all the letters and who I talked to.

About four days before Thanksgiving, Michael called. "I don't know who you talked to, but I'm getting out of here. They're sending me to Germany for substance abuse counseling." He asked his officer what that was about, and the officer said, "Shut up, Hervey, it's getting you out of here, so just take it."

Substance abuse. Are you kidding me? Michael never had a problem. But I said, "If it gets you out of there . . ." But he said he had to have his gear. "They won't let me get onto the helicopter to Germany without it." Most of his gear had been blown up. It was a mixed task force. The Army has to tell the Marines to get his vest. The guy next to him had been waiting two weeks for his gear.

I asked, "Don't they have a loaner vest?" "No, you have to have your own." I called Tim Kahlor, and said, "Can Ryan help get Michael's stuff on the next convoy to Al Asad?" Tim said he'd ask. A few hours later, he told me that Ryan is going to Al Asad tomorrow and he'll take Michael's gear. When Ryan walked in, Michael said, "That was quick, how did they get the gear so fast?" Ryan said, "Your mom called." I said to Michael, "Those generals have nothing on us moms!"

He was sent to Balad. They took the stitches out of his leg. Then he was sent to Landstuhl for Thanksgiving. Within twenty-four to forty-eight hours the receiving psychiatrist figured out there was no basis for substance-abuse counseling. He asked Michael if he'd failed the drug test or what. No, no reason. To this day, I don't know why they changed their minds, whether there really was a connection I was able to make. It doesn't really matter.

Now he's back in Germany. They lost five in his unit during this deployment. I've written to four of the families. Michael didn't know the fifth guy. It's heartbreaking to me that these boys won't be coming back.

In February 2007, I went to Germany to see Michael, finally. He took me to a bar in Germany where the I-6 hung out. There was a flag on the wall that all the guys signed. In front of it there was a shelf with photos and obituaries of the five guys they lost, and a candle burning. Throughout the night, guys would order drinks to send over to the shelf, and toast their guys.

The guys all talked of the "reintegration process"—financial affairs, health screenings, etc. I said to Michael, "I realize the Army has set up a process, but the most powerful reintegration happened at that bar, sharing their experiences."

Michael showed me horrible-looking pictures of his leg after surgery. I asked if I could show people and he said no. One thing Michael was concerned about was how he'd be portrayed to the other guys in his unit. He didn't want to seem like a coward. He said it might be okay for me to say things, but he couldn't.

I was able to speak in D.C. in January. I've done a talk in Des Moines on the fourth anniversary of the war. I'm constantly having to make sure I don't say anything that would offend Michael or appear to be putting words in his mouth.

I asked Michael how he feels about me speaking out. He says he and Ryan tease each other about their parents being old hippies. He says, "Why should this be any different from other issues?"

Sometimes Tim and I talk about how tired we are. How long will we have to do this? When the Democrats won the [2006 mid-term] election I thought, "Thank God, they'll take care of it now." But now . . .

*[I ask what she says to people who question how she can support the troops without supporting the war.]* I'm so tired of hearing that. We are the families of these kids on the front lines. Who more than us supports the soldiers? The fact that they're still risking their lives, getting between Sunnis and Shiites, should show everyone that it's Bush and Congress that don't support the troops. They're choosing to use our soldiers for political gain. They're willing to use our kids on the front lines to leave their legacy. How is that supporting our troops?

# Chapter 25
# Tim Kahlor

*Tim and his wife live in California. Their son Ryan has done two tours of duty in Iraq with the Army First Armored Division.*

I'm originally from Oklahoma. My wife is from California. We just have the one child. Ryan was raised with his mom and I and his grandmother. His grandmother was an amazing person; she was a dancer in Hollywood in the '40s. She only had the one child and one grandchild. Her whole life was around Ryan.

Ever since Ryan was little, he was an outdoor kid. He had all the army toys, he was always into the military thing. My dad called him "Sarge." Our street is all retired Navy and Marines. We're right behind Camp Pendleton. When they use weapons we hear it. When they move helicopters, they come right over where we live.

Ryan was kind of a jock in high school, started playing football, got hurt, and went into wrestling. He always did things one hundred percent, 120 percent really, never went half-way. He was probably in every ER room in southern California, growing up. Once he stuck a piece of hard gum up his nose. I don't know why. He'd ask, "How much is this going to cost? What's the co-payment?" He thought he was the parent. He's always been very mature for his age.

Ryan is dyslexic. He had to do special classes, but he is so determined, he was in the honor society by the time he graduated high school. He started his freshman year in college in 2002. He said he was tired of working harder than everybody else in school. So he started going around to the recruiters. The Army was offering him twelve thousand dollars if he went in the infantry. They said they'd guarantee that he could live in Germany.

He wanted some adventure, some travel. I guess I was just naïve. I bought into the whole thing. I said, "If you join the military, we'll support you all the way. The main thing is, you should be happy." His mom was never behind it. She just wanted him to go to college.

He signed with the Army delayed entry, because he still had braces on his teeth. That's when it hit me how young he was. The reality was, he had to have his braces removed for this job.

Ryan left for basic March 18, 2003, the day they announced we were going into Iraq. I cried like a baby. But my wife and I thought the war would be over before he was out of basic. We thought it would be a quick action, and he would be in Europe.

He came home for a month after basic. He got a tattoo that said "Duty, Country, Honor" on his leg. When they get home, they are so polite. He was opening doors for ladies. He looked really neat in his uniform. We had this feeling, maybe everything is fine. We still thought this was going to end. We were naïve about what was going on over there.

He was told he was going to be put in a nondeployable unit in Hohenfels, Germany, training personnel before they went to combat. We thought he'd be safe. He got to Frankfurt, and they told him if he went to Iraq, he wouldn't have to pay taxes on his wages and he'd get ranked quicker. That totally appealed to him. He always has to go for the brass ring. He wants to succeed. Everything is a challenge. He tells me, "Dad, I am going to go to Iraq." I said, "What? You're supposed to be in Germany!" They put carrots out there, and he went for it.

At first he was in the Green Zone on guard duty. It was a pretty safe area. He got to a phone one night in the middle of the night: "Mom, Dad, you won't believe this. A car bomb just went off. Watch the news." So we watched and saw it on the news.

Once, he called and said, "This is PFC Kahlor. I have someone else's cellphone and I just wanted to tell you I love you." This officer would randomly hand his cellphone to soldiers and tell them, "You'll talk to your parents as long as you want and tell them you love them."

He was starting to journey out more. He told us that one of his buddies from Germany was killed, November 8, 2003. He was in a Humvee that didn't have side panels.

Before that, he seemed like a kid on an adventure. In this email, he said he'd seen an Iraqi man, accused of talking with Americans, whose throat was slit, and he was left to bleed out in the street. Kids were playing soccer in the street. His whole tone changed. All the reality of what war is came home.

Usually before they go on a mission, they let them call home for ten minutes. The first time, his voice was different. I asked why. He said he couldn't talk about it. It dawned on me he was going into combat. That was really hard. I kind of isolated Laura from it. It was too much for her to deal with. Her mom was starting to show signs of Alzheimer's. She carried around a photo of a soldier she cut out of the paper that she thought was Ryan.

In April 2004, the First Armored Division had been there a year. Ryan joined the group later. They were supposed to be coming home, they were packed and ready. Bush announced he'd extend the tour 120 days. My neighbor's son-in-law had seen them. He said they were so ticked off and disappointed. The same week, Bush went on vacation.

I drive a van pool for the university part-time to save money. I was in the van and my sister called me: eight soldiers in the First Infantry Division from Baumholder had been killed. My sister said, "Don't let Laura turn on the news." Laura said, "Why?" I said "Trust me." I got to work, shut the office door, and just started crying.

The next day I was mowing the yard and I wouldn't turn around if I heard a car coming down the street, in case it was the military. Ryan called and we found he was okay. We were really happy, but it hit home. Eight people didn't get that call.

We've been through more horrible things. But to this day, I can feel all those same emotions. I keep thinking about those families. It's not just the one soldier: it's a huge ripple effect, whole families destroyed.

Then Ryan finally got home from the first tour. We were standing at LAX, his grandmother, mom and I—he'd never been away from home before. We were so excited, waiting and waiting, but he's not coming down the escalator. Of course he had to do something different. He came up behind us. He said we looked older.

That weekend they had a block party for him. We put a table of traditional Iraqi things he brought home out for the kids so they could learn about Iraq. I don't know how many steaks he got that day. He was the star.

A few days in, we were at the mall. People had showered him with gift certificates. We met this lady we knew from church. She realized Ryan just got back from Iraq. She says, "Did you kill anybody?" It floored us. A grown woman to ask such a thing! I looked at her and said, "I never will ask my son that question." He just walked away. Later he said, "Just take me home, I feel weird." He wanted to be left alone for a few days. He said he didn't feel comfortable not holding a weapon.

He went back to Germany. He convinced us to have Christmas over there. We met his new girlfriend, who is now his wife. We had a wonderful time. The following year, Ryan was out of the war, in Germany. He and his best friend went all over Europe and Russia.

We went back for the next Christmas, 2005. He was leaving for Iraq in January 2006. He got married to Naomi, and we got to know our daughter-in-law. His wife bought him a GPS [global positioning system] for Christmas. I said, "Doesn't the Army give you that?" He said the last time, his GPS didn't work.

We sent him Q-tips, stuff for cleaning his rifle. People were shocked that they didn't give that stuff to them. In a tank unit, all the money went into the tanks. It became a joke. They'd never get anything. They'd go to other units and trade out.

When he went back to Iraq, he told me more and more. I found out they didn't have current body armor. They had to share night goggles. I said, "This is ridiculous."

I wrote over thirty letters to the Armed Services Committee. It snowballed from there. I started going to marches and rallies. This is when I got involved in MFSO. I started speaking out. I went to D.C.— hadn't been since I was a kid. I wanted to clear it with Ryan, being po- litical. I asked him, "Are you cool with it?" All he was worried about was me being mugged in Washington.

We've done more than twenty-four months of this, him being in combat. It's been weird. Once, he had been in a tank that had been de- stroyed. He left a message saying he was a wreck, but that he was okay. He always says, "No news is good news."

Naomi called to tell me his friend Mike was killed, someone Ryan had known from the first tour of duty. We got a letter from him. In the letter it said, "Parents,"—he used to call us Parental Units—"Yesterday my friend was shot and killed. His death has started an uproar of emo- tions in the platoon. Some have said they weren't going to fight anymore. No one understands why we're here or what our mission is. Dad, keep up your fight to bring the troops home."

It tore us up. I just went crazy. I did as much media as I could and got as much information out as I could. I was always involved and in- formed, but I am so much more now. When your kid asks you to do something . . . Once I chased a kid down the street in Huntington Beach, a rich area. The kid was around twenty. He said, "Your son's having a blast over there, like a video game." I wanted to tell him, "Mike is dead, this is no game."

I've had people tell me I was anti-American. I've gotten people in my face, letters, email, phone calls. My sister is like my watch guard. She constantly worries some one will hurt me. She found a blog saying, "If Tim Kahlor stands behind the troops, we'd rather he'd be in front of them."

I kept asking Ryan if he was okay with this. He said he was really proud of what I am doing. He says "Dad, it's your right." He supports me. My wife totally supports what I do, but the public stuff she lets me do.

People come over and say, "Your son is the reason you are allowed to do this." I say "Right. He gives me the right to do this." People wrap themselves in the flag, put up yellow stickers. It's BS. The yellow ribbons probably were made in China, a country with human rights violations.

People need to think when the U.S. does something, it's for a good cause. When you tell them the facts, it kills them. They don't want to see. September 11 pulled us together. But there was no connection between that and Iraq. Afghanistan was connected, not Iraq.

Ryan says he'd really like to see victory over there. The first tour, they had such good rapport with people. It's different now. He says they want us to leave. He says now, they'll never send enough troops to control the insurgency, control the borders. They'll never be able to do what Bush says he wants to.

People say, "Why don't they show the good happening over there?" Right after the election, I was in D.C., and I said, "Bush has the ability to order every military photographer to go and capture every good thing happening over there. It's not happening because nothing good is going on. If there's schools being built, show me. They get schools built, then they are blown up. So many contracts, billions of dollars spent to build things, and nothing comes of it."

It's craziness. There are schools in America that need funding. There is gang violence. We have horrors going on in LA that need to be addressed. Instead we're pouring money into Iraq.

I tell the press, "The Democrats won this election on the back of this war. Now they need to step up." We are harder on the Democrats than the Republicans now.

Hillary had a fundraiser at some rich folks' house. They had no family members in the war. I was yelling, "I'll even take a fifth cousin! Give me something!" It's all about winning elections right now, not about our loved ones.

My son says, "Take a southern California cul-de-sac, a typical neighborhood. Can you imagine one person on the cul-de-sac suspected of doing something illegal? And the military comes in, separates the men from the women and takes some of the men with them, and they don't tell families where they have gone or why. They search all the houses and leave. If that happened anywhere in the U.S., we'd be appalled; we'd be on every talk show. This happens all the time in Iraq. One person is suspected, and they go to every house. How can we bring democracy to people when we're not practicing it?"

These right-wing fundamentalist Christians that support Bush . . . Abortion is such a big issue. But a six-year-old in Iraq gets blown up, it's just a casualty of war. It doesn't make sense to me.

In LA, we did the Oscars for Peace, on the day of the Oscars. I always try to put a face on this war with a photo of my son. There were kids connected to the Oscars, five teenagers. I had my poster: "My son spent twenty-four months in Iraq in combat." I said, "I'll give you an example." I pointed at one. I said, "The other four are blown up and you have to pick up the pieces, put them in body bags, and then go back to work. Ryan had to do this five times. All that was left of one was the head and skin."

I want people to feel what war is. We just do this "honor the fallen heroes" thing. Go down to the VA hospital. What will you do about them?

If you see an animal that's been hit by a car, it bothers you. Can you imagine seeing children on the street like that? That's what war is: blood and guts. It's human lives out there. I try to get people to feel the human pain. When a woman bends down and picks up her child and half of it is gone: can you imagine? That child meant as much to her as any of our children do to us. That's what war is.

Right now, Ryan's unit is due back in Germany, but we haven't seen them. Until you see and hold them, you don't know. You still have that fear. Sometimes I wonder if Laura and I worry too much or not enough. Ryan's ears ran the whole year he was in Iraq. When he got back, his speech was slurred, he had balance problems, and he was shaking. They're doing brain scans. They got him a counselor. As far as I know, he's going, which makes me so happy. They're going to follow up on the brain injury. I feel good that they're taking care of him now.

They're transferring him here to California. Supposedly, if he stayed in Germany he'd have to go back to Iraq in the fall. Ryan's been struggling over going home. He kept wanting to go back to join his buddies. He's so loyal to the people next to him, he couldn't break away.

I still can't believe he came through. My wife and I just didn't think he'd come home. So many people were killed or wounded. People would get killed right before they were coming home.

A young man on his first patrol in Iraq stepped on an IED, lost his legs, and part of both hands; he was at Walter Reed. So we went to see him. Outside Walter Reed there was a pro-war group. We went out and said, "Does anyone here have kids in Iraq?" Nobody did. I said, "If you support the war, make sure the kids are taken care of when they come home."

Suddenly we were surrounded. They said we didn't have kids over there. Right then, I got a call from Ryan in Iraq. Ryan said, "Let me talk to these people. Just so long as they don't thank me." But they wouldn't talk to him. Finally one guy did talk. He couldn't convince the others Ryan was really there. They wanted to hurt me. They looked like your next-door neighbors. It scared the heck out of me.

With MFSO, you don't have to explain anything. As a parent, you have a right to raise all the hell you want. A lot of the time, wives [of the troops] can't speak out. They worry about their housing and benefits. They can't do a damn thing to me. I'll yell all I want. Just because my kid's on a combat field doesn't mean my obligation to keep him safe ends.

It is our loved ones who are fighting and dying in this war. Do not ever tell me that we do not support the troops. We want the money to bring them all home safely. We don't want to take away money to treat PTSD, or take care of them, or keep them safe.

Ryan is having nightmares. He says they're so vivid. He's trying to get someplace, get to somebody. We get our kids home, and now it's chapter two: trying to keep them safe once they're home. We have to watch how they're doing mentally. The hell doesn't end. It's just a new hell.

# Chapter 26
# Catherine Smith

*Catherine lives in Missouri. Her oldest child, Tomas, joined the Army for the second time immediately following 9/11. He is confined to a wheelchair because of injuries he suffered while serving with the First Cavalry in Iraq, and is a vocal activist against the war. Another of Cathy's sons, Nathan, a sergeant in the Army's 101st Airborne Division, is serving his second tour in Iraq.*

I was raised in the Midwest. My father was drafted during the Korean War. He was in medical school at the time; he was going to be a doctor. He worked in a hospital in Okinawa. When he went back home, he worked on a farm. He never went back to school. Korea was not a good thing for him. He was a very liberal Democrat, a pacifist. He didn't believe in killing anything—a very kind, gentle man.

I've been married more than once. I'm very happily married now. The gentleman is not the boy's father, but he's better than most fathers. They get along very well. We have a blended family: my four kids and my stepson, five altogether.

In '04, when Tomas was shot . . . I guess it happened as it was supposed to. In January that year, my middle son Nathan graduated boot camp and went to Fort Sill. At the beginning of February, my husband and I were married. At the end of February, my father passed away unexpectedly.

Tomas was shot at the beginning of April. I spent April and part of May with him at Walter Reed. At the beginning of June, he came back to the hospital at St. Louis and spent two or three weeks there. I had taken a leave of absence at work. In August, the company I'd worked for fifteen years closed down. In November, we bought a new home. All these things are considered major stressors; any one of them is supposed to be enough to make you crazy.

Now they're getting ready to send Nathan to Iraq for the second time. He's also in the Army, with the 101st Airborne. He'll be a sergeant as of July 1.

My husband is a gun-toting, "Second Amendment makes all the rest possible" Republican. We spend a lot of time arguing about this war. It makes for interesting days.

Nathan is a conservative Republican. He believes in Rush Limbaugh. Tomas is a very liberal Democrat, anti-war. They've each taken sides. Tomas was against this war before he went. He's a lot stronger than I could have been through all this.

Tomas was my first-born. He spoiled me for all the other children; he was the ideal child. He got good grades, he was gifted. He was never a problem. His teachers had to keep busy to keep him challenged. We had him in a gifted program, but he dropped out when he found it was just more work. He never tried harder than he absolutely had to. When he was a senior, he enlisted in the delayed-entry program. He did boot at Fort Leonard Wood. He did AIT a year after, and developed tendonitis in his shoulders. He had a medical discharge out of the Army. That was his first enlistment. He worked at K-Mart, waited tables, drifted for a while. He was one of those lost children. We didn't know what we were going to do with him.

Then September 11 happened. On September 13, he called his recruiter and decided to get back in the Army. He was one of the big surge that enlisted after September 11. He shipped out in January, went to boot camp in Fort Benning, Georgia, and then did infantry training in Fort Hood, Texas. He was in the First Cavalry, the same group Cindy Sheehan's son was in.

I've always had a probably strange relationship with my kids. We're very close. They talk to me about everything—things I don't want to know. That's just the way we are. Tomas and I talked a lot. I went to Fort Hood several times before he was deployed. He didn't want to go but it was his duty, he'd signed on for the job. I was proud of him but would rather he hadn't.

Tomas and I both thought this war was ridiculous. There was nothing we could do. We couldn't stop it from happening. He went reluctantly, but he went. He signed on for a supply clerk job, thinking it would keep him from fighting. He's a borderline pacifist. He signed up to go to Afghanistan and smoke the evil-doers from their caves. When he found out he was going to be used for something so wrong, it made him sick in the head.

When Tomas realized he'd be going to Iraq, he became despondent. Before they would treat the depression, they told him to talk to the military chaplain. We're lazy Methodists, at best; he's closer to agnostic or atheist now. His chaplain told him, "Wait until you get over there and start killing people. Then you'll feel better." They put him on Prozac.

He was in Baghdad for four days when he was shot. On the Monday morning after that, they called and told me my son had been shot. I thought it was a joke at first. He'd just gotten there. I hadn't even had time to get worried about him yet. At first, that's all the information they gave me.

That evening, someone called and told me the Army would pay to fly me to Landstuhl; he was considered seriously wounded. That entire week, I got no good information. One day they told me he had whiplash and a knee injury.

On the Thursday following, I was told he'd be transferred from Kuwait to Landstuhl that weekend. I applied for an emergency passport so I could fly to Landstuhl on Monday. They were supposed to call me that weekend to tell me about the transfer. On Monday, they told me they no longer considered him seriously wounded, so they wouldn't pay. Fine, whatever. I was going anyway. I paid two hundred dollars for an emergency passport out of my own pocket.

But I thought if my son wasn't seriously wounded, he would call me. So that morning, I called Landstuhl and spoke to Captain Cummings. He saved my sanity. He did a search for my son and found out that the week prior, he had already been through Landstuhl and had gone on to Walter Reed. He had been there almost a full week!

That Tuesday morning, I got a flight to D.C. and went to Walter Reed. My son had been in a medically-induced coma all week. They took him out of it about half an hour before I got there. The first thing he saw was me walking toward him through the medical ICU [intensive care unit]. The first thing he said was, "Mommy."

He had probably lost forty pounds. He looked like a cancer patient. He was gaunt, his skin was grey. He was attached to all different tubes and monitors. I still didn't know the extent of his injuries.

As soon as I got there, one of the nurses, Marty—he was wonderful—told me Tomas's spine had been severed. They have ceramic plates on their Kevlar vests. The bullet went between two of the plates, through his spinal cord.

What happened was, four days into his tour in Baghdad, they went out in an LMTV, an unarmored two-and-a-half-ton truck. It had no cover on it. They had twenty-five soldiers sitting without even a tarp over them. They drove through Sadr City. At that time, they'd just shut down the TV station. Everyone was aiming for our guys.

They went over as a peace-keeping unit. My son was trained to drive a Bradley, a tank. They only took two Bradleys with them. We didn't want to look like we were going to war. So they put all these babies into this open truck. They didn't want all these tanks rolling through the streets.

He was sitting cross-legged. A sniper was taking potshots at the truck. I have no idea how many were injured in that truck. Since he was cross-legged when he was paralyzed, he thought he was still cross-legged for the longest time. He kept trying to straighten out his legs. He was also shot in the knee. Thankfully, that was after the shot to his spine, so he didn't feel it.

He spent a month at Walter Reed. There are probably fifty nurses at Walter Reed that if I have to go back through there, they'll quit. I believe I was there to be an advocate for my son, so I had no qualms about causing a stir.

They had visiting hours; I thought that was bullshit. I was going to be there as many hours as I could. They put me up in Malone House, like a hotel for military families. I would go to the hospital at four a.m., stay until midnight, go back to the hotel to shower and sleep a couple of hours, and go back.

One morning, I came back to the hospital and my son was running a temperature of 105.6. He was delirious. They had the thermostat in his room set to eighty-five degrees. He had three blankets on him. He was literally cooking, he was so hot. The nurses knew about his temperature; they were waiting for a doctor. I said, "You have got to be kidding me. You don't need a doctor to turn the thermostat down or take the blankets off." I made all sorts of noise.

I couldn't tell you how many times a doctor told a nurse to do something and I'd come back hours later and it wasn't done, and I'd once again have to throw a fit.

I had a nurse tell me to stop doing things for Tomas because he was in rehab now. I got in his face: "I'm his mother. I'll do anything I can for him. If he wants a drink of water, I'll get him a drink of water. If he says wipe his ass, I'll wipe his ass." I can't put a band-aid on the hurt like I used to, and kiss it and make it all better.

I was trying to do everything I could to keep Tomas from killing himself. Every day he would talk about killing himself. Who could blame him? I don't know if I wouldn't have. I was grasping at straws to bring some spark to him. He looked like he had no soul left, like he was dead. He was always a very vibrant, sparkly, happy kid.

I said, "Who do you want to meet? You can meet anybody you want to in this town." He has always been very politically active. I was trying to get someone he looked up to. Rumsfeld, all the other Republican big shots came through for photo ops—Tomas didn't want to see any of them. He said "Ralph Nader," of all people. Ralph's assistant said, "Can Ralph bring a friend?" I said, "Fine, but no media." The friend was Phil Donahue. I spent six hours with him at Walter Reed.

Probably about two months later, we heard from Phil Donahue: he was coming to St. Louis for a doctor's appointment. He and Marlo Thomas came to our house. About a month after that, he called back and said he'd met a wonderful woman, Ellen Spiro, who made documentaries. "Would Tomas be interested in doing a documentary?"

The movie is called *Body of War*. It's amazing. During the backdrop of the whole movie, it shows senators talking about WMD and how Saddam Hussein was training Al Qaeda, and the roll call vote of seventy-seven senators voting for the war. At the end of the movie, Tomas met with Robert Byrd [long-time Democratic senator from West Virginia]. They talked about the "immortal twenty-three" who voted against it. He walks with two canes. They talked about mobility issues. He asked Tomas what he'd do now. Tomas said he didn't know; he wasn't in charge of his own life. Byrd said, "Me too."

Tomas left Walter Reed after three and a half weeks and went to the St. Louis spinal cord unit. He was there until June 16, 2004. They gave us a bag of pills and said, "Good luck." We left not knowing what to expect. Tomas says he got more after-care instructions when he got his tattoo.

We brought him home to our house. He no longer has control of his bladder. He has to cath internally four times a day. Otherwise, the urine doesn't all come out. If it doesn't, you can get a urinary tract infection and it can kill you. That's what killed Christopher Reeves. He has no control over his bowels. We do a bowel program every three days. He uses a suppository to go poop.

He's had one serious bedsore at home. It was awful. He had rolled over in his sleep onto a little piece of plastic. We took care of it ourselves. It took six months to heal.

He was married in August 2005. His divorce was just final. Neither one of them was prepared for all of the issues.

He has his own home now. He's doing very well. He just got back from meeting Eddie Vedder, the leader of Pearl Jam, Tomas's new best friend. He's doing two songs for the movie, the most unbelievable songs. He wants Tomas to come out to Hawaii and learn how to surf.

We have met so many amazing people. Mark Zupan (who made *Murderball*) said, he could honestly say he's glad he's paralyzed—so many good things have happened to him because of it. Tomas said the same thing the other day.

We've been to D.C. five or six times. We met with congresspeople. Tomas is in Iraq Veterans Against the War. He did commercials for several candidates [in the 2006 elections]. In one, he's in his kitchen holding his dogtags. He says, "X voted against veterans benefits. That looked good from where she sat, not from where I sit." The camera pans back to show his chair.

At the first big D.C. march, there were about fifty people on the side calling us unpatriotic. Tomas rolled up, and oh my God, what could they say. They got in a shouting match. They were his age. He said, "Why are you here? If you believe in this war, go see your recruiter."

When I came across MFSO, I was looking for a support group for mothers whose kids have been injured. There was nothing. There still isn't. There are a lot of us now. We need a club. There was no one I could call to find out what to do. The Army is no help.

Tomas' roommate Riley, who lives with him, was shot in the foot the same day as Tomas. He's from Kansas City. Just last week, Riley's cousin was hit by an RPG. Riley's mom called me and said, "What do I do?" I gave her the Landstuhl number, and that's how they found him. She got the same runaround. There ought to be someone who calls us. Nobody ever called and said, "This is what you'll run up against."

When my company closed, they gave me a very nice severance package. I could afford to stop working and help Tomas get through the VA system. It's a full-time job. We fight for everything. Now we're fighting for a wheelchair. Two weeks ago, he had a seizure: autonomic disreflexia. If you burn your hand, the autonomic nervous system tells you to move your hand away from the fire. If Tomas has pain, like a bladder infection or a stubbed toe, he doesn't react to it. His blood pressure shoots up really high and he gets a high fever. They put him on a nitro gel. Two weeks ago, they did this and he got a grand mal seizure. We had the ambulance take him to the emergency room ten minutes away, not the VA hospital forty-five minutes away. Then you have to fight so the VA will pay for it.

He's trying to go to school online. The VA doesn't want to pay for online schooling. The VA wants a competitive school environment. He wants to sit at his computer, where he's comfortable.

Every time we get a new chair, it's a six-month process. The VA is overwhelmed with all the new soldiers. I shouldn't have to call Congress every time we need something from the VA. I've done it, and it helps. It breaks my heart. What do these other vets do who don't know congressmen?

So I was looking for a military family support group, and I found MFSO. I went, "Wow, okay: these people are against this war." My problem with most groups of peace activists is, I don't believe peace is always the answer. I believe sometimes war is necessary. I don't believe in this war.

MFSO understands being proud of your son and being against this war. I have a son who's gone once and getting ready to go again. Yet people tell me I don't support the troops—people with magnetic yellow ribbons on their car. I gave my babies. I want to support them by bringing them home.

Nancy, Charley, Stacy Bannerman . . . they're wonderful people. I would love to be able to do what they're doing. I just can't. I work sixty hours a week. I'm at Tomas's every other day. I did activism for a while, when I wasn't working.

When I went to D.C. for the first time, in September 2005, I came back so empowered. I talked to Lynn Woolsey, Henry Waxman, spent time with all the people concerned. I was hunting bear. At home, I was all by myself. Here in Kansas City, all there is is peace activists. They just want to stand around and sing Kumbaya. That's not gonna stop this war.

I wish we could get loud again. We got so fractured and so quiet. It's frustrating. We go to peace rallies and do nothing but get angry. Lighting a candle isn't doing anything. I have trouble meeting anyone who's not with the choir. Like Hillary Clinton: you voted for the war, and it's your fault, you and seventy-six others. John Kerry: don't tell me how bad it is now. I can't handle it, I get so angry. We elected them for the sole purpose of going to Washington and stopping the war. We sent a thunderous call, and they used it to get elected. This war is a waste. When do we stop?

Nathan and Tomas have arguments. Tomas wants to get in his face about the war. Nathan has to believe in what's going on. He can't go there right now. I walk a fine line. I feel Nathan is most honorable for what he's doing, and I'm so proud of him. But I have to support Tomas.

It was probably harder for me to send Nathan off, because it was no longer abstract. You think your son could end up dead, but you don't think they could be horribly maimed. I don't know if I would even survive if I lost my baby. I have a lot of problems sending Nathan off again. I do not know how I'm going to get through the next fifteen months. I know what it is now; I'll go three or four weeks without talking with him. They'll have communications blackouts.

Mothers have nowhere to go for our PTSD. If you have a child that's injured, you might as well be injured yourself. "Secondary PTSD" isn't always so secondary. Fortunately, my husband is very good at listening. He supports me constantly. He doesn't have to believe in activism; he believes in me.

I have a nineteen-year-old daughter who's very good when Mama needs a hug. My stepdad was in Vietnam. He understands so much about PTSD. I'll call Mom and say, "I need to talk to Dale." When he came back from Vietnam, nobody wanted to hear his story. They couldn't handle it. PTSD wasn't known. There was no treatment. They became recluses. Recently a lot of them realized they don't have to hide; they have nothing to be ashamed of. These boys coming home owe a lot to the Vietnam vets.

Tomas's PTSD is worst when we're at the VA and something stupid happens—when he sees someone scamper out to their handicapped parking space. He has a bullhorn, which I have to take away from him frequently. He says, "What do I have to lose? Will they hit me?" No, they'll hit me!

He considers his van his palette. He has bumper-stickers all over it. "Ignorance and arrogance is a bad foreign policy." "At least in Vietnam, Bush had an exit strategy." "When love of power is replaced by the power of love, then we'll have peace." People will drive by and give him angry looks. To him, that's an invitation to roll down his window and have a conversation. They usually don't want one.

Tomas is doing very well. He's very healthy. I feel truly blessed to have my son home. So many don't. That's my salvation. He's still the same person; he's back. He still has days when he talks about suicide, but not very often. When people tell me it's God's plan, I say, "No. I think this war was carried out by very stupid people. It's been so wrong and so evil; God's not in charge of these things. We have free will. It's a terrible accident that happened." Tomas spoke in a church. He said we've perverted "in the name of God." God's not what all this is about.

We can say, "Why me?" Or try to bring some good out of it. Cindy Sheehan took her pain and made something positive out of it. That inspired me. It inspired a lot of people. With the movie, Tomas says to young men, his life should show that you should not rush into anything. Don't rush into your future. Sometimes you don't come back a hero.

Sometimes you come back and piss yourself. Maybe you'll come back with half your brain blown off. You can lose your ability to have an erection—if you're a young man, that's what life is all about. There are worse things than dying.

I was at Walter Reed for a month. I saw what war is all about. I've seen the worst war has to offer. Fortunately or unfortunately, a lot are surviving that wouldn't have survived Vietnam. Tomas wouldn't have survived twenty years ago.

This war has taken our brightest and best and changed them forever. They were patriotic, they wanted to serve, and we wasted them. For what? Nothing noble. Peace in the Middle East? That's not going to happen.

Less than one percent of the population is affected by this war. Bush said recently, he wasn't going to talk about Iraq, just make dinner table conversation. I got sick to my stomach. What do you think we talk about at our dinner table? Iraq. People are only bothered when gas goes up.

They won't listen to us. We've lain down in the street; they put us blocks away from Bush so he doesn't have to see it. He doesn't want to hear about it. He's a stubborn, arrogant man. He uses "God" like he's a man of God. Apparently we read a different Bible.

# Chapter 27
# Gilda Carbonaro

*Gilda lives in Maryland and teaches in a private middle school. Alessandro Carbonaro, her only child, was killed in Iraq in May 2006.*

All of this took me by complete surprise—both Alex's interest in the military and the war that took him away.

Alex was such a rugged individualist, so stubborn you can't imagine, not easily swayed by anybody, by his friends or his parents. After high school, his uncle offered him a job in Italy. So he went there for a year and worked in his uncle's publishing house. But he got lonely and decided to come back.

He said he was going to get a job. But I said, "Alex, if you're going to get a job, you'll have to make it on your own, get your own house and car. Why don't you just go to college?" I had already gotten an application from Georgetown for him. He had a good chance to get in; he had good SATs. He said he wasn't going to write a glowing essay about himself. He said it was BS, he wouldn't do it. A week later, he said, "What if I joined the military?" I wish I could rewind. . . . He had made this difficult decision by himself, so we honored that.

When his five years were almost up, I asked what he'd do. He'd already decided to re-up, get into reconnaissance. I practically threw myself at his feet. I said, "Alex, why would you do that?"

Once Alex was accepted in reconnaissance, it was an even more pressing issue for us. I began a life of constant fear, crying at the drop of a hat. That continued until the day all my fears came true.

Before his fifth year was up, 9/11 happened. After the event, I can imagine all those kids wanted to be part of this vengeance or whatever you want to call it. They wanted to go and defend the country from evil terrorists.

All this time, my husband and I were insanely writing letters to anyone who'd listen about how wrong the war was going to be, what a mistake it was going to be. The title of Fulvio's letter was "Pandora's Box." In the end it did no good. The war happened so quick. The tide came in and took everybody away.

I joined MFSO right away at a protest in D.C. I saw two women standing with photos of their sons, at the front of a group of women. My eyes went to the posters of these young men, and I went over. I burst out crying right there on the street. It was as though I saw my future.

I marched in every event MFSO did. I would have done anything to save Alex, to save all those kids. If the Marines had taken me instead of Alex, I'd have gone. I knew he was heading toward a conflagration it would take a miracle for him to come back whole from.

I come in contact with a lot of people who are able to wield influence. Some said, "Tell us what you want us to do, we'll get Alex out." But Alex was a very successful Marine. He'd built a lot of confidence through his "band of brothers." How could I destroy him by saying, like he was a little boy, "I'm taking you out"?

I live in a world where no one has a child in Iraq. I go to dinner parties where people complain about kids not washing their own clothes. I couldn't get people to lift their lazy hands and write a frigging letter. They are responsible for the deaths of these kids. They were asleep at the wheel. We are the governed, but we have a voice, we have a duty to these kids that we put on the firing line like that.

Alex met a student from George Washington University at our house in 2002. They were very much in love. It was beautiful to see. As soon as he'd call Gildita, she'd call us. She always understood our worry; she didn't keep him to herself. One day, she said he'd asked her to buy him boots on the internet. I said, "Has something happened to Alex?" We found out, he hadn't even told her: he'd been in a Humvee explosion. Only his foot was injured. He was in the field hospital in Fallujah, trying to replace his own boots. Just unbelievable. He was there about eleven days, then went back to the front.

I was just dying a little bit every day, from when he got his first orders for deployment. I was a nervous wreck. If you're reading the news, reading about explosions, decapitations, children dying, Marines running amok, it's a vision of Hell.

Alex and Gilda married in May 2005. It was a beautiful wedding, a huge family reunion. A beautiful bride, a handsome, happy bridegroom. We're very compatible with her family. I'm Mexican-American, her family is from Puerto Rico; we're from that culture. When the six of us were together, it was wonderful. Alex was so happy that we loved her, and so happy that her parents loved him.

At the wedding, I heard from the Marines they'd be deployed again. Only one more year. I hoped my suffering would be over, he'd be able to stay home. He was married, he had grown up to be such a wonderful, good, honest, responsible man. He wanted to go to college. He grew up about that. His wife was going to law school; he would help her study.

Once, we were sleeping on a Saturday, about six in the morning. I hear the door downstairs opening, heard tiptoes into the house. I said, "Fulvio, do you hear that?" Then I hear loud thumping up the stairs. Alex jumps on the bed like he did as a little boy. They'd brought croissants and made coffee for us. On my birthday, they called, and they both sang a song that she'd taught him, a traditional Spanish song. They would call me to get recipes for things I've always cooked—an almond cake, Italian sauces. It was so cute to get those calls. After they visited, they always went back with Tupperware containers of frozen food I made for them.

As the second deployment drew near, he became very distant. We figured he was now a married person. A man leaves his parents, joins his wife; we understood. But it became worse. It would take him days to call me back.

Before the first deployment, we sat him down and spoke with him privately. We said, "Alex, you'll be in Iraq, among people—they're probably good men, but different from you. Just remember you're the son of Gilda and Fulvio. You know who you are, what your values are." He said, "Mom and Pop, you don't have to worry about any of that. I understand what you're saying and there should never be any doubt in your minds."

But when he came back, there was a change in him. When we heard about his second deployment, we drove down to Camp Lejeune. In the meantime, in fall, they'd bought a house. It was so neat to see your child so grownup and responsible, asking his father for advice. But this time, we arrived and he didn't come to meet us. We were so puzzled, so hurt. We couldn't get over it. His behavior was so hard to read. It was a difficult visit. He was very withdrawn, wouldn't engage in conversation. I'd look at him and he'd look sideways, not straight in my eyes.

He was poring over maps, worried about his men; as team leader, he was responsible for five men. He wanted to be as prepared as he could be. He was also obsessed with watching the news on CNN. He'd never watched the news. I'd always teased him about not reading the papers, always sent him articles, and now he was glued to CNN. He knew what he was headed for. He knew he was quite probably going to die.

So he left for his deployment. I got one message from Alex. Just one. I'd sent him a very funny video, *Cat Massage*, to give him a laugh. He responded, "I haven't had much time, mostly been down field, haven't slept more than three nights in my trailer, haven't showered in three weeks." They were exhausted, working so hard. In a letter he sent his wife, he said they were doing things by the seat of their pants. He was out in the field all the time. They keep sending them until they get killed. Absurd missions.

I'd baked his favorite almond cake, sealed it and sent it. It never reached him for his birthday. It came back after he died.

I was at school, teaching fifth-graders, when the chaplain came to my class and asked me to come out. She said the Marines had called the school. She gave me the phone number. They told me Alex had been in an explosion, ran over a bomb in his Humvee. Seventy percent of his body had second and third degree burns.

He'd been flown to Baghdad, and he was going to be flown to Landstuhl. Fulvio was able to arrive just a few hours after Alex got there. What met his eyes was something you never want to see: more dead than alive, in an induced coma, horrifically burned.

His Humvee had been carrying fuel for the whole convoy. There were five Humvees in the convoy. The first three passed over the same spot. Alex's triggered it. It was fate—destiny. We all knew, including him. I think you feel these things.

The night before I was told, I'd had this strange thing happen as I lay in bed. Fulvio was in Egypt; he's an information technology consultant and works in developing countries. I'm not religious, but I was praying, "Please don't let Alex die in Iraq." We had visited Walter Reed Hospital, seen horrible injuries: triple amputations; men with their heads flat, blind, but still alive, they can still think and know what happened to them. It's horrible, horrific what we've done to these kids. I was thinking, "Don't let that happen to Alex."

Next morning, six a.m., first thing I do is call Fulvio at his hotel. He said, "What happened?" All alarmed. I said, "Nothing, I just wanted to make sure I could reach you if I needed to." I got to school at ten a.m. When the chaplain came to my room . . . It was the worst day of my life. The chaplain drove me home. I got on the phone, six hours after my first call. Fulvio says, "So now what?" I said, "Now it's real."

I wanted to protect my son so much. Once, I dreamt I had been accepted into recon. Imagine, a fifty-six-year-old woman! It was a special brigade of older women, still in training. But because the war had taken such a bad turn, our training had been interrupted and we were sent to Iraq. Our mission every night was to go to a house that had insurgents, look through the window, break in, and walk out without waking the insurgents. Stealth training. Alex laughed so hard when I told him. But in the dream, I'd contacted him, asked him if what the Marines were doing, was it right? Kosher? He said "No, Mom, be careful, it's not right."

I had another dream. I stood on top of a tangled highway in the desert, like spaghetti, leading nowhere. Alex was in a helmet and fatigues, I was in ordinary clothes. He said, "Look, we've done a lot." I said, "No, what is this? A highway made of crushed Humvees, rubber, tires, all smashed together to make this road."

Maybe if I'd been an oo-rah Marine mom, it would have been easier. But I thought I could do something. It didn't work out that way. It's like a Marquez book, *Chronicle of a Death Foretold*. Magic realism.

Part of my healing is to do what I can to help the American people understand what a mistake they made, that we are responsible for the deaths of all these people. This country must come to terms with what was done in our name. I will make this my life's work if need be. This is how I will honor my son and keep his memory alive.

# Conclusion:
# The Damage Done, and How to Heal It

The military family members interviewed in this book have all suffered to some extent from the Iraq War. Much of their suffering would be familiar to the family of any soldier in any war. However, as Nancy Lessin says, "For those of us who believe that this war is illegal, it's immoral, it's unjust, it's unjustified, it's wrong, it should never have happened, to have our loved ones over there disrupts our lives in ways that are not comprehended by anyone else who hasn't been in our shoes." This book is intended to help bring about such comprehension.

Some families berate themselves for ever having believed the Bush administration's rationale for the war. Anne Chay says that when the war started she was in "that happy loyal American naïve mode. . . . I fell for the lies in the beginning: it's a necessary evil. Certainly 9/11 fired a lot of people up, not knowing that the people we were after weren't in Iraq." Linda Waste remembers, "When Iraq started, we bought into the rhetoric, and I don't know why we ever did, because we never did before." Since they had a personal stake in the war, however, even the most naïve families paid attention to the news, and soon discovered that they, and the majority of other Americans, had been duped.

The more families came to understand the real nature of the Iraq War, the angrier they got. Claire André says, "I thought, 'I'm going to research my way to the bottom of this, I'm going to find out what the point is.' But there's not a point. . . . It's all a tragedy, and the government is incompetent." Sarah Tyler ticks off the Bush administration's claims: "The uranium from Niger, that was a lie; the Weapons of Mass Destruction, that was a lie; Saddam and Osama bin Laden, that was a lie; the aluminum tubes, that was a lie. It was all a bunch of lies."

In addition to rejecting the premises on which this nation waged a "pre-emptive" war, the families refute the Bush administration's arguments for continuing the war. Anne Chay scorns the notion that American troops can calm a country where they are an occupying force: "If we are the enemy, what are we accomplishing?" John Fenton, whose son was killed by a suicide car-bomber, makes short work of the idea that pulling troops out of Iraq would dishonor the troops who have already died. "I need more kids to die to make me feel better? I don't get that. . . . I honor his choice to join the military. But he shouldn't have been where he was, and these other kids shouldn't be there either."

These families are willing to support the sacrifice of their troops if it is necessary for the defense of their country. But, as Chay points out, the Iraq War "was not a 'have to' by any stretch of the imagination." Larry Syverson calls it "a trumped-up war." Jessica White says, "Too many have been hurt, and for what? There's no good coming out of this war, just so much chaos." Tiki Fuhro voices resentment on behalf of the soldiers: "It seems to me that the troops know there's a lack of mission in the war. They're being sacrificed and they don't know why. . . . It's a horrible way to treat people who have volunteered for their country." Catherine Smith eulogizes all the troops who have been maimed or killed in Iraq: "They were patriotic, they wanted to serve, and we wasted them."

People are angry about more than the needless endangerment of their loved ones. Sarah Tyler rails against the draining of the nation's resources: "We could house the homeless, we could feed the hungry, we could upgrade our schools, we could develop and expand all kinds of youth programs. . . . So much money has been diverted." Tim Kahlor says, "We have horrors going on in LA that need to be addressed. Instead we're pouring money into Iraq." Linda Waste looks further afield: "Why are we not in Darfur?"

Families also decry the damage done to American freedoms by the Bush administration under cover of the war. Nan Beckwith rages, "I hate what they've done to our liberties. Don't you mess with our Constitution!" Kahlor, a passionate believer in free speech, quotes his son, asking, "How can we bring democracy to people when we're not practicing it?"

Nor do the families care only about the harm done to America. Michael Perkins notes, "If we were protecting our country from people who attacked us, that would be different. But these people didn't do anything to us, and we're killing them anyway." Anne Chay mourns, "And the Iraqis: my God, thousands and thousands. Two million have fled. Their lives are horrible. . . . Look what we've done to their country."

These families understand that true responsibility lies with the Bush administration for the harm done by the war both at home and in Iraq. Even the most anti-war among them are not anti-military. As Jessica

White says, "I was never against the people in the military, just how the U.S. government uses the institution. We can't blame the people in the military, they're just doing their job."

The families recognize and deplore the damage done to American Muslims by the administration's policies and rhetoric since 9/11. They view with repugnance the racism experienced by many Muslims over the past few years, and they know its source. Bob Watada puts it tersely: "There was a lot of fear-mongering." Dinah Mason argues, "You can't blame all Muslim people for what a few of them have done."

If politicians viewed war from these families' perspectives, they would be far less likely to jump into one. Linda Waste wonders, "How can you possibly believe that an Iraqi woman's life is any less important than mine, that her son's or husband's life is any less important than my son's or husband's?" War is not an abstraction to these families. War is horror, destruction, and death. The families express a deep need to get this reality across to others; as Tim Kahlor puts it, "I want people to feel what war is."

The failure of most Americans to pay much attention to the war is a powerful motivator for these families' activism. Over and over, the families reveal their outrage at the indifference they encounter. Gilda Carbonaro cries, "I couldn't get people to lift their lazy hands and write a frigging letter. . . . They were asleep at the wheel." Catherine Smith notes with bitterness, "People are only bothered when gas goes up."

Jessica White says simply, "The apathy is mind-blowing."

These family members have dedicated a great deal of energy to overcoming American apathy. Many feel their anti-war activism is a patriotic duty. Sarah Fuhro says, "My son is putting his life on the line for this country in the way that he thinks is right, and I need to put my life on the line for this country too, and this is how I need to do it, to get very involved with the anti-war movement." In a way, they are soldiers in a battle against the war. As Stacy Bannerman notes, "There are many kinds of warriors."

Joyce and Kevin Lucey, whose son killed himself after his discharge from the military, say they "stumbled into activism," but they "have a mission now. . . . We've got to try to do something to make people understand what this is all about." Gilda Carbonaro is equally driven by this mission: "This country must come to terms with what was done in our name."

The families believe they owe this fight to their loved ones. Anne Chay: "If we really cared for these guys, we'd get them out of the middle of a civil war and bring them home." JoAnn Gross: "I feel like if I sit here and don't do anything, and God forbid something happens to my son, I'd have to live with that regret the rest of my life." Tim Kahlor points out that "Just because my kid's on a combat field doesn't mean my obligation to keep him safe ends." Michael Perkins says, "I feel, as a country, we have an obligation to all the troops. We owe it to all the families and soldiers to speak up, so others don't get maimed or PTSD."

But they also owe the fight to themselves. Pat Alviso reports that her stint at Camp Casey saved her from feeling helpless: "I went in scared and came out angry." Melida Arredondo, whose cherished stepson was killed and whose husband has also become an activist, says that speaking out "is a very important means of therapy." Laura Kent, whose only child's PTSD resulted in his suicide, says of her outreach to other parents of troubled soldiers, "It helps me to help others." Denise Thomas finds that her soldier daughter is impressed by how activism has changed her: "She thinks I'm pretty weird, but she's proud of me. . . . I've learned how to fight back."

Stacy Hafley confides, "There are days I wish I could go back to being ignorant of the world situation, not be so involved, like ninety-nine percent of Americans." But she perseveres, because "I feel in some small way that I'm making a difference." Part of the difference she makes is in setting an example for other military spouses: "I refuse to let the military intimidate me or tell me what to do or how to run my family."

The families find that other activists come to mean a great deal to them. Linda Waste speaks for all of them when she says, "Thank goodness for all the families doing this." Brenda Hervey declares, "When I got connected to other people in my situation, it empowered me and helped me find my voice, gave me support on a level I didn't have before." Anne Sapp raves about "the wonderful, beautiful people in this movement."

They need all the support they can get, because their fight is apt to be a long one. Bringing the troops home as soon as possible—beginning the withdrawal immediately—is only one of the families' goals. The second, equally important, aim is to ensure that this country takes proper care of the troops once they come home. The families struggle to raise awareness of post-traumatic stress disorder (PTSD), traumatic brain injury, and other disorders that afflict many troops returning from Iraq. Nancy Lessin says, "Whether it was depleted uranium that could negatively impact [soldiers'] physical health for decades to come, or the psychological trauma of this war, this war doesn't end when they come home. . . . That devastation is not well understood." Bannerman warns, "This war is going to produce unprecedented numbers of soldiers with post-combat issues on a scale this country has never seen."

Catherine Smith helps to connect returning soldiers with necessary services, drawing on her experiences fighting to get help for her son Tomas. But she wonders, "What do those other vets do who don't know congressmen?" Kevin Lucey sums up his anguish for soldiers who suffer, like his late son, from PTSD: "They abandon the troops and leave them behind in the battlefield of their ravaged mind." Melida Arredondo, another grieving parent, echoes his thought: "All Marines say they don't leave their friends behind. That's what we're doing. We're not leaving them behind."

These activists are also fighting for the welfare of other military families. As Bannerman adds, untold numbers of wives and mothers are caring for soldiers with head wounds or other serious injuries, and "Who's caring for them?" Anne Sapp worries about what she calls "The things they carried: the extra duffel bag of guilt all soldiers bring home. Packing backpacks with it for kids to take to school." Sons and daughters, spouses and parents, as well as the soldiers they love, will need help for years to come, and activists are trying to make certain that they get it.

Military families against the Iraq War fit few of the stereotypes of anti-war activists. Sarah Tyler gives a general description of them: "This is just a bunch of middle-aged parents and we're sick about our kids." They are trying to bridge tremendous gaps in understanding between Americans who barely pay attention to the war and those who can rarely stop thinking about it. They tend not to come across as smug and self-righteous; they don't put themselves above the crowd. Many deliberately distance themselves from the more radical fringes of the peace movement as they seek to explain their position to their home communities and the general public. As Dinah Mason says, "We have to find the common ground where we can meet."

It remains to be seen how far the common ground will extend. After the U.S. finally withdraws from Iraq, will we remember the soldiers who fought there? Once we realize how much it will cost to take care of veterans' ongoing needs, will we find the money to do so? How we answer these questions will say a great deal about the true character of this country.

Whatever the outcome of the Iraq War, we have a deep obligation to its veterans. The troops signed up with every intention of bringing honor to our country, and for that they deserve our love and respect. It is not their fault that they were given an impossible mission. With few exceptions, they have struggled to build up a country that is tearing itself apart, make friends of those who can only see them as hostile forces, and settle differences they have little chance of understanding. Their efforts have been immense. Their frustration must be tremendous. We owe them accordingly.

No one in or out of the military can really know what our efforts in Iraq will achieve, in the long run. We ousted a brutal tyrant who held his country together by fear, but so far, neither Americans nor Iraqis have found a new way to keep peace among the country's rival factions. No one is sure of the best way to arrange American withdrawal so as to minimize the continuing bloodshed. Billions of dollars have been spent on huge and seemingly permanent American bases within Iraq, but how many of our troops will occupy them, or for how long, no one can say. Only one thing is certain: ultimately, Iraq's fate lies in the hands of Iraqis, not Americans.

Military families, whether for or against the Iraq War, hope that this country will always use its soldiers wisely and with great care. The U.S. military is the mightiest in history, yet its ability to act is limited by the principles on which this country was founded. Americans believe that we should be free to determine our own destiny, and that other countries— provided they don't threaten us or our allies—should be free to determine theirs. Americans are not out to conquer new territory. We do not see ourselves as a colonial power. It is not clear that the invasion and prolonged occupation of another country can ever be a wise use of American soldiers who share these beliefs.

Americans supported the Iraq War just so long as we were persuaded of the connection between Iraq and the attacks of September 11, 2001. Al Qaeda, the real perpetrator of those attacks, has used the Iraq War to whip up hatred of America's destructive power. Its cells are now active worldwide. Many Americans would like to see the so-called War on Terrorism focus anew on Al Qaeda and its leader, the mastermind of the 9/11 attacks, Osama bin Laden.

However, our military is not designed to discover, infiltrate, or destroy stateless networks of violent radicals. These are the functions of police or intelligence agencies, not armies. What, then, is the right use of the American military in the twenty-first century, barring an actual attack on our country by a nation-state?

Military families, even anti-war activist military families, have no single answer to this question. The one I propose here is my personal opinion. I do not presume to speak for the families I interviewed or for anybody else.

I believe we should use our soldiers always and only to demonstrate the highest American ideals. They should prevent the murder of innocents; they should treat all prisoners humanely; they should protect the transportation and distribution of food and medicine in dangerous places; they should rescue the victims of natural disasters like hurricanes and tsunamis. Wherever they go, they should show the world the best character democracy can produce. Most of them do so already, in spite of a civilian leadership that has other priorities.

A discouragingly large number of countries are ruled by powerful unscrupulous men with terrible weapons, many of which this country has sold them. In a world where both problems and solutions are increasingly global, the U.S. can not afford isolationism. If we ramp down international tensions by negotiating—and respecting—fair and far-sighted arms control pacts, peace treaties, and trade agreements, we can reserve our military power for situations where no better solutions exist. Unless and until such situations arise, we can use our troops to save lives wherever catastrophe strikes, at home or abroad. We can give our troops opportunities for heroism that will restore this country's honor in the eyes of all humanity.

Our soldiers, our nation, and our world deserve no less.

# About the Author

**Jane Collins** has had a motley career. She graduated from Radcliffe College in 1971 with a bachelor's degree in English literature, magna cum laude, and then moved to the country to live a hippie life, which she has never regretted. She has made handpuppets to sell on the street; taught video production and editing in the mid-'70s to hundreds of people in a small town in eastern Kentucky; raised baby calves on a kibbutz ranch in the Golan Heights; raised baby humans on a hill-farm in the middle of nowhere; worked as an organizer of homeless families; been an advocate, writer, and researcher in the field of human services; and done more low-level administrative work than she cares to remember. She and her husband have recently moved to Miami Beach, where they are most definitely not retired. Some of Jane's work is available online at www.janecollins.org.